Tennessee Studies In Literature

Editors

Richard Beale Davis and Kenneth L. Knickerbocker

VOLUME XV

THE UNIVERSITY OF TENNESSEE PRESS · KNOXVILLE · 1970

Tennessee Studies in Literature

Persons interested in submitting manuscripts should address the Managing Editor, *Tennessee Studies in Literature,* McClung Tower 306, University of Tennessee, Knoxville, Tennessee 37916. Contributions from any qualified scholar, especially from this state and region, will be considered. Return postage should accompany manuscripts. Papers should be no longer than five thousand words. Contributors will receive fifty offprints. Other inquiries concerning this series should be addressed to the University of Tennessee Press, Communications Building, University Station, Knoxville, Tennessee 37916.

CONTENTS

   Abstract. Three direct and relatively few indirect allusions to Burton's *Anatomy of Melancholy* appear in Melville's fiction. This work, however, exerted an important stylistic and thematic influence on him. It apparently encouraged him to use catalogues, digressions, and the form of an "anatomy," and deepened his interest in the subject of melancholy. In "Bartleby the Scrivener" the three main types, many of the symptoms, and most of the major causes of melancholy according to Burton are depicted. (NW)

   Abstract. A major plot element in Mark Twain's first novel *The Gilded Age*—Si Hawkins' purchase of 75,000 acres of Tennessee land to secure the fortunes of his children—is soundly based on fact. Hawkins is in many ways similar to John Marshall Clemens, Twain's father, who bought large tracts of land in Fentress County, Tennessee, with similar expectations. Jamestown, where the elder Clemens lived for several years, corresponds to the Obedstown of the novel. The land, some of which the family retained into the twentieth century, brought less than $10,000, far short of the expectations of Clemens or Hawkins. The major profit realized from the land was Mark Twain's: the $90,000–$100,000 he received from *The Gilded Age* and the play based on it. According to Twain this was "just about a dollar an acre." (AE)

   Abstract. Between 1827 and 1836, Robert Walsh, powerful editor of the Philadelphia *National Gazette and Literary Register* and the *American Quarterly Review,* waged a literary war against the Knickerbocker School. Most of the hostile encounters were in the pages of Walsh's two journals and in various New York newspapers and periodicals, though a large number of journals outside the New York and Philadelphia areas took sides in the editorial battles. Walsh's principal antagonists were Theodore

Sedgwick Fay, George Pope Morris, and Nathaniel P. Willis—the editors of the *New-York Mirror;* Lewis Gaylord Clark and his brother Willis Gaylord—the editors of the New York *Knickerbocker;* George King, William Leggett, and other editors of local New York newspapers. Political differences, sectional prejudice, economic factors—all had a part in the causes of the war. The principal cause, however, was that Walsh was conservative in literary taste, leaning to the "old school" of Neoclassicism, and the New Yorkers were more liberal, leaning to the "new school" of Romanticism. Walsh and his writers regularly disparaged modern American poets, which the New York writers praised. Heated editorial exchanges were numerous after Dr. James McHenry, one of Walsh's regular contributors, wrote a condemnatory critique of William Cullen Bryant and Nathaniel P. Willis, favorites of the Knickerbocker School, in March 1832. The war subsided in 1836 when Robert Walsh resigned his editorial posts and went to France; however, it was to flame again shortly afterwards when Edgar Allan Poe emerged as a critic to contest the taste of the New York coterie. (GRW)

IV. American Nationalism and Esthetics in Joel Barlow's Unpublished "Diary—1788"
By Kenneth Ball 49

Abstract. In an unpublished diary written during his first European visit, Joel Barlow reveals his American esthetics. Comments on architecture, paintings, and gardens show his awareness of the differences between American and Old-World cultures. Appreciative remarks on Gothic architecture are considerably reserved, perhaps because of a lack of sympathy with the church-state and the feudal order. The churches are the main difference he sees between the two cultures, but he appreciates the beauty of the Gothic style. Barlow's attitudes toward painting and gardening are also revealed in his "Diary." His American patriotism causes him to admire West, the Philadelphian, whose paintings were changing London tastes from the neoclassical style to the detailed style of historical representation. Similarly, Barlow's American republicanism causes him to object to the expensive court gardens, but he remains sensitive to the simpler garden of Pope. (KB)

V. *Spring and All*: The Unity of Design
By Linda Welshimer Wagner 61

Abstract. William Carlos Williams' *Spring and All* is the first of his carefully arranged prose and poetry *montages.* Techniques that seemed revolutionary in his epic *Paterson* had their beginning in 1923, as Williams illustrated his belief that prose and poetry were at times necessary to each other. Each single poem is set in prose which prepares the reader for it. Dedicated to Charles DeMuth, *Spring and All* considers the state of American art, and the poems illustrate one point or another of Williams' principles. "The Red Wheelbarrow," for example, is placed to illustrate the imagination's raising everyday experiences to art, now possible, Williams thinks, in a "new world" of spring and artistic freedom. Many of the poems in this collection have been considered fragmentary; taken without the prose that so fittingly accompanied them, the poems are very different in effect from Williams' intention. (LWW)

VI. The Masks of MacLeish's *J. B.*
By John H. Stroupe 75

Abstract. MacLeish's *J. B.* is an existential play in which gods gain definition through man and his suffering and in which man forges his own salvation. Through the use of the mask and the metaphor of acting, the play demonstrates the impotence of Deity before a man who finally sees the world and himself unmasked. To suffer is to be, and being, regardless of its pain, is more relevant to J. B. than play-acting behind assumed masks. In the play, J. B. rejects a series of literal and metaphorical masks—the complacency of the "good man," the ideologies of Western culture—and finally his need for a just universe. He recognizes that there is no justice, but that there is the dignity of choosing to be. It is this exercise of choice that finally establishes J. B.'s superiority to God. (JHS)

VII. Chaucer's Apostrophic Mode in *The Canterbury Tales*
By John Nist 85

Abstract. Linguistic science extends and intensifies the meaning of apostrophe to include "the expression of a great emotional discovery, in which the speaker/writer addresses the context of his discourse rather than his listener/reader." In *The Canterbury Tales* Chaucer uses this inventive dimension of apostrophe to state the central theme of the pilgrimage, to plumb the spiritual depths of the story-tellers on the journey, to confront the drama of their tales with the lyricism in their hearts, and to strengthen the moral conscience of the audience by letting it overhear what normally should be merely heard. In that quality of overheardness, Chaucer transmutes the rhetoric of his craft into the poetry of his art. The apostrophic mode, which he first learned to master in *Troilus and Criseyde,* is thus an alchemist in the laboratory of his style—a fact that is demonstrated by a detailed analysis of a dozen of the most outstanding *Tales.* (JN)

VIII. The Method in the Madness of *A Mad World, My Masters*
By Arthur F. Marotti 99

Abstract. In this play, Middleton departs from the practice of his earlier comedies, which have explicit judgment-scene conclusions, and builds into the dramatic action a "law of comic physics" through which extremes of behavior are punished through purely comic means. This creates a comic *concordia discors* (anticipated by some of the character names): the jealous husband is cuckolded, the stingy *senex* robbed, the young wit outwitted, the whore made blushing bride, and the libertine turned into a puritan. In this comedy reality and illusion are habitually confused. In the cases of Penitent Brothel, who mistakes a succubus for his mistress, and Harebrain, whose senses deceive him on three separate occasions, a moral blindness is behind the confusion. But, in Follywit's gulling of his uncle, the conversions of reality into illusion have a more theatrical form—in the robbery in masquing-suits, the theft in courtesan disguise, and, finally, in the play-within-the-play, which makes the audience aware of the arbitrariness of the boundary between the real and the illusory in a "mad world" which is, actually, their own. (AFM)

IX. Chesterfield's *Letters to His Son*: The Victorian Judgment
By Richard M. Kelly   109

Abstract. The negative response of the early Victorians to Chesterfield's *Letters to His Son* demonstrates their sensitivity to the hypocrisy of their own day, a vice which they saw epitomized in the Earl's teachings. The sense of moral superiority they assumed was that which the role of satirist demanded. Charles Dickens and Douglas Jerrold, through their caricatures of Chesterfield in *Barnaby Rudge* and "Punch's Letters to His Son," converted the Earl into a Victorian villain and conveyed the popular impression that he was an arch-hypocrite. Lord Mahon, in his edition of the *Letters,* attempted to restore the "real," historical Chesterfield but continued to judge him by the disapproving and absolute standards of the conventional morality. Abraham Hayward provided a new critical perspective through his evaluation of the Earl's morality in terms of the eighteenth-century milieu. The trend to upgrade both the writings and character of the Earl was continued by such critics as Sainte-Beuve, Mrs. Oliphant, Leslie Stephen, the Earl of Carnarvon, and Churton Collins, the last recognizing most clearly that the Victorians read other ages in the light of their own, and thus arrived at "most erroneous conclusions." (RMK)

X. MURRAYANA: Thirty-four Atrocious Anecdotes Concerning Publisher John Murray II
Ed. by Ben Harris McClary   125

Abstract. At the height of his publishing career, John Murray II was the object of a scurrilous attack by notorious editor Charles Molloy Westmacott. The attack, probably launched after Murray refused to pay "hush" money, took the form of a series entitled "Murrayana" and was made up of thirty-four anecdotes relating to the publisher. Appearing in 1828 and 1829 in Westmacott's *The Age,* "Murrayana" pictured its subject as a clownish entrepreneur to whom success had come in spite of his ineptitude, stupidity, and immorality. Although the validity of most of the stories is highly questionable, the series does serve as an interesting counterbalance to Samuel Smiles' family-commissioned biography of the publisher. Perhaps, however, the relationship with Murray is not the major significance of this series, collected here for the first time. It is a rare example of the Literature of Blackmail, which was no rarity at that time. (BHM)

Abstract. Although tradition holds that Tennyson's characterization of Ulysses was derived essentially from Dante's *Inferno,* there is good evidence that Byron's influence in "Ulysses" is as pervasive as Dante's and perhaps even more important in providing an understanding of Tennyson's persona. Ulysses' affinities with the Byronic Hero account for the compulsive self-analysis which informs his monologue, his disdain for his countrymen, his wife and his son, his spiritual arrogance, his longing for an intense life of feeling, and his discontent with the life of common humanity. Moreover, Canto III of *Childe Harold's Pilgrimage* (especially Stanzas 42-45) appears to be a significant source for the theme, imagery, and language of Tennyson's poem as well as for the characterization of Ulysses. The accumulation of parallels and verbal echoes and the similarities of the contexts in which these occur provide convincing evidence for Byron's effect on the poem. Such evidence also serves to reinforce the anti-Victorian and Byronic readings of the poem which have predominated in recent years. (BJL)

Abstract. A major portion of the tragic events in *Tess of the d'Urbervilles* flows from the unfortunate relationship between Tess and Alec d'Urberville. To emphasize the importance of this relationship to the central vision of his novel, Hardy employs in "Phase the First," especially, a series of symbols and metaphors that foreshadow both Alec's seduction of Tess and the disastrous consequences his act has for each of them. A seasonal cycle (from early summer to harvest) underscores the dramatic change which takes place in Tess during her residence at the Stoke-d'Urberville home. Of particular significance are the suggestions, sexual and psychological, related to fruit and flower imagery and to the slight cut Tess receives from a thorn among the roses given her by Alec. The sexual initiation of Tess is again predicted by Hardy's skillful handling of the scene in which Alec conducts Tess on a reckless ride in his gig at the time of her journey to the d'Urberville estate. This episode also foreshadows their mutual destruction, especially when brought into association with the return ride the two take in the same carriage following Tess's stay with Alec. Human tragedy is thus rendered a more insistent, compelling reality by the artistic design of the early part of Hardy's novel. (JJE)

Abstract. Michael Ransom, the central figure in Auden and Isherwood's *The Ascent of F 6,* has been generally regarded as the victim of a mother-fixation, a lust for power, or both. That interpretation is probably sound for much of Act I, but there is considerable evidence throughout the play which suggests that the authors intended to portray not a failure but a modern version of the mythical hero. The purpose of this essay is to demonstrate that intention. External evidence of this intention consists of statements about Ransom which the authors made both before and after they wrote the play. Internal evidence is the heroic pattern which the life of Michael Ransom follows. (FEH)

Abstract. Although Jiménez's influence upon García Lorca (as upon Lorca's whole generation) has long been recognized, no one has clarified Lorca's limited debt to him and the reasons for it, nor the fact that the two poets ultimately became alienated in spirit. For Jiménez, poetry was the expression of an achieved aesthetic or spiritual elevation. In a few of Lorca's beginning poems, there are echoes of the tender melancholy of the early Jiménez, but even at this point Lorca showed more kinship with Darío, Valle-Inclán and Antonio Machado. When Lorca reached poetic maturity in his great *Romancero gitano,* Jiménez was unimpressed, and attacked the book as being flashy and superficial. Jiménez completely rejected Lorca's impressive book of surrealist poetry, *Poeta en Nueva York,* and all his later poetry, which was also strident and revolutionary. Lorca in his turn published a poetic "Portrait" of Jiménez which subtly criticized his refusal to recognize the darker side of life. Moreover, Lorca later insisted that his poetry was inspired by the "daemon," the highest type of inspiration, while Jiménez's was inspired only by the "angel." The simple fact is that since the two poets were opposites in temperament and outlook, any enduring influence of Jiménez upon Lorca was impossible. (CWC)

NATHALIA WRIGHT

MELVILLE AND "OLD BURTON,"
WITH "BARTLEBY" AS AN ANATOMY OF MELANCHOLY

The very first of Herman Melville's multitudinous literary allusions was to a book which had a long, unquestionable, though not always clearly defined influence upon him. That book was *The Anatomy of Melancholy* by Robert Burton, first published in 1621.[1] In the opening sentence of "Fragments from a Writing Desk," Melville's first published work, which appeared in the *Democratic Press and Lansingburgh Advertiser* for May 4 and 18, 1839, the narrator begins his letter to "My dear M——" as follows:

> I can imagine you seated on that dear, delightful, old-fashioned sofa, your head supported by its luxurious padding, and with feet aloft on the aspiring back of that straight-limbed, stiff-necked, quaint old chair, which, as our facetious W—— assured me, was the identical seat in which old Burton composed his *Anatomy of Melancholy*.[2]

Presumably Melville first became acquainted with Burton's work through a volume containing extracts from it in the possession of his father Allan Melville: *Melancholy; as It Proceeds from the Disposition and Habit, the Passion of Love, and the Influence of Religion. Drawn Chiefly from . . . Burton's Anatomy of Melancholy* (London, 1801). Apparently it was sold, together with other books, at auction about 1825. By chance Melville purchased this volume at a bookstore in New York on April 10, 1847, but he did not notice his father's signature in it until his brother Allan called his attention to it four years later.[3] Meanwhile in 1848 he purchased a copy of the complete edition of Burton from the New York publisher John Wiley,

1

presumably that published in 1847 by Wiley and Putnam of New York and J. W. Moore of Philadelphia.[4]

It is surely significant that both these purchases were made during the period in which Melville was working on his third novel, the experimental *Mardi,* published in the spring of 1849. For that novel contains the second of the three direct allusions in Melville's fiction to Burton's work and exhibits the first distinctive influence of that work on Melville's own writing. The allusion occurs in Chapter 1, as the narrator complains of the lack of intellectual companionship among his shipmates on the *Arcturion*:

> And what to me, thus pining for someone who could page me a quotation from Burton on Blue Devils, what to me, indeed, were flat repetitions of long-drawn yarns, and the everlasting stanzas of "Black-eyed Susan" sung by our full forecastle choir? Staler than stale ale.[5]

Several other passages in *Mardi* apparently derive, at least in part, from Burton's work. The name of Babbalanja's laughing sage Demorkriti is a reference to the Greek philosopher Democritus, called the "laughing philosopher," whose fame was revived in modern times by laymen—chiefly by Burton, who assumed the name of Democritus Junior as the author of *The Anatomy of Melancholy.* Three of the catalogues in *Mardi,* moreover, and three in Burton's book contain identical items. The chapter "Time and Temples" in *Mardi* and the discussion of the cure of melancholy by mental exercise in *The Anatomy of Melancholy* (Part 2, Sec. 2, Mem. 4) have lists of "temples," both of which include the Escurial palace near Madrid, the temple of Diana at Ephesus, and Nero's Golden House in Rome. The list of maimed warriors in Chapter 24 of *Mardi* and that of deformed persons in the discussion of discontents causing melancholy in *The Anattomy of Melancholy* (Part 2, Sec. 3, Mem. 2) include one-eyed Hannibal. And in both the chapter "They Sup" in *Mardi* and the discussion of diet as a cause of melancholy in *The Anatomy of Melancholy* (Part 1, Sec. 2, Mem. 2, Subs. 2), Heliogabalus is listed among those who indulged their appetites; Burton names him three times, and Melville makes him stand out from the others by declaring that he was "surnamed the Gobbler" (IV, 337).[6]

The influence of Burton on *Mardi*—and on Melville's writing in general—is, however, not measurable by allusions or parallels. It is the sort of influence exerted on a young writer by an example of a style to which he has a natural inclination, as well as by a temperament like his own in maturity. Melville's chief literary affinity being for the English writers of the sixteenth and seventeenth centuries, it is difficult to assess the probable influence on him of several of these writers—Burton, Browne, Shakespeare, and other Elizabethan playwrights—or, indeed, to distinguish among the lessons he may have learned from them, directly or indirectly.

The antiquarianism and the learned tone of Burton, for example, which characterize much of Melville's writing as well, are also characteristic of Browne. It would seem, however, that it was Burton's use of catalogues, synonyms, divisions, and allusions which chiefly inspired Melville's use of these devices from *Mardi* on. And almost certainly the distinctive form of Burton's work influenced Melville's construction of *Mardi* and of later works.

In calling his work an "anatomy," Burton meant merely that it was, in the Renaissance sense of the word, an "analysis." In recognition of more particular characteristics of this work, however, the contemporary critic Northrop Frye has adopted the term "anatomy" to designate one of the basic forms of prose fiction. According to Frye, the anatomy or Menippean satire is a fictional form in which characters are treated essentially as embodiments of mental attitudes or ideas, erudite information is heaped up, but criticism is focused on pedantry. "At its most concentrated" it "presents us with a vision of the world in terms of a single intellectual pattern." It also has, like the form of the romance, a loose or disjointed structure. Among the works which Frye cites as examples is *Moby-Dick*, which he calls a "romance-anatomy."[7] Of the writers of anatomy whom he names besides Burton, Rabelais is the one to whom Melville seems most indebted technically, though temperamentally the two represent, as some of Melville's allusions testify, opposite poles of hilarity and gravity.

Though *Mardi* is not an anatomy, the sweeping range of its references, its satirization of learning, and its characters and islands depicted in terms of ideas or ruling passions particularly mark its kinship with this form. Indeed, many of the kings of *Mardi* seem to exhibit symptoms of melancholy as described by Burton, that is, a state which may appear gay as well as sad.

In any case, Melville did begin to experiment with the form of an anatomy in *White Jacket* (1850), which he commenced in the summer of 1849.[8] The subtitle of this novel, "the World in a Man of War," is a pun. The book not only describes life aboard a naval vessel, but also presents a comprehensive view of human nature and human activity in terms of life in the navy. Here are analyses, many of which may be matched in Burton's work, of social classes, professional duties, and eccentric natures; the institutions of religion, law, and education;

amusements, illnesses, and funeral rituals. Here also, the catalogues in the chapter "The Bay of All Beauties" survey man's world by listing some of its most scenic spots and recount his history through a listing of some of his famous battles. True, *White Jacket* is more social than intellectual in theme. It may be said, however, that erudition is represented in this work by naval lore and that an attack is made on pedantry in the form of literal adherence to the Articles of War.

Moby-Dick (1851) is, of course, more recognizably an "anatomy" than *White Jacket*—or than anything else which Melville wrote. The characters are embodiments of mental states, an encyclopedic mass of information is dispensed, pedantry is satirized, and metrical passages are interpolated in the prose. More significantly, the work as a whole presents a view of the world in terms of an intellectual pattern—that of whaling, conceived of as a profession operating in both the human and the non-human, the social and the naturalistic spheres. The division of whales as an order into families and subfamilies and the description of parts of the whale's body particularly recall Burton's division of men according to physical differences (most notably humors) and description of the parts of the body and the faculties of the soul.

Moby-Dick is also closer thematically to Burton's *Anatomy of Melancholy* than are Melville's foregoing works. Melville's own deepening somberness is indeed reflected in *Redburn* and *White Jacket*, and the narrators of these novels are subject to melancholic moods. These moods seem to be largely caused, however, by the human callousness and depravity which these young men encounter. The state of melancholy discussed by Burton is without apparent cause, being on this account a mental disease. Ishmael is clearly disposed to this disease. In his opening paragraph he explains his going to sea as a way he has "of driving off the spleen, and regulating the circulation," a course he takes whenever his "hypos get . . . an upper hand."[9] The prevailingly somber and foreboding, occasionally lugubrious tone of the story which he tells presumably derives in part from his disposition. Nevertheless the story itself tends to justify the view espoused by Burton that the lot of man is sorrowful and that all men are melancholy or mad.[10] Ishmael speaks for them all, citing one of the authorities also named by Burton, when he says:

. . . that mortal man who hath more of joy than sorrow in him, that mortal man cannot be true—not true, or undeveloped. With books the same. The truest of all men was the Man of Sorrows, and the truest of all books is Solomon's, and Ecclesiastes is the fine hammered steel of woe. (VIII, 181)[11]

It might be noted, moreover, that Ishmael and Ahab illustrate the difference between melancholy and madness (often confused in Burton's time and earlier) which Burton insisted upon: Ishmael exhibits the chief symptoms of melancholy—fear and sorrow; Ahab does not.

Melville's next novel, *Pierre* (1852), contains a few apparent echoes of Burton's work, chiefly in the passage celebrating love in Book II, iv. There love is associated with "mirth," "peace," and the youth of men and of the world, called the supreme god, and said to be the maker of all "things" good,[12] as it is in the discussion of "Love-Melancholy" in *The Anatomy of Melancholy* (Part 3, Sec. 1, Mem. 1, Subs. 2 and Sec. 2, Mem. 1, Subs. 2).[13] No significant use of Burton seems to be made in this novel, however.

Melville's next several works are more Burtonian, in tone if not in style. After *Pierre,* which virtually ended his critical reputation, he turned to writing shorter works of fiction—the short stories of 1853-1855 and the truncated novel *Israel Potter* (1855), in which characters who are failures or who have been forgotten are prominent. A state of melancholy, with sufficient cause, is common among them, though some affect an appearance of gaiety—notably the chief characters in "The Happy Failure," "The Fiddler," and "Jimmy Rose." Two stories merit special attention.

"Cock-a-Doodle-Doo!," published in *Harper's Magazine* in December 1853, contains the third and last of Melville's allusions in his fiction to Burton. The narrator, who suffers from "hypos" and "melancholy" caused by his financial straits, looks up from the window where he is "reading Burton's *Anatomy of Melancholy*"[14] and sees for the first time the even more unfortunate Merrymusk.

The first of Melville's stories, "Bartleby the Scrivener," published in *Putnam's Monthly* in November and December 1853, is his most concentrated study of melancholy and the work by him which perhaps owes most to Burton's work, both in theme and in form. It is a story whose specific meaning has caused some disagreement among critics in recent years, though the consensus seems to be that the title character reflects something of Melville's experience as a writer.[15] In any case, Bartleby (who is one of many passive or withdrawn characters in Melville's fiction) is presented as part of a comprehensive, though small design—one of Melville's smallest microcosms. The narrator (a lawyer engaged also in copying legal documents) says that he himself, his employees, business, chambers, and general surroundings are "indispensable to an adequate understanding of the chief character."[16] When all these elements are taken together, the story is in effect an "anatomy of melancholy."

"Bartleby" is too slight, of course, to be classified in form as an anatomy. It does, however, present a view of mankind as divided into types, first according to humors, then according to types of melancholy. The four main characters are humor characters, belonging to the literary tradition, which flourished in the sixteenth and seventeenth centuries, based on the long-held medical theory that the four fluids or humors of the body produce, when out of balance, dominant tempers in individuals—an excess of blood making one active, of phlegm lethargic, of choler irritable, of melancholy sad.

In "Bartleby" the narrator's original employees—the scriveners Turkey and Nippers and the office boy Ginger-Nut—have nicknames which are said to be "expressive of their respective persons or characters" (21). In terms of humors, Turkey, with his florid complexion (which deepens after noon) and his uncontrollable energy in the afternoon, is sanguine; the heat and the color of this predominant humor are insisted upon more than the characteristics of the humors of the other characters, his face and his activity being repeatedly described in terms of fire, his money being said to go for "red ink" (25), and his name evoking the image of a red head. Nippers, who has a "sallow" complexion and an "irritable" disposition (26), is choleric. The narrator, at least before the arrival of Bartleby, is phlegmatic, priding himself on never becoming excited or even very energetic. Bartleby is presumably melancholic, called "forlorn," "the forlornest of mankind," and said to be "by nature and misfortune prone to a pallid hopelessness" (27, 43, 65). This humorous temper is most clearly seen, however, in the influence of Bartleby on the narrator, in whom he produces "melancholy," "gloom," and "despondency" (40, 49, 52).

All these characters are also victims of melancholy in the broad sense, the mental disease defined by Burton as "a kind of dotage without a fever" (108), whose symptoms include an excess of any of the humors. All have dotages, the most significant being that of the narrator, who dotes on Bartleby. All but Turkey, in fact, are referred to by the narrator as ill: Nippers having a "diseased ambition," Bartleby having an "innate and incurable disorder" and being "demented" and "deranged," and himself being led by "chimeras . . . of a sick and silly brain" and "affected . . . in a mental way" as a result of his association with Bartleby (24, 42, 45, 40, 44).

The four main characters in Melville's story correspond, moreover, to the three main types of melancholy as designated by Burton. Turkey and Nippers taken together (since they complement each other, Turkey working best in the morning, Nippers in the afternoon) exhibit symptoms of "head" melancholy, whose victims have a "sanguine complexion" and are "very choleric"; Bartleby, melancholy of the "whole body," being "sorrowful . . . dejected . . . solitary, silent," like those so afflicted; the narrator, "hypochondriacal melancholy" (produced by disorders of the bowels, liver, spleen, or membrane), in that his symptoms, characteristic of this type, "are not usually so continuate as the rest, but come by fits" (248, 250).

The part of Burton's work to which "Bartleby" seems most indebted is his discussion of the causes of melancholy, which he divides into two main categories: "General" and "Particular." Of the "General" ones—God, the Devil, witches and magicians, stars, old age, and parents—only one figures in "Bartleby." Both the narrator and Turkey are "elderly," being "somewhat not far from sixty." In contrast Nippers and Bartleby are young men.

Of Burton's "Particular" causes of melancholy, the first group (to which more than half his discussion is devoted) consists of what he calls "those six non-natural things . . . which are principal causes of this disease": diet, "retention and evacuation," air, exercise, "sleeping and waking," and "perturbations of the mind" (136, 137). All but two—"retention and evacuation" and "sleeping and walking"—are more or less prominent in "Bartleby."

Diet is first to be noted in the story also. The narrator thinks Nippers is subject to indigestion. He and Turkey eat scores of ginger cakes and, their work being "proverbially a dry, husky sort of business" (27), many apples (brought to them by Ginger-Nut). After drinking beer at dinner they become gentler, and Turkey recommends a quart of ale a day for Bartleby. According to Burton, ginger is one of the spices which cause "hot and head melancholy" (140), apples (like all fruit) are to be avoided by anyone inclined to melancholy, and beer is generally good for that condition because of the hops in it.

Bartleby apparently lives entirely on ginger cakes. When the narrator realizes this fact he begins to speculate on the possible effects of such a diet:

Ginger-nuts are so called, because they contain ginger as one of their peculiar constituents, and the final flavouring one. Now, what was ginger? A hot, spicy thing. Was Bartleby hot and spicy? Not at all. Ginger, then, had no effect upon Bartleby. (p. 33)

As for liquids, Bartleby drinks neither beer, tea, nor coffee. Altogether his diet seems to emphasize the cold, dry nature of his dominant humor, in contrast to the hot, dry nature of the choleric Nippers and the hot, temperate nature of the sanguine Turkey.

A second "non-natural" cause of melancholy given by Burton is bad air. When the narrator of "Bartleby" decides to move his chambers he alleges that "the air is unwholesome" there (56). Certainly their situation, facing walls at both ends and on the side—on Wall Street—can hardly allow for the control of air which Burton advocates as a cure for melancholy.

In his discussion of "immoderate exercise" as a cause of melancholy, Burton treats also "solitariness" and "idleness" as states of an opposite nature. In his work as a whole solitariness has double importance, since he treats it also as a symptom of melancholy. In Melville's story solitariness figures prominently. The narrator seems to feel that it is the chief explanation of Bartleby's behavior, at least at the time of the story, and he himself is deeply disturbed by the consciousness of it which he acquires. When he discovers that Bartleby is occupying the office on Sundays when the city is empty, he is appalled:

Immediately then the thought came sweeping across me, what miserable friendlessness and loneliness are here revealed! His poverty is great; but his solitude, how horrible! Think of it. Of a Sunday, Wall Street is deserted as Petra; and every night of every day it is an emptiness. This building, too, which of weekdays hums with industry and life, at nightfall echoes with sheer vacancy, and all through Sunday is forlorn. And here Bartleby makes his home; sole spectator of a solitude which he has seen all-populous—a sort of innocent and transformed Marius brooding among the ruins of Carthage! (pp. 39, 40)

Ultimately Bartleby's solitariness deepens, until he dies at the base of the prison wall. Incidentally, the narrator's references to Wall Street as "deserted as Petra" and to Bartleby's quarters there as a "hermitage" as well as to the prison "cell" in which he finally lives (31, 33, 51, 52, 63) evoke images of several categories of persons whom Burton lists among the victims of involuntary solitariness: "monks, friars, anchorites" and "Such as live in prison, or some desert place" (154).

As for idleness, Burton calls it "cousin german" to solitariness. Actually, Bartleby at first is an example of "immoderate exercise," copying documents without interruption. With his refusal to examine his copies, however, he becomes increasingly idle. The narrator advises him to take "wholesome exercise in the open air" (46), as Burton advises moderate exercise and a change of air by travel as cures of melancholy, but in vain. At last Bartleby refuses even to eat.

Of the causes of melancholy in Burton's sixth category—"perturbations of the mind"—two are clearly distinguished in "Bartleby":

ambition in Nippers and fear in the narrator. In Burton's work as a whole fear is doubly important, being considered as both a cause and a symptom of melancholy. In Melville's story it is of particular significance. It is induced in the narrator chiefly by his speculations on the subject of solitariness. After supposing Bartleby's feelings in the empty city on Sundays, he recalls the murder of Samuel Adams by John C. Colt in New York (an actual occurrence of the year 1841) "in the solitary office of the latter" (51) and decides that it might not have occurred elsewhere:

It was the circumstance of being alone in a solitary office, upstairs, of a building entirely unhallowed by humanising domestic associations . . . which greatly helped to enhance the irritable disposition of the hapless Colt. (p. 52)

In consequence he becomes afraid that the solitary Bartleby may harm him, confessing,

My first emotions had been those of pure melancholy and sincerest pity; but just in proportion as the forlornness of Bartleby grew and grew to my imagination, did that same melancholy merge into fear, that pity into repulsion. (pp. 41, 42)

He thus illustrates, in fact, Burton's explanation of all the perturbations of the mind producing melancholy as results of the "force of imagination" (158). The narrator's fear of Bartleby may, however, represent a fear of death in general, one of the objects of fear enumerated by Burton in his discussion of the symptoms of melancholy.[17] Melville's lawyer continually anticipates Bartleby's death, likens him to a cadaver, sees him in a winding sheet, and tends to identify all men—including himself—with Bartleby's corpse.

Most of the echoes of Burton's work in "Bartleby" are of the part devoted to the causes and symptoms of melancholy. One passage in the part on the cure of this state should be noted, however. It contains an allusion to "Bartolus the lawyer" as one of those authorities approving the consultation of wizards for such a cure (Part 2, Sec. 1, Mem. 1). Bartolus was a fourteenth-century Italian jurist, professor of civil law at the University of Perugia, and the most famous master of the dialectical school of jurists. Melville could have known of him from other sources, and in any case no direct reference to him is made in "Bartleby." It is nevertheless possible that his name in the context given it by Burton suggested that of the title character of Melville's story.

Finally, in implying that melancholy is a condition common to mankind—as Ishmael had declared earlier—the narrator of "Bartleby" agrees with Burton, who more than once states that it is. When the narrator realizes the solitariness in which Bartleby lives in the city on Sundays, he exclaims:

> For the first time in my life a feeling of overpowering stinging melancholy seized me. Before, I had never experienced aught but a not unpleasing sadness. The bond of a common humanity now drew me irresistibly to gloom. A fraternal melancholy! For both I and Bartleby were sons of Adam. (p. 40)

The same theme is implicit in his description at the end of the story of the Dead Letter Office, where Bartleby is rumored to have worked, and in his concluding exclamation: "Ah, Bartleby! Ah, humanity!"

In his prefatory "Democritus Junior to his Reader," Burton recounts the story that Democritus when found cutting up beasts explained that he was attempting to discover the cause of madness and melancholy; Burton also gives as the opinion of Democritus Junior that all men suffer from such states. He begins his work proper with a description of "Man's Excellency" and "Man's Fall and Misery" in an Old Testament context and proceeds in the same context, in the third paragraph, to "A Description of Melancholy." This paragraph consists of a quotation from the book of Ecclesiasticus—XL, 1–5, 8—and a final sentence of Burton's own. The first verse from Ecclesiasticus, which expresses the gist of the whole, is as follows:

> Great travail is created for all men, and an heavy yoke on the sons of Adam, from the day that they go out of their mother's womb, unto that day they return to the mother of all things. (p. 85)

A phrase from this verse is, in fact, quoted by the narrator of Melville's story as he identifies himself with Bartleby, though whether it is quoted from Burton—or another intermediary—or from the Apocrypha directly cannot be said.

In two other long passages Burton puts the matter in his own words. Defining "Melancholy in Disposition" (which, however, he says is improperly so called, since it is not a disease), he writes that it is

> that transitory melancholy which goes and comes upon every small occasion of sorrow, need, sickness, trouble, fear, grief, passion, or perturbation of the mind, any manner of care, discontent, or thought, which causeth anguish, dulness, heaviness and vexation of spirit, any ways opposite to pleasure, mirth, joy, delight, causing frowardness in us, or a dislike. . . . And from these melancholy dispositions, no man living is free, no stoic, none so wise, none so happy, none so patient, so generous, so godly, so divine, that can vindicate himself; so well composed, but more or less, some time or other he feels the smart of it. Melancholy in this sense is the character of mortality. (p. 93)

And he concludes his discussion of the causes of melancholy thus:

Now go and brag of thy present happiness, whosoever thou art, brag of thy temperature, of thy good parts, insult, triumph, and boast; thou seest in what a brittle state thou art, how soon thou mayest be dejected, how many several ways, by bad diet, bad air, a small loss, a little sorrow or discontent, an ague, &c.; how many sudden accidents may procure thy ruin, what a small tenure of happiness, thou hast in this life, how weak and silly a creature thou art. (p. 231)

The last of Melville's novels of his major fiction-writing period, *The Confidence-Man* (1857), is the last work of his which seems to reflect his reading of *The Anatomy of Melancholy*. The varieties of duplicity represented by the Confidence-Man in his various guises correspond to those enumerated by Burton in "Democritus Junior to his Reader." Indeed, Melville's conception of his central character in this novel as a multiple one may have been partly inspired by a passage in the same part of Burton's work describing man's ability to play several parts at once.[18] *The Confidence-Man* may also be classified in form as an anatomy. It presents a comprehensive view of human experience in terms of professional practitioners and dupes of fraud.

Certainly Burton was in Melville's consciousness during the time he was composing *The Confidence-Man*. On October 1, 1856, in New York from Pittsfield to arrange for its publication, he visited editor Evert A. Duyckinck, who recorded in his diary:

Herman Melville passed the evening with me—fresh from his mountain charged to the muzzle with his sailor metaphysics and jargon of things unknowable . . . instanced old Burton as atheistical—in the exquisite irony of his passages on some sacred matters.[19]

Several months later Melville was in Oxford, where Burton spent most of his life. There he thought of Burton, as, on May 2, 1857, he wrote in his journal:

Most interesting spot I have seen in England. . . . Learning lodged like a faun. Garden to every college . . . Each college has dining room & chapel—on a par. . . . Soul & body equally cared for . . . I know nothing more fitted by mild & beautiful rebuke to chastise the presumptuous ranting of Yankees.—In such a retreat old Burton sedately smiled at men.

In another entry for the same date he wrote: "In such a retreat old Burton composed his book, sedately smiling at men."[20]

This was Melville's last recorded reference to the author of *The Anatomy of Melancholy*. It was a book which meant most to him— like many others—for what it reflected of his own disposition: in this case, a taste for the synonymous and the heterogeneous, a tendency to melancholy encouraged by the theory of man's fallen state, and a prevailing, ultimately sedate humanistic spirit.

NOTES

1. General similarities between Melville's style and Burton's have often been noted. The review of *Mardi* in the *London Examiner* for March 31, 1849, declared the digressions had "a dash of old Burton and Sterne"; that of the same novel in *The Literary World* in New York for April 21, 1849, referred to its "quaint assemblages of facts in the learned spirit of Burton and the Doctor [Southey]"; and that of *Moby-Dick* in *The Literary World* for Nov. 15, 1851, said it opened with "a hundred or so of extracts of 'Old Burton.'" (See Hugh Hetherington, *Melville's Reviewers* [Chapel Hill, 1961], pp. 103, 113.) Merton M. Sealts, Jr., was first to point out specific echoes of Burton in Melville, in "Herman Melville's Reading in Ancient Philosophy" (Unpubl. diss., Yale, 1942, pp. 180–188). The chief critics who have found other such echoes are William Braswell, Henry Murray, and Elizabeth Foster (see below, nn. 6, 13, 18). No general survey of Melville's indebtedness to Burton, however, seems to have been made.

2. *The Works of Herman Melville* (London, 1924), XIII, 382.

3. This volume, which is now in the Houghton Library, Harvard University, bears the inscriptions: "A[llan] Melville"; "Herman Melville April 10th 1847"; "I bought this book more than four years ago at Gowan's store in New York. Today Allan [his brother] in looking at it, first detected the above pencil signature of my father's; who,—as it now appears—must have had this book, with many others, sold at auction, at least twenty five years ago.—Strange! Pittsfield July 7th 1851." (See Merton M. Sealts, Jr., *Melville's Reading* [Madison, 1966], pp. 45, 47, 48.)

4. *Ibid.,* p. 45. The present location of this book is unknown. Sealts gives the publisher as John Wiley.

5. *The Works of Melville*, III, 3, 4.

6. Possibly the key word, "suppers," in the first part of this chapter of *Mardi* was suggested by Burton's exclamation in this passage: *"Quàm portentosæ cænæ,* prodigious suppers . . . our times afford?" (*The Anatomy of Melancholy* [New York and Philadelphia, 1847], p. 142). William Braswell interprets Taji, Yillah, and Hautia in terms of the "rational," "spiritual," and "vegetal" parts of the soul as named by Burton in his analysis of the soul (Part 1, Sec. 1, Mem. 2, Subs. 5–11), though Burton himself adopts the divisions "rational," "sensitive," and "vegetal," only noting that Paracelsus and Campanella added a fourth—the "spiritual" (*Melville's Religious Thought* [Durham, 1943], pp. 86 ff). In any case, still other passages in *Mardi* are at least Burtonian in tone. Probably the mere number of allusions in the novel to astronomy and cosmology and to Chinese and Turkish history is partly owing to Burton's numerous allusions in the same fields.

7. *Anatomy of Criticism* (Princeton, 1957), pp. 310, 313.

8. The intervening novel, *Redburn* (1849), may contain an indirect allusion to *The Anatomy of Melancholy*. Redburn refers to "that theory of Paracelsus and Campanella, that every man has four souls within him" (*The Works of Melville*, V, 322), a theory which Burton cites as having been held by these men and which Sealts thinks Melville learned of from this source ("Herman Melville's Reading in Ancient Philosophy," p. 180).

9. *The Works of Melville*, VII, 1.

10. For passages in *The Anatomy of Melancholy* expressing this view, see below, pp. 21, 22.

11. Both Burton and Melville, throughout their writing, cite passages from the Wisdom Books of the Old Testament depicting the woefulness and the folly of man.

12. *The Works of Melville,* IX, 44, 45.
13. Henry Murray finds a few other such echoes in *Pierre* (ed., *Pierre* [New York, 1949], pp. 435, 441, 448, 449, 482). Braswell also allows for an influence of Burton's work on this novel, inasmuch as he interprets Pierre, Lucy, and Isabel, as he does Taji, Yillah, and Hautia in *Mardi,* as three parts of the soul as named by Burton (*Melville's Religious Thought,* pp. 86, 87, 93 ff.).
14. *The Works of Melville,* XIII, 144, 159, 161.
15. For a list of the chief interpretations of this story, see Donald M. Fiene, "Chronological Development, in Summary, of Criticism of 'Bartleby,' " in *Melville Annual 1965. A Symposium: Bartleby the Scrivener* (Kent, Ohio, 1966), pp. 151–190.
16. *The Works of Melville,* X, 19.
17. Insofar as Melville's own apparent tendency to melancholy is reflected in his writing, the evidence, as here, is that it was caused at least in part by fear of death. (For the incidence of the theme of death in his fiction and a discussion of some of the implications, see Edwin S. Schneidman, "The Deaths of Herman Melville," in *Melville & Hawthorne in the Berkshires* [Kent, Ohio, 1968], pp. 118–143.)
18. Elizabeth Foster pointed out this possibility in her edition of *The Confidence-Man* (New York, 1954), p. 298.
19. Jay Leyda, ed., *The Melville Log* (New York, 1951), II, 523. Probably Melville was referring to Burton's discussion of "Religious Melancholy." There seems no reason to question Burton's religious faith, however.
20. *Journal of a Visit to Europe and the Levant,* ed. Howard C. Horsford (Princeton, 1955), pp. 260, 267.

The University of Tennessee

THE "TENNESSEE LAND" OF *THE GILDED AGE*: FICTION AND REALITY

Mark Twain liked to write about himself. *The Innocents Abroad, Roughing It, A Tramp Abroad, Life on the Mississippi,* and *Following the Equator* are all semi-autobiographical books in which Twain himself appears as the main character. *Tom Sawyer* and in part *Huckleberry Finn* strongly reflect his boyhood environment, as does—though to a lesser extent—*Pudd'nhead Wilson.* And there is one book in which Twain makes fictional capital of the experience of the Clemens family as a whole, particularly that of his father, John Marshall Clemens.

When Samuel Clemens and his Hartford neighbor Charles Dudley Warner wrote *The Gilded Age* in 1873, they used as a major plot element the "Tennessee land," a vast acreage near the village of "Obedstown," somewhere in the "Knobs of East Tennessee." This land, bought by Si Hawkins, was intended to make the fortunes of his children and secure for them all manner of future blessings. The land itself proved to be worth very little, although it came close to earning a great deal of money for its owners and promoters through one of those corrupt schemes so common in the era to which the novel gave its name.

As is fairly well known, the idea of the Tennessee land, with its magnificent yet elusive promise for the future, was a fictional rendering by Mark Twain of a piece of family history. John Clemens was in several ways similar to the novel's Si Hawkins—and "Obedstown" resembles Jamestown, Tennessee. These matters deserve further exploration in order to see more adequately the relation between the events

15

experienced by the Clemens family and the use Sam Clemens made of
them in his first novel, *The Gilded Age*.

It was apparently early in 1827 when the Clemens family—John,
Jane, and their two-year-old son Orion—moved from Gainesboro,
Tennessee, to what Mark Twain was to call in his autobiography "the
remote and secluded village of Jamestown, in the mountain solitudes
of east Tennessee."[1] Both John Clemens and Si Hawkins had previously lived in Virginia and Kentucky. In *The Gilded Age* Twain places
Obedstown on a mountaintop but says that there is nothing to indicate
this fact because the mountain "stretched abroad over whole counties,
and rose very gradually." This is an accurate description of the topog-
raphy at Jamestown, except that the mountain rises rather abruptly
to the north and west of the town. In *The Gilded Age* Obedstown has
only fifteen houses, a figure half the actual size, for at the time the
Clemenses left Fentress County there were thirty houses in Jamestown.[2] When John Clemens moved there, however, there was scarcely any village. His house, if not the first, was one of the first substantial
buildings to be erected.[3] As a commissioner Clemens had taken a
major role in the establishment of the new county seat and had
drawn up the specifications for the courthouse and jail.[4] He was
chosen as the first circuit court clerk (some say county court clerk), a
post he held for several years, and his name appears many times in the
Fentress County records.[5] His son was probably not mistaken when
he pictured him "honored and envied as the most opulent citizen of
Fentress County." Besides his land holdings, his worth came to at
least $3,500, quite a sum for that time and place.[6] We are given no
indication that Si Hawkins played so important a part in Obedstown's
affairs. The Clemens house, unlike Si Hawkins' "double log cabin, in
a state of decay," was "unusual for its style and elegance," with two
windows in each room and the walls covered with plastering.[7] The
newfangled notion of "plarsterin' " makes its appearance in *The
Gilded Age,* but there it is Si Higgins rather than Si Hawkins who has
married a "high-toned gal" from Kentucky (as Jane Lampton Clemens was from Kentucky) and plastered the inside of his house.

John Clemens' most significant act during his residence in Fentress
County was of course his purchase of the land—allegedly 75,000
acres (the figure used in *The Gilded Age*) and perhaps as much as
100,000 acres, as Twain recorded in a note to his autobiography in
1906. The total price was apparently $400-$500. Mark Twain's impression was that the "enormous area" was bought "at one purchase,"
and he so records it in his autobiography.[8] In *The Gilded Age* too Si

Hawkins buys the land all at once. In actuality, the land was bought over a period of years stretching from 1826 to 1838, in parcels seldom larger than 5,000 acres.[9] A great deal of it was bought in 1830. A typical entry in the Fentress County records reads:

John M. Clemons Location No 392 Fentress County 100 acres on Cumberland Mountain on the waters of Obid and on the Divide between said waters and those of Clear Fork, lying on both sides of the new road Beginning on the north west side of said road

1 January 1829   John M. Clemons[10]

Undoubtedly the fact that his father owned property on the "Obid" River suggested to Mark Twain the name Obedstown, which he used in *The Gilded Age*.[11] At least a small part of the land lay not in Fentress, but in adjoining Morgan County. Not all of it was in John Clemens' name, either. In 1827 he bought 120 acres of it for the two-year-old Orion.[12]

Clemens' reason for buying the land is well known to readers of *The Gilded Age*. In his autobiography, Twain paraphrased his father's thoughts: "Whatever befalls me, my heirs are secure; I shall not live to see these acres turn to silver and gold but my children will."[13] In *The Gilded Age* Hawkins predicts that some day the land will sell for $1,000 an acre, yielding a total amount of $75 million. Of his children he declares, "We'll never see the day . . . but *they'll* ride in coaches, Nancy! They'll live like princes of the earth . . . their names will be known from ocean to ocean!" In part, the prophecy came true, but not because of the Tennessee land. What John Clemens saw in the land which he thought made it so valuable was iron ore, yellow-pine timber, grapes, grazing lands, and a good place for growing corn, wheat, and potatoes.[14] Si Hawkins speaks further of the coal deposits found on the land and of its future accessibility by steamboat and railroad. Mark Twain is inconsistent as to whether his father shared Hawkins' expectations concerning the railroads. At one time he wrote that "he said that in the course of time railways would pierce to that region and then the property would be property in fact as well as name," while elsewhere he remarked that it was "barely possible he had not even heard of such a thing" as a railroad.[15]

The land did not yield the Clemens children anything approaching the amount their father envisioned, but as Bryant Morey French points out, it was not a foolhardy venture.[16] And although Mark Twain made numerous disparaging remarks about the land and about that section of Tennessee in general—in *The Gilded Age* he declares that it "had a reputation like Nazareth, as far as turning out any good thing was concerned"—by 1897–1898 he had come to see the land's worth. "I wish I owned a couple of acres of the land now," he said, "in which case I would not be writing autobiographies for a living."[17] In 1912, Albert Bigelow Paine commented, "The land is priceless now."[18] Fentress County did not, however, turn out to be in the major lanes of transportation in the state. It lies too far north for Nashville-Knoxville traffic, too far east for Nashville-Louisville traffic and too far west for that between Knoxville and Cincinnati. Mark Twain thought when writing his autobiography that the Knoxville-Cincinnati railroad "could not help but pass through" the land, but it actually went through the counties to the east. Si Hawkins is more modest, guessing that the railroad must come within thirty miles of the land.

After a time John Clemens' fortunes took a turn for the worse. He had spent too much in his land purchases, looking toward the future, instead of making sufficient provision for the present. He was making very little in his law practice and was troubled by poor health. Like Si Hawkins, he opened a store in his house and put in a "small country stock of goods," but the venture did not sufficiently boost his finances.[19]

Seeking to better his situation, John Clemens in 1831 moved his family nine miles north of Jamestown to Three Forks of Wolf, where there was much better farming land than in the county seat. Here he built a two-story log cabin—each floor containing a single room—on the two hundred acres of land he had acquired there.[20]

From Three Forks of Wolf, Clemens moved again, to Pall Mall, also on the Wolf River, a town later known as the home of the World War I hero Alvin C. York. Here he once again kept store, also serving as postmaster from 1832 until 1835.[21] In *The Gilded Age* Squire Hawkins (Clemens too was called "Squire") serves as postmaster of Obedstown in addition to running a country store—undoubtedly the result of family stories about the elder Clemens' occupation in Fentress County. Hawkins was not, however, a lawyer or circuit court clerk. With respect to occupation and residence, then, the picture of Hawkins in the novel resembles John Clemens more in the years after he left Jamestown than when he lived there.

Clemens' finances did not improve at Pall Mall, and by 1834 he was worth only one-fourth of the $3,500 he had been a few years before.[22] Plainly something had to be done. In *The Gilded Age* a way out appeared in the form of a letter from Colonel Sellers urging Hawkins to come to Missouri. It is often said that a similar letter was written to Clemens by his brother-in-law John Quarles, but evidence for this is lacking.[23] In any case, Clemens, like Hawkins, decided to make the great move, unwilling—as Twain explained in his autobiography —to stay "among the scenes of his vanished grandeur and be the target for public commiseration."[24]

The precise date of the departure of the Clemens family from Fentress County is unknown. The county records show that John Clemens was there on April 23, 1835;[25] the presumption is that the family left within the next month, probably around the first of May.[26] Sam Clemens was born seven months later at Florida, Missouri.[27] In 1847, after the Clemens family had moved to Hannibal, and young Sam was eleven years old, John Clemens died, once more cautioning his children to hold onto the Tennessee land.[28] In *The Gilded Age,* Si Hawkins' departing words are: "Never lose sight of the Tennessee Land! Be wary. There is wealth stored up for you there—wealth that is boundless!" He dies, trying once more to say "the Tennessee Land."

Needless to say, the Clemens family did not forget Tennessee, the vast tract of land which they owned there, or the equally vast fortune which it was supposed eventually to produce for them. Fortunately the taxes were not heavy—a mere $5.00 for the whole.[29] Before his death John Clemens came back to see the land, and Orion made visits there in 1858, 1867, and 1875.[30] Jamestown legend has it that Mark Twain himself came to visit the lands his father had bought, but the story is apparently without foundation. Twain says in his autobiography that he wrote about the area "from hearsay, not from personal knowledge."[31] It seems entirely possible that the legend of a Twain visit grew out of those paid by Orion.

As the years passed, various efforts were made to sell the Tennessee land. *The Gilded Age* reflects these aborted sales. At one point an iron manufacturing company agent offers Si Hawkins $10,000 for the land —money that he desperately needs. He turns it down, asking $30,000 and confiding to his wife that he might even get a quarter of a million, though he realizes too late that he was a fool not to take the $10,000. In reality, there were times when the land was almost sold for a good price, only to have the agreement fall through. Through Orion's bungling, offers of $200,000 and later $15,000 in cash were turned down.[32] Sam Clemens, furious, wrote Orion's wife: "It is Orion's duty to sell that land . . . if he lets it be sold for taxes, all his religion will not wipe out the sin."[33] When Sam's urgings to sell went unheeded, he besought Orion "never to ask my advice, opinion, or consent about that hated property."[34]

In *The Gilded Age* matters come to a climax when a bill is intro-

duced in Congress providing that the government purchase from the
Hawkins family some 65,000 acres for the establishment of the Knobs
Industrial University, a school for training Negroes in the sciences.
The price which the government was to pay was $3 million. The op-
position moves to amend the bill by substituting as a price "five and
twenty cents, as representing the true value of this barren and isolated
tract of desolation." The narrator puts the actual worth at about
$90.00, a figure clearly too low for the actual land. The amendment
fails and the bill passes the House but is rejected in the Senate, after a
disclosure of bribery on the part of a chief sponsor, Senator Dilworthy.
Washington Hawkins, Si's son, now recognizing the land as a "curse,"
allows it to be sold for taxes. "Never mind the Tennessee Land," he
tells the visionary Colonel Sellers; "I am done with that forever and
forever."

The real Tennessee land was not sold for taxes. For the most part it
was finally disposed of in the 1870's and 1880's by Jane and Orion
Clemens. The price paid them ranged from ten to fifty cents per acre—
much more than John Clemens had paid for it, but far short of his expectations. The whole amount received for the Tennessee land did not
reach $10,000.[35] Mark Twain wrote in his autobiography, referring to
a transaction of 1894, "that ended the Tennessee land."[36] Oddly
enough it did not. In 1902, Sam Moffett, Twain's nephew, passed on to
Livy Clemens the news that a possible defect in the title might cause
some of the land to revert to the family. She advised Moffett of her husband's feelings: "He is afraid it will bring you trouble as it has brought
it to those who went before you."[37] Similarly, in *The Gilded Age* the
disillusioned Washington Hawkins declares, "I'll leave *my* children no
Tennessee land." The land was again brought to Twain's attention in
April 1906, when he was informed that a correction of old surveys
showed that the Clemenses still owned 1,000 acres. A prospective buy-
er from New York accompanied the gentleman from Tennessee who
told him this. "This time," wrote Twain, "I hope we shall get rid of the
Tennessee land for good and all and never hear of it again. It was created under a misapprehension; my father loaded himself up with it under a misapprehension; he loaded it on to us under a misapprehension,
and I should like to get rid of the accumulated misapprehensions and
what is left of the land as soon as possible."[38] Nevertheless, Paine
wrote in his 1912 biography that a corporation of Clemens heirs was
then contesting the title of about 1,000 acres previously overlooked.[39]

The only person who really made much money from the Tennessee
land was Mark Twain, and his profit was largely literary, earned from

The Gilded Age and the play based on it. From the former he received $15,000–$20,000; from the latter, $75,000–$80,000: as he remarked, "just about a dollar an acre." That the chief figure of the first chapters of that novel, Si Hawkins, closely resembles John Clemens is apparent: they were about the same age, they had lived in the same places, they had the same number of children, and they had the same unrealistic expectations of vast wealth to be eventually obtained from 75,000–100,000 acres of land. Both had begun their East Tennessee careers at the top of the social scale and had fallen far below. Both journeyed to Missouri in the hope of bettering themselves there and died with their fortunes not yet materializing. As a final note, one may say that there is something of Mark Twain himself in Si Hawkins, for as his experiences with the typesetter and with the Charles Webster publishing company show, he too had a firm belief that great sums of money could be made by wise investments. Neither, unfortunately, could always be sure what constituted a wise investment, and they were all too quick to say with *The Gilded Age*'s Colonel Sellers, "There's worlds of money in it—whole worlds of money."

NOTES

1. *The Autobiography of Mark Twain,* ed. Charles Neider (New York, 1959), p. 18. Rachel Varble, *Jane Clemens: The Story of Mark Twain's Mother* (Garden City, N. Y., 1964), p. 103, dates the move in March 1827. The Records of Fentress County, Entry Book A, 1824–1836, pp. 125, 126, show that as early as July 28, 1826, John and his brother Hannibal Clemens purchased 508 acres of land.
2. Eastin Morris, *Tennessee Gazetteer or Topographical Dictionary* (Nashville, 1834), p. 79. In the preface to this work, Morris acknowledges the assistance of "John M. Clemmens [sic] Esq., of Fentress."
3. A. V. Goodpasture, "Mark Twain, Southerner," *Tennessee Historical Magazine,* Series II, I (July 1931), 255, says it was the first structure. Dixon Wecter, *Sam Clemens of Hannibal* (Boston, 1952), p. 30, hedges a little to observe that it is "said to be the first substantial structure erected there."
4. The text of the document can be found in Albert Hogue, *History of Fentress County* (Nashville, 1916), pp. 12–13. It is now in the possession of a private collector in Knoxville.
5. Hogue, *100 Years in the Cumberland Mountains* (McMinnville, Tenn., 1933), pp. 11–13.
6. *Autobiography,* p. 23.
7. Albert Bigelow Paine, *Mark Twain: A Biography* (New York, 1912), p. 6. The house is said to have been at the northeast corner of Main and the street now called Mark Twain Avenue, on the spot where the I. R. Storie home formerly stood and where the post office is now located. Directly across Mark Twain Avenue from the site of the house is the spring where the Clemens family obtained their water.
8. *Autobiography,* pp. 18, 22. Mark Twain wrote the figure 75,000 in 1870, and then corrected it in 1906 to "above 100,000." The Fentress County

records I have examined, however, do not indicate that the property was so large. Ralph Gregory, curator of the Mark Twain Birthplace Shrine, Florida, Mo., has expressed to me his own inability to get the Clemens purchases to add up to anything like 75,000 or 100,000 acres. As to the price, the autobiography says it was about $400. Wecter, p. 278, points out that in 1870 Mark Twain put down the price as $100, then altered it to $400. Paine, p. 6, states that the amount was probably no more than $500. Samuel C. Webster, *Mark Twain, Business Man* (Boston, 1946), p. 10, puts it at two-thirds of a cent per acre, a total of $500 if 75,000 acres were purchased.

9. This information is provided by the Fentress County records. See Wecter, p. 278. It is often said that the land lay about twenty miles south of James-town, but the records show Clemens bought land elsewhere too. Among the names appearing most frequently in the records are: Crooked Creek, Mill Creek, White Oak Creek, Rock Castle Creek, and Cumberland Mountain.
10. Fentress County Records, Entry Book A, 1824–1836, p. 195. The spelling "Clemons" frequently occurs in the county records.
11. Present-day maps designate the Fentress County river as Obey, giving the name Obed to a river farther south in Tennessee. But Mark Twain thought the river was called Obeds. See *Autobiography*, p. 22.
12. Fentress County, Entry Book A, 1824–1836, pp. 164, 167. According to Varble, p. 108, James Clemens, a cousin from Danville, Ky., owned over 10,000 acres of land in the county. James Lampton and others bought 5,000 acres in 1830.
13. *Autobiography*, p. 22.
14. *Ibid.*
15. *Ibid.*, pp. 18, 23. The latter statement is the earlier, having been written in 1870.
16. *Mark Twain and the Gilded Age* (Dallas, 1965), p. 148.
17. *Autobiography*, p. 19.
18. Paine, p. 6.
19. Paine, p. 7; Wecter, p. 32.
20. Paine, p. 7; Goodpasture, p. 255; Wecter, p. 33.
21. Wecter, pp. 33–34.
22. *Autobiography*, p. 23. The task of supporting the family was further com-plicated by the birth of Benjamin Clemens in June 1832. Of the Clemens children, Orion was born at Gainesboro in 1825; Pamela at Jamestown in 1827; and Margaret at Jamestown in 1830. According to Webster, p. 44, another son, Pleasants Hannibal—named for his two uncles—was also born at Jamestown but lived only three months. Mark Twain mistakenly says in his autobiography, p. 18, that Orion was born at Jamestown. Wecter, p. 29, gives the correct information.
23. Ralph Gregory, whose research on Twain's uncle appears in "John A. Quarles: Mark Twain's Ideal Man," *Missouri Historical Society Bulletin,* XXV (April 1969), 229–235, does not believe that Quarles called the Clem-enses to Missouri but that the two moved there about the same time. One sentence of his article appears to say that Quarles did send for Clemens, but Mr. Gregory informs me that this was an editorial change and does not represent his own opinion. The character of Colonel Sellers, it should be noted, is based on Twain's cousin James Lampton (*Autobiography*, p. 19).
24. *Autobiography*, p. 23.
25. Fentress County Records, Deed Book, Volume A, 1824–1838, p. 389.
26. Hogue, *Mark Twain's Obedstown and Knobs of Tennessee* (Jamestown, Tenn., 1950), p. 1.

27. Fentress Countians like to assert that Mark Twain was conceived there, though Wecter, p. 38, and Varble, p. 120, say not so. The matter is complicated by Sam Clemens' having been born two months prematurely (Wecter, p. 43).
28. *Autobiography*, p. 19.
29. *Ibid.*, p. 18.
30. John Clemens appeared before the county clerk at Jamestown on Sept. 29, 1838, according to Deed Record C, p. 38, cited by Hogue, *100 Years*, p. 12. He may have made a later visit to the county in 1842, for he wrote of performing "the journey to Tennessee" and of trying "to effect a sale of my Tennessee lands . . ." (Wecter, pp. 74–75). Orion was in Fentress County in 1858, about the time that Henry Clemens was killed in the explosion of the *Pennsylvania* on the Mississippi River (Paine, p. 140). Wecter, pp. 29–30, mentions a visit to Jamestown by Orion in March 1867. In the Mark Twain Papers at the University of California there is a letter written by Orion from Jamestown in November of the same year. Another letter written by Orion from Jamestown on May 15, 1875, is quoted in Hogue's typescript, "John M. Clemens, the Father of Mark Twain," in the Nashville public library.
31. *Autobiography*, p. 18. Hogue too acknowledges that so far as is known Mark Twain never visited Jamestown (*Mark Twain's Obedstown*, p. 1).
32. *Autobiography*, p. 218; *The Love Letters of Mark Twain*, ed. Dixon Wecter (New York, 1949), p. 152. The offer of $200,000, made in 1866, was by a man named Camp, who proposed to turn the land into a wine-producing country.
33. Quoted in Webster, p. 87.
34. *Mark Twain's Letters,* ed. Albert Bigelow Paine (New York, 1917), I, 176.
35. Hogue, *Mark Twain's Obedstown*, p. 1; *100 Years*, p. 13.
36. *Autobiography*, p. 24.
37. Quoted in Justin Kaplan, *Mr. Clemens and Mark Twain* (New York, 1966), p. 361.
38. *Autobiography*, p. 219. Perhaps being shown the corrected surveys led Twain in 1906 to alter the figure of 75,000 to 100,000 acres.
39. Paine, p. 6.

The University of Tennessee

GUY R. WOODALL

ROBERT WALSH'S WAR WITH THE
NEW YORK LITERATI: 1827–1836

Edgar Allan Poe's famous war with the New York literati between 1835 and 1849 is well known.[1] Less known and not yet so thoroughly examined by scholars was a similar protracted struggle waged earlier against the same New York literary coterie by Robert Walsh, Jr. (1784–1859), magisterial editor of the Philadelphia *National Gazette and Literary Register* from 1820 to 1836, and concurrently editor of the influential *American Quarterly Review* from 1827 to 1836. As an active critic and editor who insisted upon regulating the standards of criticism of his contributors, Walsh was a powerful literary force in Philadelphia. He steadily resisted every effort by the Knickerbocker School to extend their influence in his domain and though disdaining editorial combat was never afraid to take up the gauntlet. His entire career was a series of skirmishes with hostile British periodical critics, censurers of his Johnsonian prose style, apologists for Lord Byron, votaries of the Lake Poets, and indulgent nationalistic critics, most of whom were in New York. James Kirke Paulding once averred that it was in England that Walsh "polished his lance and learned the arts of literary warfare."[2] Walsh was, indeed, a great disciple and admirer of the British reviewers, particularly of Francis Jeffrey, whom he counted a personal friend, but he first gained experience as a literary polemicist.[3]

Walsh's hostile encounters with many of the same New York journalists with whom Poe tilted—Theodore Sedgwick Fay, George Pope Morris, Nathaniel P. Willis, Lewis Gaylord Clark and his twin Willis Gaylord, and George King to name a few—were generally based upon

25

his insistence that *soi-disant* indigenous poets should not be puffed simply because they were Americans. He fought in every case the efforts of the highly chauvinistic critics in New York and the East who pleaded for preferred and lenient treatment of American writers as the best way to produce a truly national literature. That Walsh was not an ardent admirer of most American popular poets in his age was well known, but what was never granted him by his adversaries was that he sincerely believed that a genuine national American poetry had to be constructed upon the "old"—i.e., Augustan—school of poetry.

A good example of Walsh's editorial direction with reference to poetry criticism is evidenced in a letter to George Bancroft on September 23, 1827. After expressing pleasure that the reviewer would undertake an article on American poetry, Walsh suggested that it include such poets as Barlow, Dwight, Freneau, Paulding, Percival, Bryant, and Hillhouse. The editor stated explicitly that Percival, Bryant, and the modern poets should not be treated encomiastically. With regard to these, he charged Bancroft thus:

> All may profit by wholesome advice. It seems to me that you might touch upon the differences of every kind, between the old & new schools of British poetry, indicating the superiority of the former & exhorting our poetical aspirants to look to it rather than servilely imitate the Scotts and Byrons.[4]

Bancroft fairly well followed Walsh's suggestion. He reviewed James Gates Percival's *Clio* in an essay entitled "Early American Poetry" in the December 1827 number of *American Quarterly Review*. His attitude toward the poet was, in his own words, "comparatively a cold one."[5] He did not recommend that American poets follow writers of the "old school," in so many words; but the fact that he was indifferent to the current crop of poets showed where his sympathies lay.

Walsh himself wrote a personal expression of the inferior quality of American poetry in "American Poetry" in the September, 1829, *American Quarterly Review*. He reviewed Samuel Kettell's *Specimens of American Poetry, with Critical and Biographical Notices,* which was planned to record every American poet from the beginning who had written "with credit." Walsh derided the author's naïveté for trying to include every commonplace scribbler. He was especially displeased with the nationalistic prejudice that clouded Kettell's judgment. For example, he cited as erroneous Kettell's ranking John Pierpont as superior to Pope in the "essentials" of poetry, ranking John G. C. Brainard with Burns, ranking James Hillhouse with such religious poets as H. H. Milman, placing Timothy Dwight above the average British poet, and equating Mrs. Sigourney with Mrs. Hemans in merit.[6] Because of personal criticism that he had long suffered at the hands of John Neal, Walsh, it can be guessed, had a special reason to express irritation for Kettell's having been "deeply smitten" with, to use Walsh's epithets, "the ranting, lawless, madbrained muse of John Neal, of Maine." With an obvious relish, Walsh put the lash to Neal: "We shall postpone the perusal of his verse, as long as we can command a volume of Pope, or even of Scott. He is understood to allow his imagination and pen to run riot together, and then the workings of the muse resemble the plungings of a kite broken loose amid the clouds of a strong gale."[7] However, not wishing to incur the charge that he was hostile to all American poets, Walsh wrote:

> Let it not be concluded that we undervalue or would decry the faculties and the productions of such poets as Percival, Bryant, Hillhouse, Sands, Paulding, Willis, Eckard, and a few others who have had real "visitations of the muse," and in whom we can recognise more or less vigor of genius, nicety of taste, and excellence of culture. We only deprecate and resist the attempt to exalt them to the height of the British classics, whom they themselves have never pretended to emulate.[8]

Walsh rejected the position of Kettell that American literature had been retarded by a dependence upon British literature and maintained that for some time Americans must look to English authors as models.[9]

Provocative statements about the poverty of American poetry and the need to look to the eighteenth century might not have created much controversy or earned Walsh the wrath of the New York writers if he had not encouraged Dr. James McHenry, a Philadelphia poet and critic, to write stringent criticism of current American poets who were being puffed in New York. The conductor and his critic wholly agreed on matters of literary opinion, but McHenry was the more acrimonious. In the March 1832 number of the *American Quarterly Review* he wrote an essay entitled "American Lake Poetry." It was destined to incite a major literary war that was to go on for about three years. The principals openly involved were Walsh, his son Robert Moylan, and McHenry in Philadelphia. Theodore Sedgwick Fay, George Morris, Charles King, Lewis and Willis Gaylord Clark carried the battle in New York. Behind the scenes were William Cullen Bryant, Robert Sands, William Leggett, Gulian Verplanck and other New Yorkers, plus a few lesser known Eastern journalists. The battleground was mainly Walsh's *National Gazette and Literary Register* and *American Quarterly Review,* Charles King's *New-York American,* Colonel William L. Stone's *New-York Advertiser,* William Cullen Bryant and William Leggett's *New-York Evening Post,* Willis Gaylord Clark's Philadelphia *United States Gazette* and Lewis Gaylord Clark's New York

Knickerbocker, and George P. Morris and Theodore Fay's *New-York Mirror.* Other journals were involved, but most editorial shots were fired in these.

Dr. McHenry's inflammatory review is a very good example of the tomahawk criticism which was prevalent in the age. In vituperative language he damned William Cullen Bryant's *Poems,* and Nathaniel P. Willis' *Poems delivered before the Society of United Brethren, at Brown University, on the day preceding Commencement, September 6th 1831.* The central theme of the condemnatory critique was that Bryant and Willis, especially the latter, were guilty of borrowing the worst excesses of the British Lake Poets. They should, declared the reviewer, be stigmatized as bad examples for other American poets. "We will," McHenry said, "hold up their works as beacons by which future pilgrims, on the path to poetical fame, may be warned to avoid the snares into which they have fallen, too deeply, we fear, ever to rise again, and become disentangled from their error."[10] The critic claimed that the two poets had been seduced to follow the British Lake School by specious thinkers, whom he designated "newspaper critics," "literary petitmaitres," "good-natured editors," "parlour loungers," "idlers in society," "affected sentimentalists," "injudicious patriots," "hireling-puffers," and "easy-conscienced critics."[11]

While ridiculing the poem, the main poem in Willis' volume, that Willis had read before the Society of United Brethren at Brown University, McHenry questioned whether the Society could not have found a better poet in New England. "By the bye, we fear not," he answered; and then he categorically discredited all New England poets: "Poetry is not the pursuit in which the truly enlightened inhabitants of that section of our country seem to excel . . . . Theirs is the land of practical sound sense, industry, enterprise, acuteness, and persevering research, rather than a keen feeling, or glowing and active imagination. If our brethren east of the Hudson are not content with this praise, we cannot help it. Justice will not permit us to accord to them, in addition, that of poetic excellence."[12] Having dispatched with a single savage stroke New England poets, whom he equated with the British Lake School, the Doctor dissected Willis' poems piecemeal, attacking primarily the faulty diction and obscure imagery in them.[13] After condemning "The Dying Alchymist," "The Leper," and "Parrhasius," McHenry closed his consideration of Willis' volume, declaring that it was the most unpleasant that he had ever read and that the author's mind had carried him beyond the bounds of common sense.

Turning to Bryant's volume, he found the same faults in it as in Willis', but to a less "Fanatical extent." It was said to be prosaic but to have the redeeming feature of lucidity, which was more, the critic felt, than could be said for the poetry of Shelley, Keats, Willis, and Percival. The dull aspect of Bryant's poetry struck the critic unfavorably, as he explained: "Page after page may be perused, if the reader has sufficient patience, with dull placidity, or rather perfect unconcern, so that the book shall be laid aside without any single passage having been impressed on the mind as worthy of recollection. A vague remembrance may be left of many passages abounding in good sense, and correct in their moral tendency; but on the whole, rather common-place, and encumbered with verbosity."[14] This statement was to become a major point of dispute by Bryant's defenders who understood McHenry to mean that Bryant had never written a line worth remembering. Many would have forgiven McHenry's harsh treatment of Willis but never his thinking of Bryant as a common scribbler and his proscribing both the poetry and criticism in the East.

Response to the "American Lake Poetry" article was immediate and positive. It was to incite the New York writers to editorial combat even more quickly than Poe's *Norman Leslie* review a few years later. Charles King, the editor of the *New-York American,* on March 10, 1832, rushed to Bryant's defense: "Our big brother is here so ruthless and indiscriminate in his slaughter of bardlings, such a remorseless Herod in his murder of innocents, that it makes our flesh creep to mark the operations of his tomahawk. And indeed, we feel like flinging the weapon back upon his invisible sconce, when he buries it in the head whose laurels should have protected it from the blow. Mr. Bryant, one of the American poets whom we are willing to recognize as such, is treated as a negative, while Mr. Willis at least has the satisfaction of being cut up at his own table."[15] The editor challenged the contention that Bryant's poetry was prosaic, quaint, sentimental, and sluggish. He further questioned the logic that Bryant's poetry was not good because it had not drawn attention in Philadelphia. Countering with his own sectional authority, the *New-York American* editor cited the *New England Quarterly*'s high opinion of Bryant's poems.[16] In his Philadelphia *United States Gazette,* Willis Gaylord Clark, one of Walsh's most vociferous enemies, joined King, opining that "The New York American has taken hold of the article in the latest number of the American Quarterly, and handles its author without gloves. We have rarely seen a critic more cleverly criticised. We believe that, in general, readers will hold faith with the New York writer. The reviewer seemed very much inclined to serve the American poets as Major Noah wished to dispose of the State of Delaware."[17] On the afternoon of the same day that Willis Gaylord Clark approved the opinions expressed in the *New-York American,* Walsh printed a blistering reply to both newspapers:

> Of readers in our country, there are many who have improved sound judgement and natural taste by extensive acquaintance with the truly great poetry and prose of our language: and of that description there are few who would not concur with the Reviewer, concerning the productions of Mr. Willis. It is also, we believe the impression of most of them that Mr. Bryant has been overrated. The Reviewer refers to his *volume,* and pronounces on its general merit and effect. Some of Mr. Bryant's effusions are, doubtless, excellent; but others— perhaps the greater part of the volume, are trite and not above mediocrity. The panegyric which has been lavished, in New York and Boston upon his genius and performances, would be too strong for any other living bard, and might be deemed commensurate with the highest possible deserts. Exaggeration reacts.[18]

In his defense of McHenry, Walsh added to McHenry's charges by attacking Willis' prose and observing that even the *New-York American's* editor admitted that one would be hard pressed to defend Willis.

On March 14, Charles King replied to Walsh's rejoinder. He asserted that Walsh had misquoted him and misrepresented his views by linking his sympathy for Bryant with sympathy for Willis and Shelley. "Upon the whole," said King, "while we agree with the reviewer in the propriety of drawing a line—and a very broad one—between literary pretension and real merit, we think he erred egregiously in placing Bryant on the side which he did."[19] On March 17, Walsh admitted in his editorial column that he had erred in reading the *New-York American,* as had been charged, but he maintained his initial opinion of Bryant and Willis. Colonel William Leete Stone's New York *Commercial Advertiser,* mainly a mercantile paper, sided with Walsh against King, though its feelings were probably not dictated by literary convictions. A writer in the *Commercial Advertiser* humorously declared that "We are afraid this valuable periodical [the *American Quarterly Review*] will be obliged to surcease. A recent scathing which it administered the namby-pamby poets, had well nigh 'done it up,' by bringing against it such a nest of stingless hornets as were never seen before. All the 'witlings and brisk fools// Who buzz in rhyme, and, like blind flies,// Ever with their wings for want of eyes,' seized their grey goose quills, and tilted away at the reviewer, like another crazy Knight Errant against a wind mill."[20]

The *New-York Mirror,* a weekly literary journal, whose pages were reserved primarily for New York and Eastern writers, was drawn into the controversy on March 17, 1832. One of the editors—either George Pope Morris or Theodore Sedgwick Fay, for Nathaniel P. Willis, the third partner in the editorship, was abroad at the time—noted in the editorial column that the *Mirror* had received a communication censuring the author of the "American Lake Poetry" article. Explaining that he did not want to make the *Mirror* an arena for an angry and intemperate quarrel, the editor said he refused to insert the letter. He maintained that silence was the best policy in such circumstances. Obviously the writer, probably Morris, had no desire to remain neutral, for he thoroughly lectured the Philadelphians:

> The writings, both of Mr. Bryant and Mr. Willis, can take care of themselves. The former gentleman, who is attacked in the Quarterly with a virulence savouring something of political malice, is present, and can take the measure of his antagonist whenever he pleases. Mr. Willis, who most likely is getting paid off now, for having in former times laid the lash on the shoulders of the critic, is luckily (or unluckily, we scarcely know which) absent. His compositions speak for themselves. The article on the Lake school of poetry could never have been written by the enlightened editor of the Quarterly, whom we respect sincerely: and the only wonder is how it found its way into that excellent journal. We are told the critic is a disappointed brother poet. We believe it. He has that air, and writes as if smarting under some keenly unpleasant recollection which urges him on till his censure curdles into a rankling hate.[21]

Willis' fellow editors never seemed too eager to come to his defense. As late as 1835 when he was still being attacked in the newspapers, Lewis Gaylord Clark wrote to Henry W. Longfellow: "Some of the newspapers—Nat. Intell., Eve. Post, Courier, &c. are using up Willis (N. P.) most tremendously, the latter especially. They treat of his breaches of confidence, want of honor,—his unAmerican bias, and his flippancies, and affectations. Morris shrinks from his defence, and says he is not responsible for what Willis does or says, don't alter, &c."[22]

The *Mirror* became more deeply involved in the controversy on March 24, 1832, when it admitted to its pages a lampoon and a letter, signed "H," traducing McHenry for his role as a poet and critic. The correspondent lashed him particularly for having damned categorically all New England poets. The letter and the lampoon were inserted with an ironic apology by the editors: "It is not our custom to admit articles like the following, but as the writer *insists* upon it, we suppose there is no appeal. We make it a point to treat old subscribers very respectfully. This is from a number of communications which have come to our hand on the same subject."[23] It is quite likely that "H" was George S. Hilliard, one of the Cambridge literati who later defended Longfellow in the *Mirror* against charges made by Poe.

The letter, poem, and editorial comment piqued Walsh exceedingly. He wrote in his editorial column on March 29 that he had seen the remarks in the *Mirror* that related to the "American Lake Poetry" critique. Walsh said that he had always regarded the *Mirror* with respect and friendship until he found that it was "infested with rhapsodies of Mr. Willis." He expressed indignation that his reviewer had been the subject of a lampoon, insisting that literary controversy should not be made personal. Observing that the editor of the *Mirror* himself expressed some doubt about the propriety of introducing the lampoon, he expounded to him what his editorial duties were:

> Truly respectful treatment consists in preventing an old or new subscriber from doing what is wrong and disgraceful; and the first law is self-respect—the first duty of editors is to the public and their journal. That *mirror* which is specially designed for the use of the refined and gentle sex, should be without flaw or stain. It should reflect no false images; no distortions, no grimaces; no caricatures—nothing meretricious or sardonic; but only the expression of sound and benignant sentiment and the "hues and colors" of chaste and elegant diction.[24]

The editor of the *Mirror* did not reply to Walsh's remonstrance in his next number, that of March 31, 1832, probably because it came to his attention after he had gone to press. He, however, continued in his present number to assail the article on "American Lake Poetry" by saying that it had been generally condemned by "intelligent people." Further, he charged that the *American Quarterly* had applauded the virulence of the *Edinburgh Review* in its severe attacks upon the British poets. He closed his discussion by attributing the malignity of McHenry's article to sectional prejudice and cited as examples of fair reviews of Willis and Bryant those that had appeared in the *North American Review* and the *Southern Review*.[25] By the following week the *Mirror*'s editor had fully absorbed Walsh's lengthy article of March 29. He replied in length on April 7, 1832. Protesting his reluctance to engage in literary warfare, he explained that he had to reply to the article which Walsh had written in the *National Gazette* of March 29, as well as to articles of a similar nature which had appeared in the Philadelphia *United States Gazette* and other papers. He defended himself first of all for inserting the lampoon on McHenry. He reminded Walsh that it was Walsh himself who had sanctioned ridicule as a proper device for literary chastisement. Admitting the possibility of error for permitting the lampoon to be inserted, the editor said that two wrongs did not make a right and that the editor of the *National Gazette* could not have been more surprised at the doggerel on McHenry than the editors of the *Mirror* were at the nature of the reply of the editor of the *National Gazette*.[26]

Having dispatched the faults of McHenry as a critic, the editor of the *Mirror,* with irony, paid Walsh the following compliment: "But if we have gone too far in respect to the reviewer, we must acknowledge the moderation and courteous bearing throughout, of the editor of the National Gazette. He has conducted himself with a propriety which confirms our previous sentiments of respect. We acquiesce in the full force of the gentle and beautiful rebuke with which he takes leave of his subject."[27] But the editor had yet a few more words before he was done with Walsh and McHenry. He encouraged them at length to employ a benign and instructive criticism.[28] The editor had no more to say about Walsh or McHenry until June 16, 1832, when he favorably reviewed the whole of the latest issue of the *American Quarterly*. Noting that all of the articles had been written with "spirit, candour, and ability," he said that this evidenced that the author of the "American Lake Poetry" article, which had "disgraced" the *American Quarterly*, had no part in writing any articles in the present number.[29] With this note the *Mirror* lapsed into silence on the controversy for a while.

Dr. McHenry was to feel the sting of three Eastern journals, most likely for having felled all New England poets with one stroke. *The New-England Monthly Magazine* repaid him with a review of his works. The author of the essay entitled "Irish-American Literature" flayed without stint his fiction, poems, and plays. Typical of the reviewer's sentiments are his closing lines on the Philadelphia "Aristarchus": "He has been endeavouring to obtain notoriety for some years, by the most indecent exposures. Such is his taste, and he has an undoubted right to enjoy it. If he should construe our well-meant intentions unfavorably, we can only say, that we have much mistaken his character; for we have always believed that nothing gave him so much pleasure as to see one of the minnows of Helicon impaled alive on the barbed hook of criticism."[30] Professor Sidney Willard's *American Monthly Review* handled McHenry quite as badly in a review in its May 1832 number. Again, resentment of McHenry's proscription of all New England poets was the underlying cause.[31]

The Baltimore *Gazette* entered the altercation with an article on March 16, 1832, in which the author said that the essay in the *American Quarterly* negated Walsh's pretensions at decency in which he prided himself. The writer charged that Walsh had a history of using a harsh style such as was employed in the "American Lake Poetry" critique. Citing as an example an article on Lady Morgan's *France* that had appeared earlier in the *American Quarterly*, the writer said the harshness was unforgivable because the author was a lady. But quite as bad, he went on, was McHenry's article, which was unjust, ungenerous, and violent because it was written at a time when Willis was abroad and unable to defend himself.[32] Walsh professed surprise that the writer in the Baltimore paper would assume such an "unsensible" attitude. He then defended himself and the articles in the *American Quarterly*. He assured his detractor that the decencies and charities of life are not violated by the use of satire in literary productions. As was always the case, he had authorities and precedents at hand: "The great satirists, such as Dryden, Boileau, Pope, Gifford, the author of the Pursuits of Literature [Thomas Mathias], the Reverend Sydney Smith, have received—what they fully merited—the applause and thanks of the republic of letters. Some of the writers who were most severely handled in the Dunciad, possessed more talents and had produced better things, than Mr. Willis."[33] Walsh dismissed his critic's claim that he had been unduly severe on Lady Morgan, saying that she forfeited her right to be treated as a lady by disregarding feminine decencies in her book. He swept aside the charge that Willis had been unfairly treated for having been criticized when he was out of the country by explaining that Willis was ever at home in his verse and, moreover, that the poet's poems were simply reviewed in the first number of the *American Quarterly* after they were published, with no thought to the whereabouts of the poet.[34]

The most significant things in Walsh's reply to the writer in the Baltimore *Gazette* was his confession that he concurred fully with the article on "American Lake Poetry," that it had been written at his encouragement, and that he had encouraged the author to undertake a similar work "upon the school of prize tale writers, lackadaisical and horromanical."[35] The fact that Walsh was directly responsible for the offensive article was overlooked by most of Dr. McHenry's critics, but, as will be seen, William Cullen Bryant was aware that Walsh was responsible for the origin of the article. Walsh, however, was not without a newspaper supporter in Baltimore. The Baltimore *American* wrote that the article in the *American Quarterly* had drawn out the "overzealous champions of the Lakists."[36]

A new champion of American poets arose when the *Knickerbocker; or New-York Monthly Magazine* was founded in January 1833. It immediately began to praise and defend the poets of New York and New England and to take the war to the Philadelphians. In its life it was edited respectively by distinguished literary men: Charles Fenno Hoffman (1833), Samuel Daly Langtree (1833), Timothy Flint (1833–1834), and Lewis Gaylord Clark (1834–1860), who was assisted by his brother, Willis Gaylord (1834–1841). Willis Gaylord

Clark, who resided in Philadelphia while he assisted his brother, labored as editor of the Philadelphia *United States Gazette*. Boasting some of America's most popular and successful New York authors of the time as contributors (e.g., Irving, Cooper, Bryant, Halleck, Sands, Willis, Paulding, and Verplanck),[37] the *Knickerbocker* had an obvious economic interest in spreading a panoply over its area writers. Walsh and McHenry learned long before Poe did that an outside critic attacked a New York writer only with trepidation. In a laudatory review of Bryant's *Poems* in the October 1833 number, a *Knickerbocker* critic said: "We would love to examine the crania, (and we have furnished such in our country,) of those *writers, critics! poets!* who could find in their hearts to vilify, belittle, or damn with faint praise William Cullen Bryant."[38] After Lewis and Willis Gaylord Clark, more pugnacious writers than most, assumed charge of the *Knickerbocker*, the war between the literati of New York and Philadelphia became more vigorous.

The *Knickerbocker* might not have been drawn so quickly into open hostility with the *American Quarterly* except that in the June 1834 number McHenry, with his editor's blessing, wrote to his "American Lake Poetry" a sequel entitled "The Decline of Poetry." He reviewed respectively five volumes of poetry, all written in 1833, by Charles C. Pise, Solyman Brown, Willis Gaylord Clark, M. J. Chapman, and Charles O. Apperly. The central opinion of the review was that American poetry had not only declined but collapsed. Or, to put the plight of American poetry in McHenry's own words: "Of the good, we have had none at all; and of the bad, so little, that, had it not been for the occasional performances of a few adventurous Lakers, the lash of poetic criticism might have entirely forgotten its occupation."[39] As it turned out, McHenry's greatest mistake was his severe treatment of Willis Gaylord Clark, because Willis had at his disposal the *Knickerbocker* and the local Philadelphia *United States Gazette* as instruments of defense—and, to Walsh's and McHenry's regret, he made full use of them. In "The Spirit of Life," the main poem in Clark's volume, the critic found nothing praiseworthy. "This poem," wrote McHenry, "is throughout in the genuine Lake Style. It is as dreamy, misty, confused, quaint, and, in many parts, as incomprehensible as anything that ever came from the cogitations of N. P. Willis himself; nay, we question whether Shelley ever produced anything more intellectually impalpable."[40]

Willis Gaylord Clark read Dr. McHenry's critique, fumed, and vowed revenge, as one of his later letters showed. He vented his wrath in the July 1834 number of the *Knickerbocker* in an essay entitled "American Poets, and their Critics." The attack was a personal assault upon McHenry in which his failures as a novelist, poet, dramatist, and finally as a critic were traced in detail. Clark, in the course of lambasting McHenry, treated Walsh sarcastically, asserting: "The American Quarterly has struggled through the hands of different publishers, until the present time. The conductor of the work, very properly, has always refrained from laying any claim to consideration in the matter of poetry. It has never interested his mind, nor occupied his attention; he professes to experience none of its soul; and while the other departments of his periodical are sustained with a very laudable degree of talent, that of poetical criticism has been usually consigned to a person so utterly unfit for that office as to excite surprise and derision wherever his agency in this division of the Review is known."[41] In the same number of the *Knickerbocker,* however, the latest issue of the *American Quarterly* was well reviewed except for the "Decline of American Poetry," which was said to have been written by Dr. McHenry—"a person qualified, by his own melancholy experience, to speak both of the Decline and Fall of Poetry."[42]

Willis Gaylord Clark's pique at McHenry's article was expressed privately in a long letter that he wrote to his friend Morton McMichael a short time after he (Clark) had answered McHenry in the *Knickerbocker*: "I can stand reasonable criticism, from a sensible American, even if it be adverse, . . . but to be sweepingly lampooned, by an old Lamp whose every effort has been damned beyond redemption, is really 'beyond my continent.' "[43] From an undated letter that Willis Gaylord Clark had written earlier to McMichael, it can be surmised that Clark had at an earlier time reviewed some of McHenry's works unfavorably. He asked McMichael to send him a copy of McHenry's play *The Usurper* since it would be needed in the "anatomical process" upon which he was about to begin.[44] Possibly this "anatomical process" was the essay "American Poets, and their Critics," much of which dealt with *The Usurper*. From the letter it is quite clear that McMichael himself had been in the habit of "riding over" Dr. McHenry.

In the August 1834 number of the *Knickerbocker,* Lewis Gaylord Clark heaped more fuel upon the fire of controversy by exulting over the "invariable praise" given to Willis Gaylord's "American Poets, and their Critics." He marveled that it was possible for such a universally condemned critic as McHenry to gain admission to the *American Quarterly*. With regard to McHenry's "Decline of Poetry," Clark said that "all the journals of authority" had expressed their disdain and censure.[45] One of the journals that he had in mind was the *New-York Mirror*. This journal, which had remained silent on McHenry since it condemned his first article in the *American Quarterly,* inserted the whole of Willis Gaylord Clark's essay in its number of July 19, 1834, with unqualified praise. As he had done earlier, the editor, George Pope Morris, sanctimoniously condemned severe criticism. "But there are," he said, "cases of stupidity in a writer, which we cannot overlook without tacitly compromising our own understanding; and there are instances of half-witted, conceited foreigners' denouncing, in the capacity of critics, all that belongs to American literature, which we have no patience to think of, and no disposition to spare."[46] Charles King's *New-York American* complimented the *Knickerbocker* for justly and humorously exposing McHenry as a "literary charlatan."[47] Lewis Gaylord Clark wrote many years after the whole affair that the public journals fully approved Willis Gaylord's article and that the *Knickerbocker* "literarily and literally" killed McHenry "very dead."[48] This was an overstatement.

The *Knickerbocker* article triggered Walsh to action. He wrote on August 1834 in his editorial column: "We mean to give place soon to the communication entitled *The American Quarterly Review and the Poetasters.* It is our intention to look into the number of the *Knickerbocker* to which the author of the article directs our intention [*sic*]. The Magazine has been so paltry that we have deemed it unworthy of notice, and could not apprehend any injury to the critic of the American Quarterly Review from any detraction in such a quarter."[49] Walsh, for some reason, did not place the communication that he had received in the *National Gazette,* nor did he pay attention right away to making an answer to Willis Clark's "American Poets, and their Critics." A reply to the article might never have been made if the New York writers had permitted matters to rest, but they did not. Either Bryant or, more probably, William Leggett, his associate editor, attacked Walsh and his contributors in an acrid editorial in the *New-York Evening Post* on January 29, 1835. Amidst a tirade lamenting that the *American Quarterly Review* had survived so long, the editor characterized the conductor and his writers in unequivocal language:

Mr. Walsh is one of the most arrogant, malignant, and pedantic writers in this or any other country. His mind is sluggish and indiscriminative, his style lumbering and awkward, his temper crabbed and morose. His learning consists in a huge and useless collection of musty commonplaces, to introduce which into his articles, instead of enlivening them with sallies of original wit, or just views and apposite reflections seems to be his chief object of solicitude. His principal

contributors seem chosen for their congeniality of taste, temper and erudition.
Thus, Dr. McHenry, his familiar, is scarcely behind Walsh himself in malignity
and want of true mental discrimination, and is not much his superior in point of
style.[50]

It is a good surmise that this invective caused Walsh to recall in the
March 1835 number of the *American Quarterly Review* his position on
criticizing American writers and to answer Willis Gaylord Clark's
"American Poets, and their Critics." Walsh denied the allegations of
the New York writers that he had been hostile to American writers
and thus failed to encourage a national literature. While admitting that
the *American Quarterly's* criticism had at times been severe, he
avowed that in producing a national literature there was less danger
in severity than in excessive tenderness.[51]

The *Knickerbocker* persisted in derogating the poetry criticism in
the *American Quarterly* and baiting its conductor. After Walsh and his
son, Robert Moylan, bought the complete business interest of the
American Quarterly in 1835, Lewis Gaylord Clark wished their new
business venture well but patronizingly added that "for however numerous or egregious may have been the sins of taste and spirit hitherto
exhibited in the work, we feel confident that certain lessons have been
acquired by the offenders, which will make their errors less frequent
hereafter."[52] Lewis was not to let Walsh off too lightly for venturing
to answer Willis Gaylord's article. He was particularly offended that
Walsh claimed to have supported American writers whenever he could
possibly do so. As proof to the contrary, Clark recalled as evidence
the strictures that McHenry had written on American poets, many
of whom were widely acclaimed abroad. He instanced Bryant specifically. He further declared that Walsh, who had at first agreed with
McHenry, shifted positions himself after he had found that Bryant
had been praised everywhere abroad—shifted positions in fact to the
point that he publicly declared that Bryant's poems were "excellent."[53]

Robert Moylan Walsh, the junior editor of the *American Quarterly*
since January of 1835, in an editorial communication entitled "The
Reasons of Criticism" in the *National Gazette,* rushed to the defense
of his father and the *American Quarterly*. He challenged the allega-
tion of the *Knickerbocker* that "many" American poets had been
praised abroad, but admitted, however, that Bryant's poetry had been
well received. Robert Moylan also contested his adversary's charge
that Robert Walsh had been inconsistent. Robert Moylan said that
his father had always held a single opinion of the poet and that was
the one well stated in a review of *Kettell's Specimens of American*

Poetry in the *American Quarterly* back in 1829.[54] To the *Knicker-bocker*'s charge that "native writers of merit" had been badly treated in the *American Quarterly,* Robert Moylan cited about twenty indigenous writers who had been praised in the magazine's pages.[55] Robert Walsh, who thought his son's answer more than sufficient payment for the invidious remarks made in the *Knickerbocker,* said of his son's reply: "He had supererogated, we think, as the magazine is trashy in general, though emblazoned in some of the newspapers. We presume that but few persons of adult age and intellect read it, or more of it than may happen to be quoted in those newspapers."[56]

Robert Moylan Walsh's essay stirred a correspondent (who signed himself "W") to Jesper Harding's Philadelphia *Inquirer* to answer on April 16, 1835, in an essay captioned "A Rejoinder." The "Rejoinder" was essentially a repetition, though put at greater length, of the *Knickerbocker*'s charges that the *American Quarterly* had been hostile to all American poets. Again the case of McHenry's having called Bryant's poetry prosaic and negative in quality was cited as proof of the hostility. The writer concurred with the justness of the *Knickerbocker*'s cause in defending American poets. Robert Moylan Walsh immediately issued a reply in the *National Gazette.* The principal points in his answer were denials of certain "incontestable" facts related in the "Rejoinder," viz., that the *American Quarterly* had vilified American poets and that Bryant's poetry possessed not a line worthy of remembrance. In addition to these denials, Robert Moylan accused the *Inquirer*'s critic of garbling statements made in several *American Quarterly* articles over a period of years so as to pervert the truth.[57] Robert Walsh expressed pleasure with his son's rebuttal, declaring that the junior editor had again "supererogated." Walsh ended: "As to the admirers of the Knickerbocker and the effusions of the *soi-disant* poets, which he derides, we leave them unenvied to the enjoyment of their taste. When Diogenes was told that his townsmen had condemned him to live out of Sinope, he answered— 'And I condemn them to live in Sinope.' "[58]

Walsh's statement might have been his last in the controversy, but his son still had much to say. In the morning issue of the *Inquirer* on April 20, 1835, both the editor of the *Inquirer* and "W," who had written the "Rejoinder," reasserted the earlier charges that Bryant had been unfairly treated in the *American Quarterly.* They then rested their case. Robert Moylan took the statements of the two as a retreat in the argument, and in the afternoon issue of the *National Gazette* of the same day exulted that he had routed the enemy: "It requires a good many sonorous words under certain circumstances, to express a simple thing—witness two articles in the Pennsylvania Inquirer of this morning, one of some thirty lines from the editor, and another fifteen or twenty from 'W.,' the whole amount of which might have been said in a single short phrase: 'W.' having nothing more to say, thinks it better to withdraw.' A wise and commendable resolution."[59] It is possible that "W," the correspondent in the *Inquirer*, was none other than Willis Gaylord Clark himself, for on May 9, 1835, Lewis Gaylord Clark wrote to Henry W. Longfellow: "The touch at the Am. Q in the April no. drew out Walsh and his son in three or four long articles in the Nat. Gaz. Willis met them finely, and proved everything, with a skill *before* the former number on McHenry, even."[60]

Though Robert Moylan Walsh thought that he had caused the Philadelphia apologists for Bryant to withdraw from the contest, the matter was not permitted to rest. On April 22, 1835, a lengthy extract from Walsh's "American Poets" that originally appeared in the September 1829 number of the *American Quarterly Review* was inserted in the *National Gazette*. No editorial comment accompanied the article, but it was probably a reminder of Walsh's continued lukewarm attitude toward American poets. More calculated to give the *Knickerbocker* writers no respite, however, was in the same number of the *National Gazette* a long article copied from the New York *Mercantile Advertiser* in which the *Knickerbocker* was reproved for its illiberal and unjust attacks upon Walsh. "There is a coarseness," said the *Advertiser*'s writer, "in the language, of which the editor of the Washington Globe himself might be ashamed, and is so little in keeping with the usual tone of the *Knickerbocker,* that we are prone to suspect there must have been 'some time or other' a collision between its author and Mr. Walsh's high standard of criticism."[61] The political affinity between the *Advertiser* writer and Walsh is here evident. Francis P. Blair, who edited the Washington *Globe* (a Jackson organ), was a political adversary who frequently attacked Walsh in the most virulent language. But that the *Advertiser*'s antipathy for the *Knickerbocker* was based on more than political differences is indicated by its writer's spirited encouragement to Walsh to continue his present course of criticism:

It is too obvious from the unworthy temper of the Knickerbocker that the crying sin of the American Quarterly is the austerity of the Review toward the common scribblers of the day, now dubbed native writers of merit—as if the circumstances of nativity should excuse the presumption of ignorance. What will be the state of American literature when *nativity* and not *scholarship* is the standard whereby an author is to be adjudged "a writer of merit." We cannot sympathise with the *Knickerbocker* in its complaints against the American Quarterly—but on the contrary, we must be excused for unqualified approbation of the course of Mr. Walsh—and again conjure him to lash all poetasters and scribblers of fiction who shall presume to come before the public in a careless and ungrammatical dress.[62]

The *Knickerbocker* editors did not retreat. In the May 1835 number they introduced a series of three articles entitled "American Literature" in which American writers were exhorted to write genuine American literature. In the course of his appeal, the author of the articles criticized "certain" American periodical publications for their failure to encourage native productions and was pleased that most of them were passing away.[63] In the same number a more blatant attack was made upon Walsh personally and the *American Quarterly* specifically when one of the bellicose brothers Clark, at the expense of all other American literary reviews, extolled the *North American Review* as being "eminently in the van of American periodical works." The writer clearly had Walsh and the *American Quarterly* in mind, for he quoted a statement that Walsh had made in the *National Gazette* on April 10, 1835, "that a survey of our periodical literature of every kind, is needed on many accounts." The author declared that it was only in the *North American Review* that such a survey should be made. The writer blasted the *American Quarterly* and its editor thus:

It is impossible that a dull man should make a just or spirited periodical. When we meet a self-erected but unrecognized dictator; one arrogant and oracular, without one true claim to the deference of literary men; one strikingly deficient in both fancy and judgment,—who, confined intellectually to a narrow round, treads that round with a pompous stride and stiffness that would become the Colossus of Rhodes,—one whose style, lumbering, bloated, and inexpressive, is the very model of what correct English should *not* be,—one, in short, whose only merit is a mass of undigested reading, displayed with more ostentation than judgment, and quoted with more labour than elegance,—when, we say, we meet with such a man at the head of a periodical . . . imbuing it, not merely with a concentrated and irresistible drowsiness, but with a settled, deep, and malignant hostility against every thing produced by *young* Americans,—we cannot but hope, most ardently, that the Boston Review, acting as a counterpoise, will continue to give its regular and just surveys of our rising literature.[64]

Walsh, who was ailing at the time, made no editorial reply to the *Knickerbocker*. A writer for the *New York Evening Star,* however, noticed that the *Knickerbocker* had continued its hostility against the *American Quarterly Review*. He did not care for the *Knickerbocker*'s hostile methods, but he was not too sympathetic to Walsh: "Though we cannot refuse our sympathy to the American Quarterly Review for its misfortune in lying under such maledictions, we are unable to deny that it has itself provoked them. It can therefore expect no vindication; and since its editor has violated scripture and sense by throwing his pearls in a prohibited direction, he cannot reasonably be surprised at meeting from the recipients of such unprofitable favors the customary and characteristic return."[65]

While the war between the *American Quarterly Review* and the New York journalists raged in the open, the whole affair was much a part, quite naturally, of their private conversations. Bryant revealed his state of mind on the stormy reception of his volume of poems in Philadelphia in a letter to his friend and fellow poet R. H. Dana on April 9, 1832: "The review in the 'American Quarterly' was written, it is said, by Dr. McHenry, author of 'The Pleasures of Friendship, and Other Poems': but Walsh has said, in his paper, that it was written at his particular request, and adopted by him as soon as he saw the manuscript. It is supposed, also, that it received some touches and additions from his pen. Walsh has a feeling of ill nature toward me, and doubtless [was] glad of an occasion to gratify it, but I believe that, as you say, the article will do me no harm."[66] Unquestionably Walsh had an ill feeling for Bryant, because Bryant and the *Evening Post* were political supporters of General Andrew Jackson, whom Walsh bitterly opposed after he was elected to the Presidency. Often the recriminations in political matters between the editors of the *Evening Post* and the *National Gazette* were bitter.[67] Nevertheless, it was upon philosophies of literary theory and taste that the two men disagreed quite as much as upon politics. As early as November 7, 1821, Walsh condemned a modest review of Bryant's poetry in the *North American Review* as an "inordinate panegyric,"[68] and thereafter he never mentioned Bryant very favorably in the *National Gazette*.

In the summer of 1827, when Dana sent his "The Buccaneers" to Bryant for ciriticism, Bryant passed a generous opinion on the work and anticipated that it would be respectfully received, but he reminded his friend that "there are yet a great many who count the syllables on their fingers—*e.g.,* Mr. Walsh and all that class of men."[69] When Dana published his volume of poems in November 1827, Walsh praised his talents, sensibility, and poetic style; but he was careful to admonish the poet to an "unremitted devotion to models of the old school of verse" if he wished to be successful.[70] Bryant would hardly have been surprised at Walsh's advice to Dana, but he must have been surprised when Dana's poems were praised in a review in the March 1828 number of the *American Quarterly Review*. George Ticknor, the author of this review, found no faults with the poet's work.

At the insistence of Jared Sparks, the editor of the *North American*

Review, Bryant reviewed Dana's volume for the January 1828 number of the *North American Review.* Bryant wrote a good, but reserved, review of his friend's poems. Walsh read the critique and offered the opinion that they were "too broadly and strongly eulogized."[71] Bryant read Walsh's comment and offered another opinion on Walsh as a critic: "Mr. Walsh, to be sure, says that your poems are 'too broadly and strongly eulogized,' but Mr. Walsh's opinion on poetry is not worth anything, and although it yet passes for more than it is worth, its real value is beginning to be better understood, than formerly. Mr. Walsh is the greatest literary quack of our country, and deserves to be taken down a peg or two. It would do him good, for the creature really has some talent; and, if he would be content to drudge in a plain way, might be useful."[72] Though uncertain, it was probably Bryant's review of Dana's poetry that Gulian C. Verplanck, Bryant's close friend and then New York congressman in Washington, had in mind in a letter to Bryant on January 9, 1828: "I am sorry to tell you that, although from 'The North American Review' we have learned the merits of your work, yet as Mr. Walsh thinks the praise given by the eastern critic too high, we are altogether at a loss to decide on your literary rank, not a single copy of your *coup d'essai* having reached us."[73]

Bryant and his New York friends lost no opportunities to condemn Walsh's critical pronouncements and poke fun at his editorial errors. Henry William Herbert—the New York poet, novelist, and magazinist—wrote an "Ode for the Eighth of January" to celebrate General Jackson's election triumph. Gulian C. Verplanck read and praised the poem. On January 17, Walsh published it and commented that Verplanck's eulogy on the work was "far too lofty."[74] Several weeks later Bryant related to Verplanck that Herbert was pleased with his poem's fine reception until he heard that Walsh had said that it was too highly eulogized and that Charles King had called it prosaic. Bryant said, however, that a couple of recent articles in the *New-York Enquirer* had done justice to Walsh and his "Jack Rugby" and had once again restored the "usual serenity to the features" to Mr. Herbert.[75] Another time, Bryant related, with some pleasure, to his friend Verplanck how Walsh had copied from the *Evening Post* an "Ode to Miss Wright" and had even praised it, assigning the authorship to the poet Halleck. Bryant gloated that he himself had written and inserted the poem as a prank.[76] Such private jokes at Walsh's expense were commonplace among the New York literati.

The animosity the New York writers bore Walsh led them to stigmatize him as a hack who was hired by Carey & Lea, the Philadelphia publishers of his *American Quarterly Review,* to puff their books. When a "Northern" writer openly accused Walsh of puffing Cooper's novels simply because they were published by Carey & Lea, Walsh vindicated himself by commenting that Cooper had never been made the object of a review in his quarterly.[77] On another occasion, William Cullen Bryant's *New-York Evening Post* accused Walsh of unworthy mercenary motives for accepting articles on controversial issues, such as slavery and bank questions, so that they could be published separately by the publisher for profit. In a kinder language than was called for, Walsh satisfactorily answered the charges.[78] The hypocrisy of the New York writers, themselves notorious for puffing each other's works, was monumental. At the very time, for example, when William Cullen Bryant, Robert Sands, and Gulian Verplanck were making elaborate plans to promote their *The Talisman,* a giftbook begun in 1827 in New York in competition with the Philadelphia *Atlantic Souvenir,* Robert Sands—anticipating a cool reception by Walsh—wrote to Verplanck: "We shall embrace every opportunity of having him described . . . as he truly is, a hack of Mr. Carey hired to puff only his own bookseller's publications, including his own magazine."[79]

Failing health throughout 1835 and early 1836 forced Robert Walsh to curtail his literary activities. He relinquished the editorship of the *American Quarterly Review* on January 1, 1836; on the following July 1, he turned over the editorship of the *National Gazette and Literary Register* to his publisher and old friend William Fry. On the same day he sailed for France, never to return to America. Robert Moylan Walsh blamed journalistic calumniators for contributing to the deterioration of his father's health.[80] Though the Philadelphia leader had quitted the scene of battle for health's sake, the New York literati found little reason to rejoice, because he had left a young admirer in the person of Edgar Allan Poe who, as much as he, hated their puffery, cliquishness, and chauvinism and who was quite as unafraid to carry the battle to them in the pages of public journals.[81] In the *Southern Literary Messenger* of December 1835 just as Walsh was retiring, Poe opened his campaign against the New Yorkers with his blistering, and now-famous, review of Theodore Sedgwick Fay's *Norman Leslie.*[82] Poe's opening shot was but one in a war that long been prosecuted by Walsh against the New York literary establishment.

NOTES

1. The most comprehensive treatment of Poe's editorial encounters with the

New York literati is Sidney P. Moss' *Poe's Literary Battles: The Critic in Context of his Literary Milieu* (Durham, 1963).

2. James Kirke Paulding, *John Bull in America; or, the New Munchausen* (New York, 1825), p. 165.

3. See my "The Relationship of Robert Walsh, Jr., to the *Port Folio* and the Dennie Circle: 1803–1812," *The Pennsylvania Magazine of History and Biography*, XCII (1968), 195–219.

4. Letter, Robert Walsh, Jr., to George Bancroft, Sept. 23, 1827, George Bancroft Papers, The Massachusetts Historical Society.

5. "Early American Poetry," *American Quarterly Review,* II, 485. Walsh's *American Quarterly Review* will be cited as *AQR* hereafter in the notes of this article.

6. "American Poetry," *AQR,* VI (1829), 255. William Snelling declares in his *Truth; New Year's Gift for Scribblers* (1831) that Walsh criticized Kettell's work severely because Kettell did not include him in his anthology. William Snelling, *Truth; A New Year's Gift for Scribblers* (Boston, 1831), pp. 48–50. Not too much importance should be attached to Snelling's opinion. His satire condemned almost every American poet of the time, and he in turn was condemned. Walsh published a few poems in the *National Gazette and Literary Register* from time to time, but he made no serious pretense at being a poet. *National Gazette and Literary Register* cited as *NGLR* hereafter.

7. "American Poetry," *AQR,* VI (1829), 255–256.

8. *Ibid.,* 261.

9. *Ibid.,* 262.

10. "American Lake Poetry," *AQR,* XI (1832), 155.

11. *Ibid.,* 155–156.

12. *Ibid.,* 158–159.

13. Several years later either Walsh or his son, Robert Moylan, severely criticized Willis and this same poem in *NGLR,* Feb. 6, 1836, p. 2, col. 2.

14. *Ibid.,* 173.

15. *The New-York American,* March 10, 1832, p. 2, col. 2.

16. *Ibid.*

17. Copied in the *NGLR,* March 13, 1832, p. 4, col. 1.

18. *NGLR,* March 13, 1832, p. 4, col. 1.

19. *The New-York American,* March 14, 1832, p. 2, col. 4.

20. Copied in the *NGLR,* April 17, 1832, p. 1, col. 3.

21. *The New-York Mirror,* X (March 17, 1832), 295.

22. Letter, May 9, 1835, in *The Letters of Willis Gaylord Clark and Lewis Gaylord Clark,* ed. Leslie W. Dunlap (New York, 1940), p. 89.

23. *The New-York Mirror,* IX (March 24, 1832), 303.

24. *NGLR,* March 29, 1832, p. 1, cols. 1–2.

25. *The New-York Mirror,* IX (March 31, 1832), 311.

26. *The New-York Mirror,* IX (April 7, 1832), 318–319.

27. *Ibid.,* 319.

28. *Ibid.*

29. *The New-York Mirror,* IX (June 16, 1832), 397.

30. "Irish-American Literature," *The New-England Monthly Magazine,* II (1832), 498–499.

31. "Note to the Review of Bryant's Poems in No. IV," *The American Monthly Review,* I (May 1832), 430. A writer in the *Boston Literary Magazine* said that he was sorry to name the article in the *AQR* as the single one

that did not acknowledge Bryant's great merit. He was pleased that the critic had got what he deserved— "the censure of every wise and sensible man." "Bryant's Poems," *The Boston Literary Magazine,* I (1832), 147–148.

32. *NGLR,* March 20, 1832, p. 2, cols. 3–4. "Lady Morgan's France in 1829–30" appeared in the *AQR,* IX (1831), 1–33. It was written by Walsh.

33. *Ibid.*

34. *Ibid.*

35. *Ibid.*

36. *NGLR,* Feb. 29, 1832, p. 1, col. 4.

37. Frank Luther Mott, *A History of American Magazines: 1741–1850* (New York, 1930), p. 608.

38. *The Knickerbocker, or New-York Monthly Magazine,* III (1833), 319.

39. "The Decline of Poetry," *AQR,* XV (1834), 449.

40. *Ibid.,* 467.

41. "American Poets, and their Critics," *The Knickerbocker, or New-York Monthly Magazine,* IV (1834), 13.

42. "Literary Notices," *The Knickerbocker, or New-York Monthly Magazine,* IV (1834), 77.

43. *The Letters of Willis Gaylord Clark and Lewis Gaylord Clark,* ed. Leslie W. Dunlap (New York, 1940), p. 63.

44. *Ibid.,* p. 64. Willis Gaylord Clark solicited the aid of his Philadelphia friends in publicizing the ineptness of Dr. McHenry. To John J. Smith and Adam Waldie, publishers of *Waldie's Select Circulating Library,* he wrote: "Have you received the Knickerbocker? I hope you have; and I hope too, that you will be good enough to suggest to the public that it is a fair sketch. . . . I hope you will take notice of the Critic's inconsistencies, for the benefit of the cause." *Ibid.,* p. 70.

45. "Editor's Table," *The Knickerbocker, or New-York Monthly Magazine,* IV (1834), 160.

46. "Literary Criticism," *The New-York Mirror,* XII (July 19, 1834), 14.

47. "Editor's Table," *The Knickerbocker, or New-York Monthly Magazine,* LIII (1859), 424.

48. *Ibid.,* 423. Robert E. Blanc, McHenry's biographer, says that Willis Gaylord Clark's "American Poets, and their Critics" was full of lies and misrepresentations. Robert E. Blanc, *James McHenry (1785–1845): Playwright and Novelist* (Philadelphia, 1939), pp. 98–99.

49. *NGLR,* Aug. 2, 1834, p. 2, col. 4.

50. *The New-York Evening Post,* Jan. 29, 1835, p. 2, col. 2.

51. "Rombert: A Tale of Carolina," *AQR,* XXXIII, N. S. (1835), 232–233.

52. "Editor's Table," *The Knickerbocker, or New-York Monthly Magazine,* V (1835), 355.

53. *Ibid.,* 356.

54. *NGLR,* April 10, 1835, p. 1, cols. 4–5.

55. *Ibid.,* col. 5.

56. *Ibid.,* p. 2, col. 2.

57. *NGLR,* April 18, 1835, p. 2, cols. 1–3.

58. *Ibid.,* col. 3.

59. *NGLR,* April 20, 1835, p. 2, col. 2.

60. Dunlap, ed., *The Letters of Willis Gaylord Clark,* p. 89.

61. Copied in the *NGLR,* April 22, 1835, p. 1, cols. 3–4.

62. *Ibid.,* col. 5.

63. "American Literature," *The Knickerbocker, or New-York Monthly Magazine,* V (1835), 383–384.

64. "Editor's Table," *The Knickerbocker, or New-York Monthly Magazine,* V (1835), 464.
65. Copied in the *NGLR,* May 15, 1835, p. 2, col. 3.
66. Letter in Parke Godwin, *A Biography of William Cullen Bryant with Extracts from His Private Correspondence* (New York, 1883), I, 275.
67. The following editorial note by Walsh is fairly characteristic of his exchanges with the *New-York Evening Post:*
    "The New York Evening Post styles the National Gazette a 'bitter opposition paper.' All truth is bitter to those against whom it operates. The part which we take in opposition is pursued with bitter chagrin at the necessity which a sense of duty to the country has produced. We have been as well disposed, personally, toward General Jackson, as to any other public man; we would as cheerfully promote the interest and gratify the wishes of some or many of his coadjutors and of his advocates, as those of any of his political adversaries. We should be not less devoted to his 'person and government' than the Evening Post, if we consulted alone our private or personal advantage in any respect; but there are public obligations which we cannot infringe nor overlook." *NGLR,* March 10, 1832, p. 1, col. 1.
68. *NGLR,* Nov. 7, 1821, p. 1, col. 2.
69. Godwin, *Biography of William Cullen Bryant,* I, 233.
70. *NGLR,* Nov. 29, 1827, p. 2, col. 1.
71. *NGLR,* Jan. 8, 1828, p. 2, col. 4.
72. Godwin, *Biography of William Cullen Bryant,* I, 235.
73. *Ibid.,* 243–244.
74. *NGLR,* Jan. 17, 1828, p. 1, col. 2.
75. Godwin, *Biography of William Cullen Bryant,* I, 243–244.
76. *Ibid.,* 239. Bryant heard Frances Wright, the free-thinker and reformer, in her first lecture in New York in 1829. He thought that she was a sensationalist who had nothing new in her philosophy. In the *Evening Post* of Jan. 17, 1829, he inserted his "Ode to Miss Frances Wright." In this poem he poked fun at Col. William L. Stone (a friend of Walsh) of the *Commercial Advertiser.* See Charles I. Glicksberg, "William Cullen Bryant," *American Literature,* VI (1935), 427–432. Walsh did not agree with Miss Wright's philosophy, but he deplored the abuse that the New York papers were heaping upon her. See *NGLR,* Jan. 15, 1829, p. 2, col. 2; also Jan. 31, 1829, p. 2, col. 5.
77. *NGLR,* March 3, 1832, p. 1, col. 1.
78. *NGLR,* Oct. 1, 1833, p. 1, col. 2.
79. Letter, Robert Sands to Gulian C. Verplanck, Dec. 23, 1827, Miscellaneous Papers, New-York Historical Society.
80. *NGLR,* Feb. 23, 1836, p. 1, col. 1.
81. Shortly after Walsh left the country in 1836, Poe wrote a highly favorable review of his *Didactics.* He praised Walsh as a scholar, writer, and critic. Edgar A. Poe, "Walsh's 'Didactics,' " in *The Works of Edgar Allan Poe,* eds. Edmund Clarence Stedman and George Woodberry (New York, 1914), VII, 146.
82. Sidney P. Moss calls the *Norman Leslie* Review the "first shot" in Poe's campaign against the New York clique. Moss, *Poe's Literary Battles,* p. 38.

Tennessee Technological University

KENNETH BALL

AMERICAN NATIONALISM AND ESTHETICS IN JOEL BARLOW'S UNPUBLISHED "DIARY—1788"

After Joel Barlow arrived in France at Le Havre-de-Grâce in the summer of 1788, he recorded various observations in his "Diary" about his introduction to European society. His comments range from incidental remarks on travel to perceptive analyses of the current political developments in London and Paris on the eve of the French Revolution. This paper concentrates on only one aspect of the unpublished "Diary," and although some general information may be found in the biographies, no similar examination has been previously accorded to it. Barlow's remarks are significant because of his reputation as one of the group of poets called the Connecticut Wits and because he had just come to national prominence with the publication of a long epic, *The Vision of Columbus* (1787). The "Diary" of 1788 also provides insight into the American provincialism and patriotism of the late eighteenth century. Upon his arrival Barlow contrasts the public works and churches at Le Havre, at Rouen, and London with the American scene. The Congregational churches of New England, even ancient ones such as North Church at Boston, could form but a poor comparison to the antiquity and magnificence of Notre Dame at Paris or St. Paul's in London. Barlow's impression of massive stonework is not confined to the cathedrals but is also shown in his astonishment at the man-made seaports or the stone walls of the cities such as Le Havre. By constantly comparing his American experiences with his new ones in Europe, Barlow becomes aware of the inferior cultural development of the United States; but throughout the whole of the "Diary" of 1788, there is a strong sense of Yankee pride in American

49

accomplishments. While this fundamental optimism is the key to Barlow's cultural orientation, he does not disguise his admiration for European church architecture or for the gardens he sees in Paris and London. At the same time, he criticizes the English gardens as being wasteful expenditures on luxury. With typical irreverence he also comments humorously on the dirtiness of the cathedrals and with national pride rejoices at seeing the paintings of the American artist, Benjamin West, in Windsor Castle. In the same vein, Barlow is never slow to point up advantages such as the superiority of America's natural harbors over the artificial ones of Europe.

In each of these instances as in others, the pattern of cultural ideas in Barlow's "Diary" converges on a point of American nationalism and practicality, sometimes to the point of disparaging the European society. His nationalism derives in part from his own participation in the American Revolution as chaplain and is reflected in his patriotic poem, *The Vision of Columbus*. Because of this ebullient patriotism, the magnificence of the European scene represented to him the old political order, decayed and crumbling in its social significance and soon to give way, he thought, to the more perfect and actively progressive American spirit. As Barlow arrived in France, he was prepared to move into the circle of liberals who were contemplating the first steps of revolution in Europe. Jefferson and Lafayette in Paris, and Paine and Priestley in London were soon to become his friends and associates. They were interested in freeing the Old World from feudalism and in constructing a new social order with its foundation in the broad base of the people. In the context of the "Diary," Barlow views the art, architecture, and gardens of Europe with a skeptical political eye, but with an appreciative esthetic one.

The cathedrals of Europe, with their long importance to the intellectual history, have affected American thinkers differently at different times. To Barlow they seemed less objects of reverence than they did material objects to be measured with a Yankee's practical eye, or on a different level they seemed symbols of feudalism and despotic church-state alliances. Instances of this separation of American and European social traditions around 1800 are evident in Barlow's "Diary." The isolated and primitive condition of the nation as described by Henry Adams in his *History of the United States of America* is illustrative of the importance of society in conditioning the attitudes of the Americans. Barlow's "Diary" succinctly summarizes the attitudes of the New World toward the Old: "On approaching the shore at Havre I was presented with the first clear view of the old world. The first thing that strikes an american Eye is a certain air of antiquity which renders every object venerable. Not a tree upon the coast but what seems to have furnished colonies from its branches; as they are generally trimmed & taught to grow in a particular manner, to answer some purpose of the owner."[1] This brilliant sentence tells in itself the attitude of the colonies toward the European owners who thought they existed to be shaped and trimmed for the benefit of the mother countries.

In another instance, Barlow observes the town of Le Havre, saying it is "enveloped with high walls, which in the days of ancient fortification were necessary against invasion, and are now necessary against smuggling." By extension he says that the walls represent the separation of the people and the kings: "This is generally the case thro' Europe; wars of conquest are turned into wars of revenue, & the contests between sovereign princes or states, are now contests between the prince & his people."[2] In this manner the first European city he sees gives him the impression that the Old World is culturally as well as politically much different from America. At Le Havre he notes that a wall a mile long is being built to hold back the tide, and that "all the public works in the United States taken together, aside from what we call *buildings,* I am positive would not equal those of the small town of Havre de Grace."[3] The significance of this simple contrast in the "Diary" can be seen in light of a modern critic's concept of American culture in Barlow's day: "As Americans stood poised in 1800 for the great western expansion, they were still rural-minded, racially homogeneous, economically differentiated, regionally oriented, unprepared for the onslaught of technology. They lived in a clear architectural tradition of neat domestic buildings in which a city was only a larger village."[4]

In a more immediate, eyewitness account, Barlow's "Diary" reveals the point of view of the American villager who is accustomed to simplicity, cleanliness, and frugality. The churches give an impression foreign to his experience: "The church at *Notre Dame* is in the gothic style & very ancient. It is certainly much larger than any works of the kind in America & crouded with saints & angels; but it is kept so dirty that it would require an uncommon weight of devotion to bring a well drest man upon his knees in it."[5] Barlow's wit is characteristic, but his use of the term "Gothic" in the passage above is especially interesting in a reference to the general understanding of church architecture at this time. Its meaning is clarified by one authority: "During the eighteenth century, in the course of a slow process of development, a more positive view of the Gothic style was reached, and, with it, the concept of what was Gothic changed . . . . The Gothic style was said to possess a picturesque quality, a quality of infinity, a vegetal quality, a romantic quality. All these different concepts were first formulated in the eighteenth century and then were considered more closely in the nineteenth and systematically bound into one unified concept. Some of these concepts were also applicable to sculpture and painting, and the concept of what was Gothic was widened to include, not only architecture, but also the fine arts."[6]

Barlow's own recognition of the great difference between the meaning of the American and the European architecture is indicated by his comments on the cathedral at Rouen: "Nothing gives me more pleasure in these old places than the contemplation of their Gothic cathedrals. The style of building is so totally unlike what can be seen or ever will be seen in America that it is impossible to form the least idea of it but by the eye. This church struck me with such an air of solemnity & magnificence, & being so much larger than any I had before seen, that I should have taken the dimensions of every part, were it not that I expected to see those that were larger & more worthy of notice at Paris & London."[7] It is perhaps worthy of notice, in assessing his attitude as he first came upon the European scene, that he was neither inclined to worship in these great churches nor to revile them as emblems of religion. The thing which occurs to him is to measure them, as Jefferson or Franklin would have done. As the narrative continues, Barlow shows that while he may respond to the esthetics of the architecture of the churches, he does not respond spiritually. When he is told that the bell which he is taken to see is the largest in Europe, he is skeptical. After being told that the bell weighed 40,000 pounds, he writes, "it only induced me to take its dimensions that I might calculate its weight at my liesure. It is ten feet deep, fourty four feet in circumference, the shell eleven inches thick, the tongue is said to weigh 4200 pounds—"[8]

With a Yankee's inquisitive, practical attitude toward the world, there is little wonder that Barlow does not pause to make metaphysical speculations about the spiritual world to which the bell summoned people. He seems at this stage of his acquaintance with the Old-World architecture to have had little sympathy for its meaning. As a modern writer on architecture has said, "to understand the meaning of a Gothic church, one must understand both the meaning of religion and, more specifically, the meaning of Christian religion during the age of Gothic architecture . . . ."[9] The concept may have escaped Barlow because, as an American of the Congregational and Deistic eighteenth century, he is not prepared to accept the church hierarchy. In the language of Paul Frankl, both social and ecclesiastical distinctions are indicated by the spatial arrangements of the Gothic cathedrals: "This idea embraces both the eternal, that is the timeless and placeless, existence and omnipotence of God, and his temporary and earthly existence in Man and the works of Man. The building of churches on earth as the seat for religious services is, at the same time, always a symbol of the transcendent kingdom of God. Church architecture may mark the contrast between pope and emperor or between monks and laymen . . . but these functional divisions always reflect the differences between certain social strata, or at least strata of responsibility within the *Civitas Dei,* which remains an immutable idea to which any division is subordinate."[10]

A lack of comments upon the spiritual hierarchy as symbolized by the Gothic cathedrals may argue for Barlow's opposition to the Church, but it does not argue that he is esthetically insensitive. Part of his description of the beauty of Rouen is representative of his life-long attachment to France:

> The hill on the N.W. of the town 2 miles from the centre presents a agreeable prospect of the town[.] I spent some time on it in the morning; but when I come to proceed toward Paris in the after noon & rise the hill on the east it was with greatest reluctance I quitted it, for I never yet in any country have seen so charming a prospect. The hill is at least 400 feet in height & you have the whole town under your feet, Beautiful waters of the Sciene for about 6 miles in a meandering direction court the eye by concealing half their charms in the poplar groves that play upon their banks. thousands of acres of rich meadows are covered part with grain, part with verdure & part with bleaching calicoes & linnens; while the surrounding hills at unequal distances seem loath to terminate the scene. On a point of land a little below the town is the place where William the conqueror embarked when he sailed for England.[11]

In Barlow's description of the natural beauty of the countryside, he has generalized rather than given minute detail. He has given perspectives which contrast the town and the river, and he closes upon a suitably ancient historic spot to evoke the atmosphere of the past and to add to the nostalgic memory of his recent view.

The Gothic style of architecture, however, had made an enduring impression upon Barlow. Within a few weeks after his arrival in France he traveled to England. On one of his sightseeing jaunts, he says the Tower of London is about the size of Fort Putnam in America, but he adds that "it is a curious monument of Gothic Architecture, of which we form no idea in America, & of which you meet thousands in Europe. I should be glad to see them preserved to the End of the world—meerly for their style."[12] One other example of Barlow's favorable reaction to the architecture of Europe will illustrate his familiarity with current esthetics. The following passage from the "Diary" is the most extensive and most appreciative he makes on any church. In observing St. Paul's Cathedral in London, Barlow avoids his usual practical attitude and elaborates upon his feelings:

> I have been taking a through [sic] view of St. Pauls. This Cathedral is built, as far as I know, in a style peculiar to itself. It is not Gothic, nor ancient nor modern. It is vastly more magnificent than *Notre Dame* at Paris or any other building I have seen. Indeed the character of Notre dame and of all other Gothic Cathedrals is *solemnity*; the character of this is pure *sublimity*. To attain this end it is built with admirable contrivance. None of its beauties strike the beholder at first view. It is so proportioned as to decieve the eye of an inattentive observer in every direction. In passing the streets you would not think it so high as several other churches, because the prodigious size of every part makes it appear much nearer than it is. Neither does the full size at first appear because the height prevents you contemplating the distance. But when you come near and contemplate it step by step, it swells into the skies to an astonishing height, & covers a proportionate quantity of ground. It is like a distant mountain seen in company with nearer hills, where you have nothing to distinguish distances but the colour thro' the atmosphere. Modern churches aim at the sublime, but they never attain it. They strut like a young soldier, & show their full height and magnitude by the slenderness of the spire. The true and the false sublime are not more distinguishable in the writings of Milton and Blackmore, than in the style of St. Pauls & common churches.[13]

With this comment on the "sublimity" of St. Paul's (and Barlow uses the term correctly to indicate astonishment as the proper reaction to "immensity")[14] one comes again to the point that the church architecture is the most striking symbol of the difference between American and European culture. In addition, Barlow distinguishes the style of St. Paul's from the Gothic style of Notre Dame in Paris. His comment is accurate and reflects his neoclassical taste, for Christopher Wren's design of St. Paul's is a blend of the Gothic and Roman.[15] In Barlow's contrastive metaphor, the New England churches are strutting pretenders to beauty, but one should not assume that he approves the social and religious hierarchy which the European church symbolizes. The idea of the hierarchy as a politically immoral force in the church is sufficiently evident in Barlow's *Advice to the Privileged Orders* to prevent any such question. Yet the beauty of Gothic architecture is a theme in Barlow's "Diary" which emphasizes the cultural inadequacies of America in comparison to Europe. Barlow is not the only early American writer who thinks that the architectural styles are the most important difference in the two scenes. As James Fenimore Cooper says, "There is one feature of European scenery, generally, more prevalent, however, in Catholic than other countries, to which we must allude before we close. The bourg, or town, with its gray castellated outlines, and possibly with walls of the middle ages, is, almost invariably, clustered around the high pointed roofs and solemn towers of the church. With us, how different is the effect! Half a dozen ill-shaped and yet pretending cupolas, and other ambitious objects, half the time in painted wood, just peer above the village while the most aspiring roof is almost invariably that of the tavern."[16] Cooper's statement corroborates Barlow's observations remarkably well.

At the same time, Barlow's fervor for things American can cause him to stare with great interest at the paintings of Benjamin West and hardly glimpse those of Rubens and other masters hanging nearby, so strong is his desire to find the praiseworthy achievements of America. Perfectly illustrating the pride of the new American nation is the incident of Barlow's visit to Windsor Castle. He notes that the rooms of the King and Queen "are richly ornamented with paintings, the works of Raphael, Rubens, & a great variety of other masters. The presence room is devoted to those of Mr. West."[17] Barlow had previously known of West's paintings as well as those of Copley and others and had praised West in *The Vision of Columbus*:

> See, West with glowing life the canvass warms;
> His soverign hand creates impassioned forms,
> Spurns the cold critic rules, to sieze the heart,
> And boldly bursts the former bounds of Art.
> No more her powers to ancient scenes confined,
> He opes her liberal aid to all mankind;
> She calls to life each patriot, chief or sage,
> Garb'd in the dress and drapery of his age;[18]

As a point of national pride, the importance of West's art is evident in Barlow's poetry and in the list he makes of West's paintings in notes to *The Columbiad* where he gives the locations and titles of two hundred and ninety-nine of West's paintings. Barlow comments on the influence and quality of West's art by saying that "his early works in London, *The Death of Wolfe, The Battles of the Boyne, Lahogue,* &c. engraved by Woolett and others, not only established his reputation, but produced a revolution in the Art. So that modern dress has now become as familiar in fictitious as in real life; it being considered essential in painting modern history."[19] In judging the quality of West's work, Barlow refers to the opinions of his contemporaries and compares West to Raphael: "The critics find fault with the coloring of Mr. West. But in his works, as in those of Raphael, we do not look for coloring. It is dignity of character, fine expression, delicate design, correct drawing and beautiful disposition of drapery which fix the suffrage of the real judge. All which qualities can only spring from an elevated mind."[20] In *The Columbiad* Barlow also praised the American artists Copley, Trumbull, Taylor, Stuart, and Brown; in them he saw evidence for an important and growing national art.

Barlow's comments about West in his "Diary" and in *The Columbiad* have additional cultural interest. The terms of his criticism are those which are appropriate to the "grand style" of art, meaning the Roman School. Sir Joshua Reynolds explains the terms in *Discourses on Art,* particularly in "Discourse IV" in 1771. Barlow has used most of the terms which are explained by Reynolds. Of the five criteria, "Invention," "Composition," "Expression," "Colouring," and "Drapery," the last is the most relevant because of the controversial manner in which it was portrayed by West in *The Death of Wolfe.* Reynolds in "Discourse IV" argues that in the grand style, particularities should be subordinated to the general concept of reality, so that "perfect form is produced by leaving out particularities" and "in the same manner as the historical Painter never enters into the detail of colours, so neither does he debase his conceptions with minute attention to the discriminations of Drapery."[21] In rebelling against this use of drapery West painted historical costumes in detail.

A modern historian of art says that West's *Death of Wolfe* is important in "marking the turning-point from the old style of history painting to the new," breaking with the European tradition by painting the figures in contemporary costume.[22] To account for this innovation, another critic stresses the importance of West's Philadelphia background as part of a growing nationalism in art: "In the earlier stage, they had tended to patronize native artists only when foreigners were not available; now they wanted to startle the London connoisseurs by making an American painter as skillful as any Englishman."[23]

The story of the reception of *The Death of Wolfe* again stresses the idea of the change which was occurring in art because of West's influence: "John Galt made up a story that was accepted and spread far and wide by William Dunlap. This is the story: When Sir Joshua inspected the canvas he was shocked to find that West had painted the British soldiers in their actual uniforms. But after West explained that Quebec was located in a region unknown to Greeks and Romans and that the battle was fought at a time when warriors did not wear the costume of antiquity, Reynolds surrendered with these words: 'West has conquered. He has treated the subject as it ought to be treated. I retract my objections. I foresee that this picture will not only become one of the most popular, but will occasion a revolution in art.' "[24] The anecdote speaks for the spirit of the age. When Barlow came to choose the subjects for the famous engravings for his *Columbiad,* however, he preferred the old style of classical robes, pedestals, and columns in his format.

Like his topics of art and architecture in the "Diary," Barlow's comments on European gardens indicate his direct republican attitude toward esthetics. He contemplates the church architecture neither as symbolic of the heavenly city nor emblematic of a garden of Eden. In the words of one critic, "the interpretation of a church as a symbol of the garden is a rare one, although some scholars see an allusion to paradise in the foliage on the capitals of Reims, and in the framework of tree-trunks which appeared in church architecture after 1490."[25] The whole idea is out of keeping with Barlow's American background and is significant in pointing up that contrast. In America at that time there was some formal gardening, representing order, rationality, and the desire to emulate Europe.[26] Barlow's own preference for the English gardens, as shown in his "Diary," is neither metaphysical nor formalistic but according to his neoclassical taste has literary associations. After visiting Pope's garden at Twickenham he says: "the whole is in the truest English style of gardening, rather more solemn & gloomy than what is common, but perfectly harmonizing with the turn of mind that most distinguished the Planter. The trees are all said to be planted by Mr. Popes own hand; &, what is much to the credit of Sir Weldbare Ellis the present owner & His father in law Mr. Stanhope the late owner, not a single tree has been violated nor a new one added since the death of Pope. The garden is perfectly well kept, clean & neat, & everything remains precisely as the Poet left it, excepting that the Statues obelisks & urns have grown rusty by time & the trees have grown larger."[27] Barlow's feeling for Pope's garden is an extension of Pope's influence on his poetry, as is evident in his remarks in the "Diary": "Not all the gloomy gothic temples, palaces, groves, alcoves & hollow sounding arches that I have entered in Europe, designed to impress the beholder with the most substantial reverence have forced themselves upon me with such silent veneration & respect as I felt upon entering the simple gardens of Pope. Perhaps the idea of the Planter might help to make the impression, but to my Eye there is as much real taste discovered here as in any of his writings."[28]

Barlow saw other gardens, formal, botanical and landscape, and there are two additional ideas to be gained here in our viewpoint through the "Diary." In one instance he comments about the royal gardens at Hampton, where he compares the artificial stream to the natural beauty of the Thames outside the palace: "Here is a vast expense of water works to make an artificial river within forty rods of the thames, which is of it self ten times more majestic & beautiful, & cannot but shame the poverty of art when she attempts to bring his works into so close a comparison with nature."[29] He sees nature as superior to Art, a thought more romantic than neoclassic. The other point is apparent in the "Diary" as Barlow objects to the size and expense of the gardens, seeing them as representing the aristocracy which owned them and lavished money on them, money that might have been better spent in social reform. Evidence of the revolutionists' general as well as specific objection to the gardens of the aristocrats is expressed by Henri Gregoire, one of Barlow's political friends, who wrote that France had offered some bad examples of morality in setting up "licentious statues" in the palace gardens.[30]

Barlow's preference for the gardens of Pope has one final implication. Although Pope's garden was becoming dilapidated when Barlow wrote about it in his "Diary," Pope had begun the change of taste away from the formal, geometrical designs to those more imitative of nature. In this latest trend, mineralogical gardens were made with walls ornamented with pebbles and shells and were diversified with canals and grottoes. Pope's grotto at Twickenham was his special pride, and his influence led in a rebellion against the old style of formal gardens.[31] A critic who disapproves this change says: "It now became the fashion to rave about nature, and to condemn the straight forward work of the formal school as so much brutal sacrilege. Pope and Addison led the way, with about as much love of nature as the elegant Abbe Delilly some three generations later."[32] Another critic argues that gardens do not deserve more appreciation as they increasingly imitate nature because questions of art and nature are judged differently. A third writer brings the charge more directly against Pope's grotto: "It would hardly lay claim to being 'natural,' for nothing more fantastical can be imagined, although in Pope's own lines to his grotto, he invites the stranger thus:—'approach! Great Nature studiously behold.' "[33] The influence of Pope's garden is expressed in a more relevant manner by Horace Walpole in 1786, however, as he refers to Kent, the first of the great landscape gardenists of the natural school: "But just as the encomiums are that I have bestowed on Kent's discoveries, he was neither without assistance or faults. Mr. Pope undoubtedly contributed to form his taste. The design of the prince of

Wales's garden at Carltonhouse was evidently borrowed from the poet's at Twickenham."[34] Speaking further of Kent's style he says: "He had followed nature, and imitated her so happily, that he began to think all her works were equally proper for imitation. In Kensington-garden he planted dead trees, to give a greater air of truth to the scene—but he was soon laughed out of this excess. His ruling principle was that nature *abhors a strait line*."[35] In accordance with similar esthetic principles Barlow objected to excesses in gardens such as Hampton because he thought art could not excel nature and because of his republican attitudes toward gardening. His expressions of approval of West's painting and Pope's garden are enlightening passages from his "Diary" which provide insight into eighteenth-century esthetics and politics. They lead from American nationalism to the French Revolution.

NOTES

1. Joel Barlow, "Diary—1788," Harvard Ms. The manuscript is dated but is without pagination and is hereafter cited simply as "Diary—1788." The "Diary" is approximately 16,250 words in length and has forty-one entries covering a period of time from May 29, 1788, to October 11, 1788. The best biography is James L. Woodress, *A Yankee's Odyssey* (Philadelphia, 1958). I am grateful to the Houghton Library for their assistance.
2. "Diary—1788."
3. *Ibid.*
4. John Burchard and Albert Bush-Brown, *The Architecture of America: A Social and Cultural History* (Boston, 1961), p. 71. See also Russel B. Nye, *The Cultural Life of the New Nation 1776–1830* (New York, 1960), pp. 268–294.
5. "Diary—1788."
6. Paul Frankl, *Gothic Architecture* (Baltimore, 1962), pp. 218–219.
7. "Diary—1788."
8. *Ibid.*
9. Frankl, p. 226.
10. Frankl, p. 231.
11. "Diary—1788."
12. *Ibid.*
13. *Ibid.*
14. John Steegman, *The Rule of Taste from George I to George IV* (London, 1936), pp. 60–62.
15. Hugh S. Morrison, *Early American Architecture* (New York, 1952), pp. 280–283.
16. James F. Cooper, "American and European Scenery Compared," in *The Home Book of the Picturesque: Or American Scenery, Art, and Literature* (1852) with an introduction by Motley F. Deakin (Gainesville, Fla., 196.'), p. 69.
17. "Diary—1788."
18. Barlow, *The Vision of Columbus* (Hartford, Conn., 1787), Book VII, p. 209.

19. Barlow, *The Columbiad* (Philadelphia, 1807), pp. 430–463, note 45.
20. *Ibid.*, p. 436, note 45.
21. Sir Joshua Reynolds, *Discourses on Art*, ed. Robert R. Wark (San Marino, Cal., 1959), pp. 57–62.
22. Ellis K. Waterhouse, *Painting in Britain 1530–1790* (Baltimore, 1953), p. 201.
23. James T. Flexner, *American Painting: First Flowers of Our Wilderness* (Boston, 1947), p. 193.
24. Oskar F. L. Hagen, *The Birth of the American Tradition in Art* (New York, 1940), p. 113. See also John Galt, *The Life, Studies, and Works of Benjamin West,* II (London, 1820), 46–51.
25. Frankl, p. 236.
26. Ulysses P. Hedrick, *A History of Horticulture in America to 1860* (New York, 1950), p. 167. One such American garden is described in a letter received by Manasseh Cutler who was a business associate of Barlow's in 1787.
27. "Diary—1788."
28. *Ibid.*
29. *Ibid.*
30. Henri Gregoire, *Critical Observations on the Poem of Mr. Joel Barlow, 'The Columbiad'* (Washington, D.C., 1809), pp. 12–13.
31. Rose S. Nichols, *English Pleasure Gardens* (New York, 1902), pp. 254–256.
32. Reginald Blomfield and F. Inigo Thomas, *The Formal Garden in England* (London, 1892), p. 81.
33. Alicia A. Rockley, *A History of Gardening in England* (London, 1896), p. 247.
34. Horace Walpole, *Anecdotes of Painting in England to which is added The History of the Modern Taste in Gardening,* IV (London, 1786), 294–295.
35. Walpole, IV, 298.

University of Kentucky

LINDA WELSHIMER WAGNER

SPRING AND ALL: THE UNITY OF DESIGN

In 1921, William Carlos Williams included a prose piece, "The De-
licacies," among the poems of *Sour Grapes*. The study alternates between descriptions of the food at a dinner and of the people eating it—
"The hostess, in pink satin and blonde hair" is set against "the great
silent bald head of her little-eyed husband!"[1] Then Williams describes
the herring salad: "delicately flavoured saltiness in scallops of lettuce
leaves." Some of the food demands as much exuberance as the pretty
women ("Salz-roles, exquisite!"), although there is no question but
that the poet's title relates as much to the woman with hair "like some
filmy haystack" as to the "masterly caviare sandwich."

Williams' inclusion of this prose in a book of poems set the key for
his writing practices in the next decade. Between 1921 and 1934,
Williams was to publish no poetry. The seven books and several shorter selections published in magazines are all either prose or mixtures of
poetry and prose, extending the techniques he had introduced in the
1920 *Kora in Hell: Improvisations. Spring and All,* the collage of
prose commentary, typographical jokes, and untitled poems, appeared
in 1923, as did Williams' attempt at a stream-of-consciousness novel,
The Great American Novel (Joyce's *Ulysses* had been published in
1922). In 1925 appeared the twenty essays of *In the American Grain,*
Williams' great testimony to the efficacy of organic form in prose as
well as in poetry. In 1927 and 1928 he published mixed selections in
the two volumes of *American Caravan,* prose and poetry coupled and
titled as one piece of writing. Worksheets show that he was also writing
as prose the poems which later appeared in "The Descent of Winter"

61

(1927). In 1928 Williams published *A Voyage to Pagany,* his first novel; and in 1929, his translation from the French of Philippe Soupault's *Last Nights of Paris.* Not until 1934 were the poems of the period published as *Collected Poems, 1921–31,* following the 1932 *A Novelette and Other Prose* and Williams' first short stories, *The Knife of the Times.*

Surely this is a decade of prose for Williams. Yet the question remains, why? *Kora in Hell* had not received so much attention that Williams felt compelled to continue with prose. True, it was a period of great interest in fiction—Fitzgerald had published *This Side of Paradise* in 1920, *The Beautiful and The Damned* in 1922, and *The Great Gatsby* in 1925; Hemingway's short stories had achieved much notice even before *The Sun Also Rises* appeared in 1926; Gertrude Stein's 1914 *Tender Buttons* and 1925 *The Making of Americans* were exciting writers in much the same way The Armory Show had aroused painters in 1913. In 1921 Sherwood Anderson won *The Dial* Award for his two collections of short stories, *Winesburg, Ohio* in 1919 and *The Triumph of the Egg* in 1921. Dos Passos' experimentation in his 1921 *Three Soldiers* and the 1925 *Manhattan Transfer* helped to emphasize the innovation in technique, used also by e.e. cummings, not only in his poetry but in his 1922 novel, *The Enormous Room.* Joyce's *Ulysses* in 1922; Dreiser's *An American Tragedy* in 1925; D. H. Lawrence's *Lady Chatterley* in 1928; Sinclair Lewis' news-making novels, six or seven in the decade—the affluent public was buying books, and the books they were buying (and talking about) were novels.

Set against these—for the most part—exciting works of fiction (technically exciting as well as thematically), the production in poetry during the twenties was most disappointing—to Williams, even defeating. Eliot was the central figure: *The Waste Land* in 1922 created as much furor in one way as did *Ulysses.* Williams said of "the great catastrophe to our letters," *The Waste Land* "gave the poem back to the academics. We did not know how to answer him."[2] Then in 1925 came Eliot's *Collected Poems,* and the same year, the first book of Pound's *Cantos* (1-16) followed with Numbers 17 to 27 in 1928. It was a dismal showing for poetry, dismal because, in Williams' words, much of it was a "looking backward." Of Eliot, a "conformist," Williams writes,

I felt he had rejected America . . . . I knew he would influence all subsequent American poets and take them out of my sphere. I had envisaged a new form of poetic composition, a form for the future. It was a shock to me that he was so tremendously successful; my contemporaries flocked to him—away from what I wanted.[3]

In one sense, Williams' writing throughout this decade is an exploration of his comment about Eliot, that he had rejected America. Like *The Great Gatsby* and Hart Crane's *The Bridge,* many of Williams' books attempt to define the spirit of America. (As Williams acknowledged in his *Autobiography,* "Mencken's *The American Language* [1919] stood in the background as a sort of formal liturgy."[4] Art was everywhere concerned with the newness of this land and its promise, a promise dimmed if not tarnished by World War I and the disappointing peace.) The essays of *In the American Grain* study some of the best-known figures of American history—some good, more evil; *A Voyage to Pagany* is almost Jamesian as the American Dev Evans searches abroad for his identity, his allegiance. Though less patently "explorations," *The Great American Novel* has many passages dealing with history—and the title makes any discussion of American art relevant. *Spring and All* deals in large part with the art and thought of Williams' contemporary America.

Williams the poet-physician was even more conscious than usual of the world of literature during the early twenties, because he had become a magazine editor. With Robert McAlmon, he edited *Contact* for three years, from December 1920 to June 1923. Publishing such writers as Marianne Moore, Kenneth Burke, Marsden Hartley, Wallace Stevens, H. D., Ezra Pound, and Kay Boyle, he worked to bring the *new* into focus. As he wrote in the second issue of *Contact*: "In answer to all criticisms we find the first issue of *Contact* perfect, the first truly representative American magazine of art yet published."[5] An American magazine, Williams continues, must emphasize "an indigenous art." Based on Williams' deep-rooted belief that an artist must "become awake to his own locality" before he can join "the main body of art," *Contact* was established to "develop among our serious writers a sense of mutual contact," and to "emphasize the local phase of the game of writing."[6]

By the third issue of *Contact* (1923), Williams was more defensive. He realized that not all young talents mature into "major" ones, but even that premise was to him essential to American art and criticism:

It is young. It is not necessarily inexpert . . . but it is necessarily young. There is no long chain of sophistication to engage us . . . . Our processes are for the moment chaotic but they have the distinct advantage of being able to claim no place of rest save immediacy.[7]

Issue IV brought a further clarification of Williams' artistic rationale: "*Contact* has never in the least intimated that the American artist in preparing his position 'should forget all about Europe.' On the contrary the assertion has been that he should acquaint himself with everything that he can gather from European sources."[8]

Immediacy and the local; the great unity of all art; "naked attention to the thing itself"—the principles Williams had emphasized in *Kora in Hell* and in his frequent writing for *Contact* grew to even fuller expression in the 1923 *Spring and All*. Kora (Persephone) had returned from her winter sojourn in hell. The prose and poetry of *Spring and All* testify to a new mood, a new theme, for the poet.

I. Art as NEW

Dedicated to Charles Demuth, *Spring and All* reads in its opening paragraphs like a continuation of Williams' *Contact* essays. The appreciation of experiment, the need for contact, the artist's realization that he will not be understood:

> If anything of moment results—so much the better. And so much the more likely will it be that no one will want to see it.
> There is a constant barrier between the reader and his consciousness of immediate contact with the world . . . .[9]

The predicament: that men are out of touch, with themselves as well as with art. The artist's solution: to write for the imagination rather than for himself or for others. Williams' dedication: "To refine, to clarify, to intensify that eternal moment in which we live there is but a single force—the imagination. This is its book" (p. 3).

Spring and All is no "beautiful illusion," Williams tells us, but a book of violence. How else to make the world new (*Kora in Hell*'s pervasive theme)? How else to make art new, but to start from the beginning? The real theme of *Spring* lies in this idea of violence, expressed so forcefully in the eleven-page opening essay:

> The imagination, intoxicated by prohibitions, rises to drunken heights to destroy the world. Let it rage, let it kill. The imagination is supreme . . . . To it now we come to dedicate our secret project: the annihilation of every human creature on the face of the earth. This is something never before attempted. None to remain; nothing but the lower vertebrates, the mollusks, insects and plants. Then at last will the world be made anew. Houses crumble to ruin, cities disappear . . . . *A marvellous serenity* broken only by bird and wild beast calls reigns over the entire sphere. *Order and peace abound.*
> This final and *self inflicted* holocaust has been *all for love, for sweetest love* . . . . and it is spring—both in Latin and Turkish, in English and Dutch, in Japanese and Italian; it is spring by Stinking River where a magnolia tree, without leaves, before what was once a farmhouse, now ramshackle home for mill-

workers, raises its straggling branches of ivorywhite flowers. (pp. 5–6) [Italics mine]

The results are worth the catastrophe, Williams' emphasis seems to prove, as he brings his proposal down to the specifics of the local (Stinking River, millworkers, straggling branches). The obvious parallel with spring's violence as a season is the apparent unrest of innovation in modern art. Later in the essay, Williams concentrates on the new in painting: Charles Demuth and Juan Gris seem to take the lead, to break with pictorial reality and find imaginative truth.

Again and again Williams returns to this point—the artist's responsibility to create the new, the meaningful. Again and again his practices within the book show the value of innovation, as he uses the poems of *Spring and All* to both illustrate and substantiate his prose theories. Frederick J. Hoffman describes *Spring and All* as "one of the most important volumes of modern poetry published in the 1920's. It is a veritable 'book of examples' of the principles (implicit and explicit) that governed the making of it."[10]

The first poems in the book are vivid evocations of the title. "By the Road to the Contagious Hospital" and "Pink Confused with White" represent both the spirit of spring and the even less concrete spirit of art. Williams leads into the poems with a grand affirmation of newness, intensified by spacing and capitalization:

... at last SPRING is approaching ...

THE WORLD IS NEW.

I.

By the road to the contagious hospital
under the surge of the blue
mottled clouds driven from the
northeast—a cold wind. Beyond, the
waste of broad, muddy fields
brown with dried weeds, standing and fallen

patches of standing water
the scattering of tall trees . . . . (p. 11)

This poem, with its more than realistic detail ("clouds driven from the / northeast," "muddy fields / brown with dried weeds") emphasizes not the "beautiful illusion" of spring but the tortuously slow awareness:

Lifeless in appearance, sluggish
dazed spring approaches—

The process of growth is presented almost as if an artist—a graphic

artist—were drawing the poem. "One by one objects are defined— /
It quickens: clarity, outline of leaf . . . ." Just as the prose leading to
the poem has been slowed by Williams' positioning of the lines, so
do his word choice and line arrangement help maintain the sedate
tempo of the conclusion:

> But now the stark dignity of
> entrance—Still, the profound change
> has come upon them: rooted, they
> grip down and begin to awaken.

"The Pot of Flowers," the poem paired with "By the Road," is
another picture—in fact it seems to be a literal "painting" of a painting. Much as he is to do forty years later with Pieter Brueghel's pictures, Williams at least starts with his own description of the model
painting:

> Pink confused with white
> flowers and flowers reversed
> take and spill the shaded flame
> darting it back
> into the lamp's horn . . . .
> (p. 14)

Progressing as would the eye, Williams' poem moves—in meaningful rhythm—down the picture to the leaves of the plant and, finally
(and perhaps not too "poetically") to the pot:

> petals radiant with transpiercing light
> contending above
> the leaves
> reaching up their modest green
> from the pot's rim
>
> and there, wholly dark, the pot
> gay with rough moss.

The prose which follows these two picture poems opens with a
phrase that relates quickly to the opening of "The Pot of Flowers," its
motif of confusion. "A terrific confusion has taken place," Williams
begins, speaking once again of the need for genuine art in modern
man's life (one of Williams' pervasive themes). "No man knows whither
to turn . . . . Emptiness stares us once more in the face." And the image
of the hoop snake, later to appear frequently in *Paterson*, "Has life its
tail in its mouth or its mouth in its tail?" (p. 14).

The poet's despairing tone modulates in a comment that hope "long
asleep" is now "aroused once more," and Williams gives his purposely
earthy description of the imagination, a description consistent with the
two "unpoetic" poems already presented:

The imagination, freed from the handcuffs of "art," takes the lead! Her feet are bare and not too delicate. In fact those who come behind her have too much to think of. Hm. Let it pass. (p. 15)

The next section concerns "Demuth and a few others" who "do their best to point out the error [of tradition], telling us that design is a function of the IMAGINATION" (p. 16). Before the next two poems, Williams comments that he is joining the "battle" now, with "these few notes jotted down in the midst of the action, under distracting circumstances...."

"The Farmer in deep thought" does seem to be almost a "note." It ends with a brief descriptive phrase (linking Demuth, Williams, and the idea of battle with the farmer):

> Down past the brushwood
> bristling by
> the rainsluiced wagonroad
> looms the artist figure of
> the farmer—composing
> —antagonist

Just as this is not the "typical" picture of a farmer, neither is its companion poem the usual re-creation of a spring night. "Flight to the City" opens traditionally enough:

> The Easter stars are shining
> above lights that are flashing—
> coronal of the black—

before the poet breaks in:

>   Nobody
> to say it—
>   Nobody to say: pinholes

"Coronal" is poetic; perhaps "pinholes" is more nearly truth. Williams goes on later, "Burst it asunder / break through to the fifty words / necessary"—and then in the poem comes the "breakthrough" itself, the poet, free, letting his imagination "see" the night as it wants to, the images juxtaposed grotesquely, in the immensity of the poet's view:

>   a crown for her head with
> castles upon it, skyscrapers
> filled with nut-chocolates—
>
>   dovetame winds—
>
> stars of tinsel
>
> from the great end of a cornucopia
> of glass.

Despite the fact that these may not be finished poems—as Williams' prefatory comment suggests—each one accomplishes what the poet's immediate aim in *Spring and All* seems to be: here, to break with the traditional associations, the usual poetic views of a subject. What more common subjects for poetry than night, a farmer, spring, or flowers? Williams' choice of topics seems to parallel some of his typography (the opening of *Spring and All* is numbered Chapter 19, followed by Chapter XIII, which is printed upside down). Critics had been objecting to the topics for his poems (a few years later Wallace Stevens is to make the "anti-poetic" statement); now Williams is meeting an even greater challenge, proving he can make *new* poetry from the most worn of poetic subjects.

In the next section of prose, Williams makes the point that the farmer and the sky might "rediscover or replace demoded meanings" (p. 19), and then he expands this idea in a passage attacking "crude symbolism" (p. 20). He questions the practice of equating objects on a one-to-one basis. Why does anger have to be represented by lightning? Why do flowers have to connote love? As the following poems illustrate, "the word must be put down *for itself,* not as a symbol of nature but a part, cognizant of the whole—aware—civilized" (p. 22).

> Black winds from the north
> enter black hearts. Barred from
> seclusion in lilies they strike
> to destroy—

Trying to break the usual associations, Williams moves into more didactic comment: "Hate is of the night and the day / of flowers and rocks. Nothing / is gained by saying the night breeds / murder—it is the classical mistake." At the end of this poem—admittedly difficult to follow without reference to the prose—Williams lapses into a more traditional image, only to bring himself up short with the observation,

> How easy to slip
> into the old mode, how hard to
> cling firmly to the advance—

The following poem, "To Have Done Nothing," seems to answer "Black Winds." Despair about his work sets the tone, in a Gertrude Stein-like pattern of repetition,

> No that is not it
> nothing that I have done
> nothing
> I have done

is made up of
nothing
and the diphthong

ae

To clarify Williams' meaning would require italicizing the phrases in
lines three and four, six and eight. Words used as words. Williams is
taking his own advice, to put down the word "for itself." This gram-
matical study "proves" that "everything / I have done" is the same as
"nothing / I have done," leaving the poet in "confusion / which only
to / have done nothing / can make / perfect."

   Back to art, this time to a concentration on Juan Gris and his use of
"things" presented imaginatively rather than realistically. As Williams
writes just before his poem "The Rose," "the attempt is being made to
separate things of the imagination from life, and obviously, by using
the forms common to experience so as not to frighten the onlooker
away but to invite him" (p. 30). Williams' re-creation of Gris' rose
("metal or porcelain," as the poet describes it) begins with the dog-
matic, "The rose is obsolete." In much the same way "At the Faucet of
June" describes a scene using the same artistic techniques. Williams'
sly references to "a Veronese or / perhaps a Rubens" help the reader
keep his place—it is art we are speaking of—and bring the poem back
to its conclusion to a restatement of Williams' basic artistic principle,
"no ideas but in things":

Impossible

to say, impossible
to underestimate—
wind, earthquakes in

Manchuria, a
partridge
from dry leaves.

Williams, like Gris, is concerned with things—familiar and simple—at
the same time, with detaching them from ordinary experience. As he
writes in the prose which follows the poem,

Thus they are still "real"; they are the same things they would be if photographed
or painted by Monet, they are recognizable as the things touched by the hands
during the day, but in this painting they are seen to be in some peculiar way—
detached . . . .
   Here is a shutter, a bunch of grapes, a sheet of music, a picture of sea and
mountains (particularly fine) which the onlooker is not for a moment permitted
to witness as an "illusion." One thing laps over on the other, the cloud laps over
on the shutter, the bunch of grapes is part of the handle of the guitar . . . . All
drawn with admirable simplicity and excellent design—all a unity. (p. 34)

Williams does, in fact, run the poem directly into uncapitalized prose, a device which emphasizes vividly the continuity between the poems and prose in *Spring and All* (a practice much like his later technique in *Paterson*).

II. The Artist and His Medium

Edgar Allan Poe is the next subject for the prose of *Spring*. As Williams' essay in *In the American Grain* was to show, Poe is one of Williams' favorite artists because of his "close identity with life . . . . Poe could not have written a word without the violence of expulsive emotion combined with the in-drawing force of a crudely repressive environment" (p. 36). Recurring themes for Williams—the tortured artist as involved man, the alienating culture—lead the poet into more personal statements ("No man could suffer the fragmentary nature of his understanding of his own life," p. 38) and his poem "Young Love":

> What about all this writing?
>
> O "Kiki"
> O Miss Margaret Jarvis
> The backhandspring
> I: clean
>   clean
>   clean: yes . . . New York
>
> Wrigley's, appendicitis, John Marin:
> skyscraper soup—
>
> Either that or a bullet!

This is the opening of the longest poem from *Spring and All,* a poem admittedly autobiographical. This poem recounts truly, *cleanly,* the montage of the poet's experience—the model; the young nurse; New York—where Williams interned at Old French Hospital—with its dime stores, skyscrapers, and the painter John Marin (to whose work Williams wrote a tribute in 1956). It must be "clean" or—"a bullet." As the poem continues later

> Pah!
>
> It is unclean
> which is not straight to the mark—

The love scene that follows makes use again of the things involved in the emotion:

> Your sobs soaked through the walls
> breaking the hospital to pieces
> Everything

—windows, chairs
obscenely drunk, spinning—
white, blue, orange
—hot with our passion
wild tears, desperate rejoinders
my legs, turning slowly
end over end in the air!

The poem ends with an ambivalent contrast. Williams repeats the central word *clean* in the next-to-the-last stanza, then introduces the last five lines with *but* to imply that the love scene was only supposition.

Clean is he alone
after whom stream
the broken pieces of the city—
flying apart at his approaches

but I merely
caressed you curiously
fifteen years ago and you still
go about the city, they say
patching up sick school children
(p. 41)

The earlier theme of poetic violence comes to mind again, as well as the later image of Paterson approaching his city, before Williams dwindles —rhythmically at least—into *truth*. The prose which follows this poem states simply: "Understood in a practical way, without calling upon mystic agencies . . . it is that life becomes actual only when it is identified with ourselves" (p. 41).

With few exceptions, many of the remaining poems from *Spring and All* have to do with Williams' concern with this real experience and with the things of the poet's locale as ways into those real experiences (this theme also dominated many of McAlmon's writings in *Contact*). "The Eyeglasses" (which opens with a line about "the universality of things"); "The Right of Way" ("The supreme importance / of this nameless spectacle"); the red paper box of "Composition"; cathedral spires; a conversation with a barber in "Death the Barber." In "Light Becomes Darkness" Williams reiterates the theme, "destruction and creation / are simultaneous."

Three of the most popular poems from this collection—"To an Old Jaundiced Woman," "Shoot it Jimmy!" and "To Elsie"—are prefaced with the comment that art "places a value upon experience" (p. 61). The idea of the imagination raising everyday experiences to art underlies the next group of poems which includes "Horned Purple," "The Sea," "Quietness," and the much-anthologized, much-maligned wheelbarrow poem. Prefacing these poems with his usual emphasis on "a

new world" and its "freedom of movement and newness" (p. 69) in
contrast to the present "stale" age in literature, Williams is free to write

> so much depends
> upon
>
> a red wheel
> barrow
>
> glazed with rain
> water
>
> beside the white
> chickens.

Many critics have made ambitious defenses for this poem, though perhaps the best defense is that it is so similar to many other of the poems
in *Spring and All* that it evidently suits what Williams wants a poem to
be at this time, as the prose statement following it would suggest: "The
same things exist, but in a different condition, when energized by the
imagination" (p. 75). And, further on, "life is absolutely simple" (p.
76). In this simplicity of his real experiences, Williams has again and
again found the materials for his poems.

Williams' concern toward the end of *Spring and All* is increasingly
with the form best suited to his writing. He frequently touches on the
differences between poetry and prose: "prose has to do with the fact of
an emotion; poetry . . . with the dynamisation of emotion into a separate form" (67); and "prose and poetry are not by any means the same
IN INTENTION" (p. 78). Williams, here, in the midst of writing each
form, comments that prose has a single purpose, "to clarify, to enlighten
the understanding . . . . There is no form to prose but that which depends on clarity. Poetry is something quite different" (p. 78). Then, a
note that he is to repeat later in his career, that there is little metrical
difference in the two, that poetry and prose may be "both, phases of
the same thing" (p. 83). And finally, back to an earlier theme, the
freedom of words (in poetry more than in prose) to act as separate en-
tities, without "impositions." The closing poems of *Spring and All* seem
to illustrate this freedom; every word is somewhat unexpected, though
apt. In "Rapid Transit," slogans and maxims are juxtaposed ("Cross
Crossings Cautiously"); "At the Ball Game" pictures an "alive, venom-
ous" crowd; and "The Wildflower" presents a unique image of the
black-eyed susan.

> rich
> in savagery—
>
> Arab
> Indian
> dark woman.

The stark expression of these poems, the intense focus, the care in choosing the single word—in 1924 Williams won the Guarantor's Award from *Poetry* and in 1926, *The Dial* Award. The working out of his theory—and his years of thinking about and scrutinizing poetry for *Contact*—had brought Williams to some of his strongest, least derivative poems. No Ezra Pound, no Keats—just Williams, a local and, yet, not parochial Williams, now writing with what Marianne Moore was to call "authoritativeness" and "wise silence" (also "compression, colour, speed, accuracy and that restraint of instinctive craftsmanship").[11]

Yet, taken without the prose that so fittingly accompanied them, the poems of *Spring and All* are very different in effect from what Williams intended. Like halves of any book, any painting, the poems cannot be separated from the prose—without reducing the whole to fragments. As conscious as Williams was about the unity of design in modern art, it is grossly unfair to have disregarded the unity of his design in *Spring and All*.

NOTES

1. *Sour Grapes* (Boston, 1921), p. 40.
2. *The Autobiography of William Carlos Williams* (New York, 1951), p. 146.
3. *I Wanted to Write a Poem*, ed. Edith Heal (Boston, 1958), p. 30.
4. *Autobiography*, p. 147.
5. "Comment," *Contact*, II (Jan. 1921), n.p. Reprinted in *Selected Essays of William Carlos Williams* (New York, 1954), p. 27.
6. *Ibid.*, pp. 28–29 *passim*.
7. "Yours, O Youth," *Contact*, III (n.d.), p. 14. Reprinted in *Essays*, p. 34.
8. "Sample Critical Statement, Comment," *Contact*, IV (n.d.), p. 18.
9. *Spring and All* (Dijon, France, 1923), p. 1. Hereafter cited in text.
10. *The Twenties* (New York, rev. ed., 1962), p. 209n.
11. "Review of *Kora in Hell*," *Contact*, IV (n.d.), pp. 5, 7.

Michigan State University

JOHN H. STROUPE

THE MASKS OF MACLEISH'S *J. B.*

In the theatre reality can be represented in a factual or a fantastic form. The actors can do without (or with a minimum of) makeup, appearing "natural,"and the whole thing can be a fake; they can wear grotesque masks and represent the truth.

Bertolt Brecht

In the almost twelve years since Archibald MacLeish's *J. B.* was first performed in 1958, far too much attention has been given to its Biblical source. Critics then as now continue to view the play against the model rather than seeing the Bible merely as a suggestive framework for the action of the drama. Early critics including Kenneth Tynan and Robert Brustein focused on the theological implications of *J. B.* and found it nothing more than "the book of Job retold,"[1] and "another adaptation."[2] Others approached the play as a "parallel to Job,"[3] a "brilliant re-creation of the *story* of Job,"[4] or as a work which "truly reflects the Bible" and serves as an illustration "of man's existence within the Christian tradition."[5] And though more recent critics have recognized that MacLeish "has significantly departed from the Biblical text which he employed," they dwell upon the "deeply religious nature of the drama," affirm that MacLeish "offers only human love" in place of "the later Christian answer of Christ's atonement for man's sins,"[6] argue that *J. B.* is "a caricature of Job," and that "Not only does Mac-Leish fail to see the real problem of Job, he fails also to understand God as the author of the Book of Job understands him."[7] My argument is that such contexts lead to misreadings of the play, for the world view developed by MacLeish provides the kind of meaningfulness found in the Book of Job plus an answer—a contemporary and existential one in which God gains definition through man and his suffering and in which man forges his own salvation.

Certainly the original problem posed in the Book of Job has in-

75

trigued countless generations. The Biblical account of a good man tested by God in a series of blows any one of which could conceivably crush the spirit has always left us with the unsolvable problem of human suffering and purpose. In other parts of the Old Testament we are reassured by the spectacle of the wicked being cut down, but here we have the spectacle of the good being destroyed. And in an age of Dachau and Buchenwald we have been pressed down on the hot fire of what seems to be an unaccountable horror. Nickles, who plays the part of Satan in MacLeish's play, mockingly points up our own dilemma in a jingle:

> If God is God He is not good,
> If God is good He is not God;
> Take the even, take the odd . . .

But the reason for MacLeish's interest in the problem of Job goes beyond this, a point we must remember as we see the play unfold.

"What attracted me to the story of Job in the first place," writes MacLeish, "was the end of the book of Job—a part of the myth that the theologians, for obvious reasons, neglect or disparage. And what excited me about the end was something that is obviously there but is omitted from the Biblical account—Job's action."[8] *J. B.* does address itself to the problem of human suffering and purpose, but as MacLeish suggests, they are J. B.'s suffering and J. B.'s purpose. Moreover, MacLeish's avowedly basic interest in Job's action suggests that his play will supply a theologically relevant answer about truth and love which the Book of Job, to MacLeish's regret, does not supply—except in a possibly apocryphal chapter whose dubious implications, according to MacLeish, "the theologians have tried again and again to explain away."[9] The emphasis in the play, then, falls upon J. B.'s recognition of his own particular worth; and guilt and "God" become tangential abstractions before the "heart coals" and "forsythia" which symbolize his redemption. Human responses are the central concern of *J. B.*, and it is the incredible fact of man and his persistence for life that fascinates MacLeish much more than the problem of unexplainable horror.

MacLeish's use of the mask in *J. B.* supports his concern with human responses in an indifferent cosmos. The masked Zuss and Nickles as "God" and "Satan" are blind actors, and their donning of the masks only takes them that much farther from the reality of J. B.'s experience. Zuss' Godmask is described as a *"huge, white, blank, beautiful, expressionless mask with eyes lidded like the eyes of the mask in Michelangelo's* Night." In contrast, the Satanmask is dark and open-eyed, and the eyes, *"though wrinkled with laughter, seem to stare and the mouth is drawn down in agonized disgust.*" In an age of violence and horror the benign Godmask is an affront; yet it represents the only vision of God available to contemporary man: God the Creator, visible in the grandeur of His created world but blindly indifferent to the human scene. The audience is inclined to agree with Nickles when he observes:

> I'd rather wear this look of loathing
> Night after night than wear that other
> Once—that cold complacence . . . .

Nickles is particularly offended by the lidded eyes of the Godmask which have seen everything in creation but are lacking in human awareness. He asks of Zuss: "What would they make of a man, those eyelids?" And Zuss' answer reflects the full extent and limitation of God's relationship with man. "Make of him! They *made* him." But Nickles is "aware," or so he would have us believe; he has "seen" man's suffering and seeking, and he has seen the Godmask empty of human meaning; his definition of hell would suit an Oedipus: "I know what Hell is now—to *see*. / Consciousness of consciouness." The eyes of his Satanmask are open and staring:

> They see the *world*. They do. They see it.
> From going to and fro in the earth,
> From walking up and down, they see it.

According to Zuss, though, Nickles' mask sees only "beneath the trousers / Stalking up the pulpit stair: / Under the skirts at tea— wherever / Decent eyes would be ashamed to." And Nickles' next vision —that of the lovers in a parked car—substantiates Zuss' judgment of his counterpart. Nickles, with his staring eyes, wrinkled with laughter, plays voyeur. Zuss with lidded eyes screens himself from what is not decent. In short, neither mask truly *sees* and neither figure is. The Satanmask and Godmask underline the fiction of creator and devil and at the same time heighten the reality of J. B., the man who refuses "to act." The metaphorical blindness of God and Satan are ironic counterpoints to the physically blinded J. B., who gains the only true vision in the play. And it is to the further glory of J. B. that he gains his vision through his own efforts and his own suffering.

The images of the play work with the masks in supporting this notion of a plastic deity made in man's image. Presented by two broken-down actors of no consequence who believe, themselves, that the play "*is* the Book of Job and that one of them is acting God and the other Satan,"[10] J. B.'s story must gain its significance from what he can contribute to it. "Oh, there's always / Someone playing Job," Zuss tells Nickles at the outset, but to the disgust of both actors, J. B. refuses to act. Zuss says of J. B., "He didn't / Act," and Nickles agrees: "He can't. He's not an actor." The seriousness with which Nickles and Zuss approach the necessity of acting, of wearing masks proper to the situation, is a motif which recurs throughout the play. For acting is the one compensation they find in existence. They treat the art of acting seriously—especially Nickles, who is despondent over the absolute determinism of the world "which allows only the freedom of pretense."[11]

J. B. on the other hand rejects the pretense of acting even though reality brings suffering. His plastic creator has asked only for someone who will speak the scriptural lines correctly—and J. B. obliges, to the consternation of both Nickles and Zuss. Recalling the story of Job, we are not surprised that Nickles is defeated by J. B.'s devotion to his "part," but we see a new side to the traditional Job when we recognize, with Zuss, that J. B. has become—to carry the metaphor further—director of the piece. Zuss says to Nickles at the culmination of J. B.'s suffering:

> Then, he [J. B.] *calmed* me!
> Gentled me the way a farmhand
> Gentles a bulging, bugling bull!
>
> . . . . . .
> That's just it!
> *He* repented. It was *him*—
> Not the fear of God but *him*!
>
> . . . . . .
> . . . As though Job's suffering were justified
> Not by the Will of God but Job's
> Acceptance of God's Will . . .
>
> . . . . . .
> . . . In spite of everything he'd suffered!
> In spite of all he'd lost and loved
> *He* understood and he forgave it!

J. B. has spoken his lines correctly, not through God's choice, but his own; in Nickles' words, "Job has chosen how to choose." Shed of initial Zuss-like complacency, then, J. B. ultimately gives the creator an existence and rejects Nickles' nihilism with forsythia and heart-coals. This emergence of J. B. as a man who chooses how to choose can be traced throughout the play.

Scene One shows J. B. and Sarah debating their differing but equally ludicrous illusions about God and His relation to man. Sarah clings to the notion of a kind of cosmic scoutmaster who awards or withholds merit badges based on individual performance, while J. B. is blissfully confident in his nonexistent Providence.

J. B.   But I believe in it, Sal, I trust in it.
            I trust my luck—my life—our life—
            God's goodness to me.
Sarah: *trying to control her voice* Yes! You do!
            I know you do! And that's what frightens me!
            It's not so simple as all that. It's not.
            They mustn't think it is. God punishes.
            God rewards and God can punish.
            God is just.

But J. B.'s faith at this point is not a result of seeing, of reason, but is of a lidded, instinctive nature, in complete harmony with the role implied by the wearing of the Godmask. All that J. B. perceives in the world has been filtered metaphorically through the eyes of the Godmask which only perceives mechanical order and the law of retribution.

        Of course He's just.
        He'll never change. A man can count on Him.
        Look at the world, the order of it,
        The certainty of day's return
        And spring's and summer's: the leaves' green—
        That never cheated expectation.

For this reason, it is only natural for him to testify that "since I learned to tell / My shadow from my shirt, not once, / Not for a watchtick, have I doubted God was on my side."

Neither Zuss nor Nickles is pleased with J. B. in this scene, especially since they recognize that he is not acting but is simply and completely deluded. Though somewhat gratified by J. B.'s love of life, Zuss can hardly rejoice in the praise of such a fortunate and unenlightened man. Nickles is merely sickened by J. B.'s blindness and piety. Both require awareness from J. B., which will be achieved through suffering. J. B.'s trials are about to begin and the conflict between Zuss and Nickles grows more heated. As they anticipate the kind of awareness J. B. will gain, the tension between the two assumes the form of a question: how will J. B. respond? Once he understands the nature of his existence, how does man continue? The contest is thus waged between the two extreme positions of orthodox belief and nihilism, stated in the form of predictions about the outcome of J.B.'s experience. Zuss is confident, and orders Nickles:

        Get your mask back on! I tell you
        Nothing this good man might suffer,
        Nothing at all, would make him yelp
        As you do. He'd praise God no matter.

Nickles is equally confident in predicting J. B.'s final response:

> Shall I tell you how it ends?
> Shall I prophesy? I see our
> Smug world-master on his dung heap,
> Naked, miserable, and alone,
> Pissing the stars. Ridiculous gesture!—
> Nevertheless a gesture—meaning
> All there is on earth to mean:
> Man's last word . . . and worthy of him!

J. B., however, must first be tested, and as each senseless tragedy occurs, he remains unwilling to question the justice of what is happening to him:

> Shall we . . .
> Take the good and not the evil?
> We have to take the chances, Sarah:
> Evil with good.

Only with the loss of his last daughter does J. B. face the injustice and destructive nature of existence. At this point, symbolically, "The canvas walls dissolve into distance, the canvas sky into endlessness," and J. B. reasons that *he* must be guilty; without his guilt, he concedes, there would be no justice and therefore no God:

> Guilt matters. Guilt must always matter.
> Unless guilt matters the whole world is
> Meaningless. God too is nothing.

It is appropriate that J. B. must now face three contemporary explanations of the nature of guilt in the form of three comforters, the purveyors of easy answers, men righteously armed with absolutes. Zophar is a fat, red-faced man who wears the wreck of a clerical collar, his garb suggesting the battered forces of the various orthodoxies. Eliphaz is lean and dark, wears an intern's jacket which once was white, and represents science in general and Freud in particular. The third comforter is Bildad, a squat, thick man in a ragged windbreaker who is the Marxist with his rigid code, his messianic zeal, and his ardent belief in the thesis of the end point of history. These grisly three expound their doctrines in their attempt to explain to J. B. about his suffering. J. B. says movingly:

> J. B.:   God is just. We are not squeezed
> Naked through a ridiculous orifice
> Like bulls into a blazing ring
> To blunder there by blindfold laws
> We never learn or can, deceived by
> Stratagems and fooled by feints,
> For sports, for nothing, till we fall
> We're pricked so badly.

Bildad: *all park-bench orator* Screw your justice!
History is justice—time
Inexorably turned to truth!—
Not for one man. For humanity.
One man's life won't measure on it.
One man's suffering won't count, no matter
What his suffering; but All will.
At the end there will be justice! —
Justice for all! Justice for everyone!

Guilt to Bildad is a sociological accident whereas to the Freudian Eliphaz it is a

Psychophenomenal situation—
An illusion, a disease, a sickness:
That filthy feeling at the fingers,
Scent of dung beneath the nails . . .

while to an outraged cleric-like Zophar it is the old explanation:

Guilt is illusion? Guilt is reality! —
The one reality there is!
All mankind are guilty always!

But J. B. is not convinced. To accept their explanations would be a retreat merely to another form of self-deception. Man, he says, has forgotten pity. Mankind has become so involved in restrictive disciplines and militant ideologies that it has lost its concept of love. Till he dies, J. B. says, he will not violate his integrity:

I'd rather suffer
Every unspeakable suffering God sends,
Knowing it was I that suffered,
I that earned the need to suffer,
I that acted, I that chose,
Than wash my hands with yours in that
Defiling innocence. Can we be men
And make an irresponsible ignorance
Responsible for everything? I will not
Listen to you!

J. B.'s concern has shifted significantly. He no longer struggles for a rationalization of God's injustice. That abstraction, like those of Bildad, Eliphaz, and Zophar, is cold comfort, and as J. B. realizes in this moment of awareness, only his own integrity and the love of other men provide reasons "why." J. B. acts, suffers and chooses, and in doing so, he *is*. Predictably, God, in the form of a distant voice—significantly more distant at this point—tries to lead J. B. to resume the metaphoric Godmask which he wore at the beginning of the play and urges him to return to his acceptance of the fact that God simply does not give answers to man:

> Who is this that darkeneth counsel
> By words without knowledge? . . .
> Where wast thou
> When I laid the foundations of the earth . . . .

And Nickles, who has completely identified with the Satanmask, offers an alternative, arguing that J. B. must refuse God's offer of a new life because of what he has seen. Seeing, for Nickles, is, of course, hell, while sight for J. B. must be quite another thing. Neither God nor Satan, then, offers satisfactory answers and their futile attempts to coerce J. B. reveal the impotence of Deity before a man who sees the world and himself unmasked. God needs a masked J. B., but J. B. unmasked can stand without the distant voice. God is perhaps not dead, but he is, for the sighted J. B., irrelevant to life.

Sarah says as much in the final scene of the play. Returning to J. B. with "forsythia / The first few leaves" in her hand, she says:

> Then blow on the coal of the heart, my darling . . . .
> It's all the light now . . . .
> Blow on the coal of the heart.
> The candles in churches are out.
> The lights have gone out in the sky.

Orthodoxy is gone and God is not in his heaven. J. B. is left with his own integrity, the heart coals of love and the flower's promise of natural renewal. And these, MacLeish would evidently have us believe, are a valuable legacy, for J. B. chooses to live, to begin again *after* he has come to a total awareness of life's horror. It is this exercise of choice, knowing what he knows of human existence, that finally establishes J. B.'s superiority to God. Insofar as he cares and is moved by the sufferings of his struggles, he differs from and rises above the impersonal, merely fateful deities who put him to the test.

NOTES

1. *New Yorker* (Dec. 20, 1958), 72.
2. "The Theatre of Middle Seriousness," *Harper's Magazine* (March 1959), 60.
3. Henry Hewes, "The Poet and the Press," *Atlantic Monthly* (March 1959), 42.
4. Samuel Terrien, *The Christian Century* (Jan. 7, 1959), 9.
5. Andrew MacLeish, "The Poet's Three Comforters: *J. B.* and the Critics," *Modern Drama*, II (1959), 228–229.
6. Sheldon A. Grebstein, "J. B. and the Problem of Evil," *University of Kansas City Review*, XXIX (1963), 260. One critic who finds the Book of Job of little help in understanding the play is Parlay A. Christensen, and his "J. B., the Critics, and Me," *Western Humanities Review*, XV (1961), 111–126, details J. B.'s movement from theist to humanist.
7. Charles M. Bond, "*J. B.* is not Job," *Bucknell Review*, IX (1961), 272–280.

8. "The Men Behind J. B.," *Theatre Arts* (April 1959), 61–62.
9. From MacLeish's comments about his play, New York *Times*, Dec. 7, 1959.
10. *Ibid.*
11. For an interesting discussion of the rhetoric of Zuss and Nickles, see Marion Montgomery, "On First Looking Into Archibald MacLeish's Play in Verse, *J. B.*," *Modern Drama*, II (1959), 231–242. My essay on MacLeish was made possible by a Faculty Research Fellowship from Western Michigan University.

Western Michigan University

JOHN NIST

CHAUCER'S APOSTROPHIC MODE IN
THE CANTERBURY TALES

As defined in literary criticism, apostrophe is a figure of speech in which "a dead or absent person, or some abstract quality or non-existent person is addressed directly as though alive and present or as capable of human understanding." As seen by linguistic science, the verbal exchange that constitutes communication consists of the following six elements: the *speaker/writer* and his *listener/reader,* the *message* sent and its *context,* the *code* of the message (its language ultimately) and its *contact* or method of delivery (e.g., speech over the telephone or print in a book). From this insight of linguistics, then, we may extend and intensify the meaning of apostrophe by saying that it is "the expression of a great emotional discovery, in which the speaker/writer addresses the context of his discourse rather than his listener/reader." As a dramatic shift to lyricism, therefore, apostrophe is intended to be *overheard* rather than merely heard. Through its very quality of overheardness apostrophe becomes, in the hands of a literary genius, a powerful esthetic instrument for plumbing the emotional and emotive depths of a human being under the stress of a situation that tests his character to the full. In *The Canterbury Tales,* Chaucer handles apostrophe with such rhetorical mastery and poetic finesse that it becomes a major mode in the strategy of his art and the tactics of his craft.

In a cry that is one of the greatest lines in the history of English literature, the Wife of Bath epitomizes her philosophical claim that experience constitutes its own authority and reveals at the same time the emotional wisdom of a romantic heart so authorized:

85

Allas! allas! that evere love was synne!
(*WBP*, 614)

Sublimity in miniature, this direct address by Dame Alice to the context of her public confession is—even more importantly—a summative ironic comment on the central message of *The Canterbury Tales,* as inscribed upon the gold broach of Madame Eglentyne, who in her aspiration to become a perfect lady remains an imperfect nun: *Amor vincit omnia* (*GP*, 162). Throughout the infinitely expanding moral universe of his vision, then, Chaucer constantly brings the quality of the *amor* into question, for he knows explicitly what the Wife of Bath has learned implicitly—namely, that love itself evolves with every phase of man's spiritual development and that like the triune other world of Dante's *La Commedia* this same love exists in three fundamental forms: the profane, the secular, and the sacred.

Though a representative of sacred love himself, the Knight (who has never said a villainy to anyone in all his life and who acts as the charitable peacemaker between the Pardoner and Harry Bailly) tells a story about secular love in the courtly tradition of a medieval romance in an ancient setting. The apostrophes in *The Knight's Tale* reveal the true nature of each of the three principals in the eternal triangle and forecast the eventual outcome of the plot. Once Palamon sees his sweet foe Emily and his heart is no better than a target for Cupid's arrows:

And therwithal he bleynte and cride, "A!"
As though he stongen were unto the herte.
(1078–79)

Because he thinks her a goddess, Palamon's address to Emily becomes an apostrophe to Venus. In that metamorphosis, of course, the speech shows the depths of Palamon's naïve idealism and tender innocence. And so this unintentional apostrophe serves, according to the rules of the game, as a foreshadowing of Palamon's romantic triumph over Arcite, who knows very well that Emily is merely a beautiful young woman.

After Arcite's long apostrophe to Palamon, Fortune, and Emily (1223–74) is answered by Palamon's long apostrophe to Arcite and the cruel gods (1281–1333), Arcite returns to Thebes and, disguised as Philostrate, becomes a page in Emily's chamber. Tormented with frustrated desire, Arcite laments his wretched lot in an extended apostrophe to Juno (1542–71). Palamon, who has just recently escaped from prison, overhears this lament—and the duel is on. Whereupon the gentle Knight himself addresses Cupid in an apostrophic complaint over the violation of charity between the two cousins and sworn blood-brothers:

> O Cupide, out of alle charitee!
> O regne, that wolt no felawe have with thee!
> Ful sooth is seyd that love ne lordshipe
> Wol noght, his thankes, have no felaweshipe.
> Wel fynden that Arcite and Palamoun.
>   (1623–27)

Duke Theseus echoes the Knight's sentiments in an exclamation about the overwhelming power of erotic love (1785–90), and Palamon proceeds to prove him right by addressing his prayer—a reverential form of apostrophe—to Venus (2221–60). It is this prayer, motivated by desire to possess the beloved, that wins out over the other two: Arcite's prayer to Mars for the grant of victory in battle only (2373–2420) and Emily's prayer to Diana for the gift of a lifetime of chastity (2297–2330). Because Palamon is the faithful servant of love, he gets the girl and his rival gets an infernal fury sent from Pluto.

As a representative of secular love, the mesomorphic Miller tells a fabliau about a profane example of courtly love (a lower-class parody of *The Knight's Tale*) that by virtue of the execution of its poetic justice becomes a laughter-induced purgation of both pornography and obscenity. In that purgation, of course, lies the sacred lesson of the story—namely, that we must not exploit the sanctity of the human person by making it a pawn on the chessboard of selfish desire. And the one apostrophe in *The Miller's Tale* shows why its practical-minded narrator is capable of such profound insight: even though slightly inebriated, the Miller knows that it is the imagination of man, in alliance with his feelings, that leads him into sin. Appalled at the utter lack of common sense in the old carpenter John, who helps make the bed for his wife's infidelity, the Miller cries out:

> Lo, which a greet thyng is affeccioun!
> Men may dyen of ymaginacioun,
> So depe may impressioun be take.
>   (3611-13)

Because his imagination leads him into both pride and superstition, John is the most severely punished of the three male principals in the triple love triangle become a burning diamond of revenge in the hot plowshare of Gerveys. The apostrophe of the Miller himself offers both the forecast of and the rationale for this outcome of all the hanky-panky trafficking in Noah's Flood.

The injudicious use of the apostrophic mode in *The Man of Law's Tale* labels it as pious melodrama and its narrator as a conventionally narrow-minded and long-winded rhetorician, who truly seems esthetically busier than he is. In answer to the example of the patient Dame Custance, of course, the irrepressible Wife of Bath launches into her *Prologue,* which shows, in its championing of women's rights in a male-dominated world dictated to by a male-dominated Church, that the best defense is a good offense. And yet despite all her gaining of the upperhand in marriage, Dame Alice has been happily married only once out of five times—perhaps a low percentage even by medieval standards. At any rate, as she remembers how she mistreated her first three husbands, she laments:

> O Lord! the peyne I dide hem and the wo,
> Ful giltelees, by Goddes sweete pyne!
> (384–385)

Upon thinking of her fourth husband, who kept a mistress, the Wife of Bath recalls her own vengeful lechery and the mood of her next apostrophe shifts and becomes a dramatic confrontation between her former youth and her present age:

> But, Lord Christ! whan that it remembreth me
> Upon my yowthe, and on my jolitee,
> It tikleth me aboute myn herte roote.
> Unto this day it dooth my herte boote
> That I have had my world as in my tyme.
> But age, allas! that al wole envenyme,
> Hath me biraft my beautee and my pith.
> Lat go, farewel! the devel go therwith!
> The flour is gon, ther is namoore to telle;
> The bren, as I best kan, now moste I selle,
> But yet to be right myrie wol I fonde.
> (469–479)

That confrontation is intensified by her recounting the ups and downs of her fifth marriage, the one that forces her to admit the deepest religious truth inherent in her past concupiscence:

> Allas! allas! that evere love was synne!
> (614)

A truth which unites with this last apostrophe in her *Prologue*:

> By God! if wommen hadde writen stories,
> As clerkes had withinne hire oratories,
> They wolde han writen of men moore wikkednesse
> Than al the mark of Adam may redresse.
> (693–696)

and leads her into the theme of her *Tale*: redemption of the worst offense a man can make against the sexual sanctity of a woman's person —rape.

Proving that gentle is as gentle does, in her *Tale* the Wife of Bath projects herself psychologically into the ugly old hag, who is the Queen of the Fairies in disguise. In that projected role, Dame Alice lectures the rapist knight, and through him all young men who are the living equivalents of her learned but dead fifth husband, in the virtues of poverty, chaste fidelity, and reverent obedience to the wisdom of experience that is age. As a silent answer to this ironic apostrophe of the knight, who is mortified at the thought of having to marry the poor witch who has saved his life by telling him what women supposedly desire most:

> "Allas! that any of my nacioun
> Sholde evere so foule disparaged be!"
> (1068–69)

the Wife of Bath counters with the knowledge that *since love is its own torment, no object of itself can give offense, and therefore to be beloved is to be beyond all need of asking if we are forgiven.* That is precisely why she ends her *Tale* upon the ecstatic union of the sacred love of charity with the secular love of eros. Pardoned with his life and suddenly the husband of a woman whose inner fidelity matches her outward beauty, the rapist knight bears witness to the fact that the Wife of Bath knows, despite all her loud protest to the contrary, that women do not desire to take the upper hand in marriage nearly so much as they desire to have marriage take the upper hand in love, so that this misdirected cause of sin may become the properly motivated redemption of it. In that redemption, of course, the eyes of spiritualized love will see the old, gat-toothed, partially deaf, and self-advertised nymphomaniac in menopause as the ravishing yet chaste bride of her *Tale*— that is, exactly as the woman that Dame Alice, in the hunger of her soul, wishes she could be.

As an answer to the Wife of Bath's *overt* philosophy of marriage, the learned and inexperienced Clerk tells the unbelievable tale of the patient Grisilde, a woman so perfect, of course, that she is not a woman, but rather a medieval symbol of the meek and obedient Bride of Christ—the Church. Forgetful of his allegory and carried away by an emotional reaction to the literal foreground of his story, the Clerk apostrophizes the fickleness of public opinion, now turned against the heroine, in this thinly masked direct quotation of "saddle folk":

"O stormy peple! unsad and evere untrewe!
Ay undiscreet and chaugnynge as a fane!
Delitynge evere in rumbul that is newe,
For lyk the moone ay wexe ye and wane!
Ay ful of clappyng, deere ynogh a jane!
Youre doom is fals, youre constance yvele preeveth;
A ful greet fool is he that on yow leeveth."
(995–1001)

The theme is a minor obsession with Chaucer himself, who thus expresses his opinion behind a double mask. This apostrophe is a forecast, therefore, of the greater apostrophe upon which *The Clerk's Tale*
ends: the deliberately ironic "Lenvoy de Chaucer" (1177–1212), addressed to all sharp-tongued followers of Dame Alice.

In the "Lenvoy," of course, Chaucer enjoys the mock cynical tone
with which he advises modern fourteenth-century women to prove to
their long-suffering husbands that wifely patience and humility have
died in Italy with Grisilde. Prove how? By windjammering contention
for the last word in any family quarrel. By making their husbands
jealous through the shameless advertisement of their beauty or, if
they are ugly, through the prodigal expenditure of funds upon their
friends, who are as light-hearted and empty-headed as they:

Ne dreed hem nat, doth hem no reverence,
For though thyn housbonde armed be in maille,
The arwes of thy crabbed eloquence
Shal perce his brest, and eek his aventaille.
In jalousie I rede eek thou hym bynde,
And thou shalt make hym couche as doth a quaille.

If thou be fair, ther folk been in presence
Shewe thou thy visage and thyn apparaille;
If thou be foul, be fre of thy dispence;
To gete thee freendes ay do thy travaille;
Be ay of chiere as light as leef on lynde,
And lat him care, and wepe, and wrynge, and waille!
(1201–12)

Chaucer's genial apostrophic satire, a realistic corrective to the unfeel-
ing business of medieval marriage on the one hand and to the overly
emotional romanticism of courtly love on the other, results in this implicit tragicomic assessment of the secular relationship between a man
and his woman: *before you decide that you cannot live without her,
first be sure that you can live with her.* Ay, there's the rub, not only
with the Host, but also—and more especially—with the Merchant.

In *The Merchant's Tale*, a piece of public psychotherapy for its
narrator, who is already the victim of two months of marriage to a
shrew, apostrophe plays a central role in the depiction of the character

of Januarie, a whoremaster who at the age of sixty thinks that the great sacrament of matrimony can not only redeem his past but also turn his present life into an earthly paradise. That Januarie is in for a rude awakening from his spiritual blindness the Merchant knows only too well, for Januarie is a guilt-ridden and self-hating projection of the Merchant's own shame: the failure to achieve salvation from a licentious past in the holy bliss of wedlock. Thus Januarie's simpleminded optimism in this apostrophe feeds the cynicism of the Merchant's newly acquired misogyny:

> "O blissful ordre of wedlok precious,
> Thou art so murye, and eek so vertuous,
> And so commended and approved eek
> That every man that halt hym worth a leek,
> Upon his bare knees oughte al his lyf
> Thanken his God that hym hath sent a wyf,
> Or elles preye to God hym for to sende
> A wyf, to laste unto his lyves ende."
>
> (1347–54)

The Merchant, however, is not about to buy this sentimental and naïve idea of connubial happiness—that is why he identifies himself with the point of view of Januarie's brother Justinus (a medieval equivalent of the voice of the superego) rather than with that of Januarie's brother Placebo (a medieval equivalent of the voice of the id). That the Merchant wants to see himself now as the equivalent of the reasonable Justinus, who warns Januarie that his intended wife May is liable to prove a Purgatory rather than an Eden, is beyond even an academic debate, for the text of his story gives him away:

> "The Wyf of Bathe, if ye han understonde,
> Of mariage, which ye have on honde,
> Declared hath ful wel in litel space."
>
> (1685–87)

The words, dramatically, are those of Justinus. But he has not heard the Wife of Bath spin out her *Prologue* and *Tale*; the Merchant has.

Chaucer uses this subconscious slip on the part of the Merchant to let us see more deeply into the tormented soul of his narrator and to reinforce the apostrophes that release some of that torment into the story itself. This in Januarie's apostrophe of thought to May, the Merchant pits his own guilt against his own lust, in lyric tension:

> "Allas! O tendre creature,
> Now wolde God ye myghte wel endure
> Al my corage, it is so sharp and keene!
> I am agast ye shul it nat susteene.

> But God forbede that I dide al my myght!
> Now wolde God that it were woxen nyght,
> And that the nyght wolde lasten everemo.
> I wold that al this peple were ago."
> (1757–64)

This tension mounts in the Merchant's own apostrophe to the treason of courtly love:

> O perilous fyr, that in the bedstraw bredeth!
> O famulier foo, that his servyce bedeth!
> O servant traytour, false hoomly hewe,
> Lyk to the naddre in bosom sly untrewe,
> God shilde us alle from youre aqueyntaunce!
> O Januarie, dronken in plesaunce
> In mariage, se how thy Damyan,
> Thyn owene squier and thy borne man,
> Entendeth for to do thee vileynye.
> God graunte thee thyn hoomly fo t'espye!
> For in this world nys worse pestilence
> Than hoomly foo al day in thy presence.
> (1783–94)

So overwrought is the Merchant in this crowning cry of the heart's despair that we must certainly suspect that he has not only cuckolded others in his time, but has also been made a recent wearer of the mythical horns. Hence his self-hatred, projected against the old lecherous drinker of love potions, breaks out in his apostrophe of advice to young Squire Damyan (1869–74); his personal shame and sorrow, in this terrible outcry against perfidious Fortune and the swift passing of human joy:

> O sodeyn hap! o thou Fortune unstable!
> Lyk to the scorpion so deceyvable,
> That flaterest with thyn heed whan thou wolt stynge;
> Thy tayl is deeth, thurgh thyn envenymynge.
> O brotil joye! o sweete venym queynte!
> O monstre, that so subtilly kanst peynte
> Thy yiftes under hewe of stidefastnesse,
> That thou deceyvest bothe moore and lesse!
> Why hastow Januarie thus deceyved,
> That haddest hym for thy fulle freend receyved?
> And now thou hast biraft hym bothe his yen,
> For sorwe of which desireth he to dyen.
> (2057–68)

Only when Januarie is about to get what he has courted does the Merchant sympathize with the victim, for then he fully sees himself as that victim. That vision, in turn, leads him to address Ovid (2125–31) as a poet of truth: illicit love always finds a way to fulfill its desire.

But the cynicism of the Merchant wins out, for even though Januarie regains his physical sight, the old sensualist remains spiritually blind to the fact that his marriage is, like that of the newlywed Merchant himself, a tragic travesty of the religious sacrament of love. And much of the cause of that travesty is Januarie's insatiable appetite for the object of the Merchant's grim echoic pun: *sweete venym queynte.*

If apostrophe reveals the spiritual agony of the Merchant, then this lyric mode of address also shows the serenity of the Franklin, who knows that Dorigen's apostrophe (868–893) concerning "thise grisly feendly rokkes blake" is an overly emotional reaction to the problem of natural evil:

> "I woot wel clerkes wol seyn as hem leste,
> By argumentz, that al is for the beste,
> Though I ne kan the causes nat yknowe.
> But thilke God that made wynd to blowe
> As kepe my lord! this my conclusion.
> To clerkes lete I al disputison.
> But wolde God that alle thise rokkes blake
> Were sonken into helle for his sake!
> Thise rokkes sleen myn herte for the feere."
> (885–893)

Unreasoning in her emotional immaturity, the heroine of *The Franklin's Tale* sets an impossible task for Aurelius in order to fulfill an impossible set of wishes for Arveragus: to save her husband, she would destroy her marriage. Her original apostrophe, then, ingenuously— if not innocently—motivated, generates the other apostrophes in this Breton lay. And it is in the serene sensibility of the Franklin himself that these various apostrophes in the hearts of the three principal characters of his story vent their rage for order and come to be stilled in the final peace of the Franklin's ultimate moral vision: Whose honor-keeping heart is indeed the most generous?

As for the apostrophes which lead to this final haunting question, there is Aurelius' epic prayer to Apollo (1031–79) for a miracle that will cover the rocks with a flood tide to last two whole years:

> "Do this miracle, or do myn herte breste—
> That now next at this opposicion
> Which in the signe shal be of the Leon,
> As preieth hire so greet a flood to brynge
> That five fadme at the leeste it oversprynge
> The hyeste rokke in Armorik Briteyne;
> And lat this flood endure yeres tweyne.
> Thanne certes to my lady may I seye,
> 'Holdeth youre heste, the rokkes been aweye.' "
> (1056–64)

Then there is the Franklin's own chaste lyric address to Dorigen upon her reunion with Arveragus:

> O blisful artow now, thou Dorigen,
> That hast thy lusty housbonde in thyne armes,
> The fresshe knyght, the worthy man of armes,
> That loveth thee as his owene hertes lyf.
> (1090–93)

This apostrophe, of course, becomes an ironic forecast of Dorigen's complaint to the catastrophic turn of events that suddenly now threatens her wifely fidelity:

> "Allas," quod she, "that evere this sholde happe!
> For wende I nevere by possibilitee
> That swich a monstre or merveille myghte be!
> It is agayns the proces of nature."
> (1342–45)

This lament, in turn, leads Dorigen into her seemingly interminable sad litany to Fortune (1355–1456), in which she recalls one ancient heroine after another who preferred death to dishonor—a preference which her opening lyric statement of the dilemma tells us she will certainly not make:

> "Allas," quod she, "on thee, Fortune, I pleyne,
> That unwar wrapped hast me in thy cheyne,
> Fro which t'escape woot I no socour,
> Save oonly deeth or elles dishonour;
> Oon of thise two bihoveth me to chese."
> (1355–59)

In the enormous litany which this dilemma generates, Dorigen protests too much. She banquets on emotion rather than on action and entertains mere melodrama. The weak passive nature that got her into this potentially tragic predicament in the first place will not now let her take the strong way out. And so she must rely on the mercy of Aurelius, who is left with this apostrophic complaint to his financial straits:

> Aurelius, that his cost hath al forlorn,
> Curseth the tyme that evere he was born:
> "Allas," quod he, "allas, that I bihighte
> Of pured gold a thousand pound of wighte
> Unto this philosophre! How shal I do?
> I se namoore but that I am fordo.
> Myn heritage moot I nedes selle,
> And been a beggere; heere may I nat dwelle,
> And shame al my kynrede in this place,
> But I of hym may gete bettre grace.
> But nathelees, I wole of hym assaye,
> At certeyn dayes, yeer by yeer, to paye,

And thank hym of his grete curteisye.
My trouthe wol I kepe, I wol nat lye."
(1557–70)

This lyric mode of address, of course, establishes the real ethos of Aurelius and—because it is based upon honor—finally wins his release from debt.

Just as the gentle Franklin is an example of secular love with a moral message about divine, so the eunuch Pardoner is the corrupt minister of divine love with a motto about profane: *Radix malorum est Cupiditas.* Separated from his human kind by the spiritual leprosy of his office and the impotence of his neuterdom, the Pardoner rides on the pilgrimage to Canterbury with an ironic apostrophe on his lips in the form of a medieval popular song: "Com hider, love, to me!" (*GP,* 672). Placed under a moral quarantine by the upperclass members in the party, the Pardoner tells an exemplum that is a masterpiece of organization in sermonizing against the vices of gluttony, gambling, and swearing. The *Tale,* in short, proves that the Pardoner, motivated by avarice (one form of negative love that is left his carnal frailty), is a real professional in his work. And the apostrophic mode is ever present, like the beads on a rosary, to lead the reader toward the fulfillment of the masked hunger of the castrate story-teller, *a masochistic confrontation with truth in the form of vengeful justice in order that outraged charity may let the Pardoner out of his moral quarantine and unite him with his fellow man.*

Thus the apostrophes to gluttony (498–504, 512–520), the lyric castigation of the stomach (534–540) and of the drunkard (551–559) are not mere eloquence to stir the audience into parting with its money; they are indications of the emotional starvation of the Pardoner, who seeks subconsciously to be admitted into a human heart, just as the old man of his *Tale* consciously wants to enter the womb of Mother Earth in the apostrophic prayer for death (731–736). Hence the story proper ends upon this climactic apostrophe to criminal mankind:

> O cursed synee of alle cursednesse!
> O traytours homycide, O wikkednesse!
> O glotonye, luxurie, and hasardrye!
> Thou blasphemour of Crist with vileynye
> And othes grete, of usage and of pride!
> Allas! mankynde, how may it bitide
> That to thy creatour, which that the wroghte,
> And with his precious herte-blood thee boghte,
> Thou art so fals and so unkynde, allas?
> (895–903)

Ravished for a moment by his own rhetoric, the Pardoner is tempted into his tragic overreach, and in his pride he picks upon the least likely person to respond positively to his invitation to kiss the relics of forgiveness for a grote: Harry Bailly, a heavy-humored man whose gross insult strips the Pardoner of his jocular villainy (a defense mechanism for heartbreak) and leaves the emasculated outcast from life psychologically naked and defenseless before the cruel laughter of a self-righteous world. But the Host who would not kiss the relics is moved by the gentle intercession of the Knight to kiss the Pardoner himself—an act that reconciles the eunuch with his fellow pilgrims as a divine answer to his secular cry, "Com hider, love, to me!" In this reconciliation, of course, Chaucer implies that in the universal mercy of divine love, all the sinners on the pilgrimage shall be redeemed. Not even the Pardoner can escape the kiss of peace in Christ Jesus.

If the apostrophic mode proves that the Pardoner is *not* the one damned soul on the pilgrimage, despite Kittredge's assertion to the contrary, then this lyric form of address does show that the Prioress, for all her conventional piety and medieval "Emily Post" concern for propriety and manners, is indeed in need of a spiritual circumcision of the heart. She is shamefully anti-Semitic. Neither the religiosity of her apostrophic *Prologue* (453–487) nor the sanctimony of her closing address to the recently martyred young Hugh of Lincoln in the *Tale* itself (684–690) can hide the fact that Madame Eglentyne is the victim of the Catholic bigotry of her time:

> O cursed folk of Herodes al newe,
> What may youre yvel entente you availle?
> Mordre wol out, certeyn, it wol nat faille,
> And namely ther th'onour of God shal sprede;
> The blood out crieth on your cursed dede.
> (574–578)

And it is interesting to note that in his depiction of this bigotry, Chaucer takes pains to separate himself from its moral taint—that is precisely why he inserts *quod she* into the Prioress's apostrophe to the chaste innocence of the murdered little choir boy of her story:

> O martir, sowded to virginitee,
> Now maystow syngen, folwynge evere in oon
> The white Lamb celestial—quod she—
> Of which the grete evaungelist, Seint John,
> In Pathmos wroot, which seith that they that goon
> Biforn this Lamb, and synge a song al newe,
> That nevere, flesshly, wommen they ne knewe.
> (579–585)

Since Chaucer's audience—as distinct from the other pilgrims—knows that the Prioress is speaking, the insertion of the formulaic phrase *quod she* in the stanza immediately following her attack on the Jews is a subtle way for the real author of *The Prioress's Tale* to protect his own ethos without being hypocritical or self-righteous in the defense.

In *The Nun's Priest's Tale,* a pedantic clergyman tells a melodramatic beast-fable about a pedantic cock. The result, of course, is a mock epic in which Chauntecleer himself lyrically addresses God as the uncoverer of murder:

> "O blisful God, that art so just and trewe,
> Lo, how that thou biwreyest mordre always!"
> (3050–51)

This brief apostrophe, in turn, forecasts the fuller apostrophe of the Nun's Priest himself on the triple subject of the murdering fox, the victim cock, and the flouting of predestination:

> O false mordrour, lurkynge in thy den!
> O newe Scariot, newe Genylon,
> False dissymulour, O Greek Synon,
> That broghtest Troye al outrely to sorwe!
> O Chauntecleer, acursed be that morwe
> That thou into that yerd flaugh fro the bemes!
> Thou were ful wey ywarned by thy dremes
> That thilke day was perilous to thee;
> But what that God forwoot moot nedes bee,
> After the opinioun of certain clerkis.
> (3226–35)

This three-part shift of address from the pilgrim audience to the context of the Nun's Priest's story is matched, after a brief apostrophe to the lords who are betrayed through flattery (3325–30), by a crucial series of lyric laments to destiny, Venus, and Geoffrey de Vinsauf (3338–54).

This series of laments culminates in this magnificent climax of apostrophic burlesque:

> O woful hennes, right so criden ye,
> As, when that Nero brende the citee
> Of Rome, cryden senatoures wyves
> For that hir husbondes losten all hir lyves;
> Withouten gilt this Nero hath hem slayn.
> (3369–74)

And then the very sky seems to collapse in all the lather-dither noise and esthetically appropriate cacophony of the chase of the fox (3375–3401). The chase itself, moreover, is reminiscent of the emotional hyperbole that dominates *Troilus and Criseyde,* the tragicomic masterpiece in which Chaucer first learned to play upon the apostrophic mode to perfection. But that creative lesson is far too large for the scope of this present study.

Suffice it to say that in *The Canterbury Tales,* Chaucer uses the figure of speech apostrophe to state the central theme of the pilgrimage, to plumb the spiritual depths of the story-tellers on the journey, to confront the drama of their tales with the lyricism in their hearts, and to strengthen the moral conscience of the audience by letting it overhear what normally should be merely heard. In that quality of overheardness, Chaucer transmutes the rhetoric of his craft into the poetry of his art. The apostrophic mode is thus an alchemist in the laboratory of his style.

NOTE

Abbreviations such as *WBP* for *Wife of Bath's Prologue* and *GP* for *General Prologue* are given in parentheses, often with arabic numbers, after references or quotations.

Auburn University

ARTHUR F. MAROTTI

THE METHOD IN THE MADNESS OF
A MAD WORLD, MY MASTERS

Although the title of Thomas Middleton's private theater comedy, *A Mad World, My Masters* (1606?)[1] seems at first to refer only to a wittily sophisticated attitude which both playwright and coterie audience share,[2] it has ultimately (like the title of Chapman's comedy, *All Fools*) the force of a dramatic thesis which the succeeding action proves. Basically, the word "mad" calls attention to the monomania of the characters and the playworld's comic disorder, both of which generate this comedy's recreative mirth. It is in this sense that Sir Bounteous Progress sees the outcome of his nephew's playlet in the last act as "the maddest piece of justice . . . that ever was committed" (V.ii.113–114). This is "mad" in the sense of "madcap," an apt characterization of the rapid, varied actions which fill this drama and create the game atmosphere of all the "jests" and "tricks."[3] The play's conclusion is a piece of "mad" or misrule justice; for no faults are really reproved and judgment is not passed on either the witty prodigal, the blithely unscrupulous courtesan, or the energetically degenerate *senex*. The word "mad," however, also raises deeper issues which lie beneath Middleton's light-hearted ironies; for the "mad world" of this play, like the ship of fools to which the humor characters of Marston's *The Fawn* are consigned,[4] is a dramatic conceit that satirically reflects the city world with which the private theater audience is so familiar and of which they are an integral part.[5] Middleton avoids naïve didacticism (in fact, he parodies it); but, in his analysis of the moral and perceptual complexities of *A Mad World,* he addresses himself to his audience in a profound and subtle way, making his

99

play, finally, what Jonson in *Everyman Out of His Humour* reminds us any true comedy should be, an "imitation of life, glass of custom, image of truth."

I.

In the upside-down world of this satiric comedy—in which the natural and the unnatural are inverted—one looks for some kind of a standard against which to measure the comic deformities of the characters. In his previous comedies, *The Phoenix, The Family of Love,* and *Michaelmas Term,* Middleton fashioned judgment-scene conclusions to restore ethical equilibrium to the individual playworlds and he empowered morally superior characters (Prince Phoenix, Gerardine, and an anonymous judge) to set things right.[6] But, like Jonson (who after *Volpone,* also abandoned the judgment scene and made a mockery of it in *The Alchemist* and *Bartholomew Fair*), he learned that judges and tribunals were not really necessary to comedy; for comic justice, which has its own logic, need not be heavy-handed to accomplish its ends. Although it cannot, like the various orders which critics like Irving Ribner and Robert Ornstein find in Jacobean tragedy,[7] be spoken of in traditional religious or ethical vocabularies, there is a legitimate moral order present in *A Mad World.* It is based on what might be called the law of comic physics, the ethic of comedy implicit in the play-title *Wily Beguiled,* or the statement at the end of Jonson's *Volpone:* "Mischiefs feed / Like beasts, till they be fat, and then they bleed" (V.xii.150–151).[8] It is articulated in Middleton's own work in such words as "wit destroys wit" and "deceit is her own foe; / Craftily gets, and childishly lets go" (*Michaelmas Term,* V.i.46 and V.iii.74). In *The Family of Love,* one of the frustrated lechers partially recognizes it:

> . . . sure there's some providence
> Which countermands libidinous appetites,
> For what we most intend is counter-check'd
> By strange and unexpected accidents. . . .
>   (IV.iv. 1–4)

As the induction to *Michaelmas Term* indicates, Middleton's comedies present the "familiar accidents" of the city world; but beneath these accidents rests a moral order in which extremes convert themselves into their opposites and natural balances are created.

In *A Mad World,* the oxymoronic names of some of the characters —Follywit, Frank Gullman, Penitent Brothel—are signs of the *concordia discors* which operates on a larger scale.[9] The world exists in a natural counterpoise of gulls and wits, or fools and knaves, a balance of extremes particularly evident in the relationships of the libertine Penitent Brothel and the obsessively jealous Harebrain or of the penniless prodigal Follywit and his wealthy uncle, Sir Bounteous Progress. In the latter case, Follywit and the old man represent extremes of age, sexual potency, and financial resources. In addition, Sir Bounteous himself is a kind of comic paradox. Subject to the humor of compulsive hospitality, "he keeps a house like his name, bounteous, open, / for all comers . . . he stands much upon the glory of his complement, variety of entertainment, / together with the largeness of his kitchen, longitude of his / buttery, and fecundity of his larder, and thinks himself / never happier than when some stiff lord or great countess alights to make light his dishes" (I.i.60–66).[10] This is his madness, the comic character of which is apparent in the scenes in which he over-lavishly entertains his disguised nephew with a remarkably vulgar display of music, ceremony, and luxurious accommodations (II.i.ii). Yet this mad generosity is balanced by a contradictory attitude; for, as Follywit remarks, in his description of Sir Bounteous' "humour, and the humour of / most of your rich men in the course of their lives . . . [they] always feast those mouths that are least needy, / and give them more that have too much already" (III.iii.20–23), a notion echoed in the old man's own words, "We'll feast our lechery though we starve our kin" (IV.iii.90). Follywit's stealing from his uncle, then, is comically "moral" insofar as it restores a kind of balance in nature between need and abundance.[11] It is also comically fitting in terms of another act "against nature" (IV.iii.46), Sir Bounteous' keeping of a whore in his old age. In the latter case, the comic Oedipus situation is resolved with the hearty approval of the *senex,* who is so amused by Follywit's marriage to the courtesan that he provides the dowry.

Generally, characters and forces exist in the "mad world" of this play in a shaky equilibrium; but there is one notable cause which produces this concordant discord. It is a comic principle of recoil, or the conversion of one extreme into its opposite. Midway in the action, Follywit ironically enunciates this principle which explains his own discomfiture: "craft recoils in the end, / like an overcharg'd musket, and maims the very hand that / puts fire to't" (III.iii.10–12).[12] At the end of the play, he admits "Tricks are repaid" (V.ii.261), after his cleverness, by some crazy chemistry, has turned to naïveté in his mistaking of the courtesan for "a woman as she was made at first, simple of herself, without sophistication" (IV.v.56–57). In as fast-moving a play as this, the recoils remain laughable—as in the comic transformation of the courtesan Frank Gullman into a faithful wife[13] or of Harebrain into a trusting husband.

The case of Penitent Brothel is interesting in this connection. Little more than an unreflecting lecher in the first three acts, he is brought onstage at the start of Act IV for a scene in which he is tormented by a succubus (exaggerated version of the wanton Mistress Harebrain), a *Doctor Faustus* situation turned into simple comedy. Middleton may here, as in the scene in which Penitent Brothel later schools his former paramour in a rigorous sexual morality (IV.iv), be parodying the didacticism of the popular theater for his private theater audience; but it is nonetheless clear that the scene, even in stretching the limits of laughter, is meant to be funny. The principle of recoil operates here as the libertine changes suddenly and incongruously from lecher to puritan.[14] Chapman writes in *All Fools*, "extreme diseases / Ask extreme remedies" (V.i.51–52),[15] and Sir Penitent Brothel's discomfiture— the full ridiculousness of his name by now quite apparent—like that of Sir Walter Whorehound in *A Chaste Maid in Cheapside*, is, in its extremity, undeniably comic.[16]

The drasticness of the recoil is fitting in the kind of "misordered world and lawlesse times"[17] this play reflects, in which, as Penitent Brothel himself remarks,

> None for religion, all for pleasure burn.
> Hot zeal into hot lust is now transform'd,
> Grace into painting, charity into clothes,
> Faith into false hair, and put off as often.
>   (IV. iv. 60–64)

To reconvert "pleasure" into "religion" or "lust" into "zeal" is to invert an upside-down world and reestablish some order. It is a mark of Middleton's perverse genius, however, that he makes the valid satiric point at the same time that he is also satirizing the thick-skulled moralism of Penitent Brothel and hence the high-intensity rhetoric of complaint, sermon, and formal satire itself. The repentant Penitent Brothel is ludicrously self-righteous in his new-found ethical bearings; and this is as ridiculous in its own right as his previous cliché libertinism.

II.

When he narrates for Mistress Harebrain his experience with the succubus, Penitent Brothel admits perplexedly that between the real and the illusory woman "in our natural sense, / I could discern no difference" (IV.iv.57–58); and it is in this kind of confusion of illusion and reality that we find, perhaps, the most subtle manifestation of the "madness" of the world of this play. Not only do characters in *A Mad World* find themselves in an epistemological fog; the audience itself is brought to an awareness of some of its own limitations of vision.

In the complicated city world which this play satirically mirrors, characters like Frank Gullman and Follywit practice the arts of deception; but, in one sense, all they have to do is minister to the particular blindness of other characters. In the play's first scene, the courtesan's comically devious mother emphasizes for her daughter the need for deceit as a means of survival and thus sounds the keynote for the succeeding action:

> Every part of the world shoots up daily into more subtlety.
> The very spider weaves her cauls with more art and cunning
>   to entrap the fly.
> The shallow plowman can distinguish now
> 'Twixt simple truth and a dissembling brow,
> Your base mechanic fellow can spy out
> A weakness in a lord, and learns to flout.
> How does't behoove us then that live by sleight
> To have our wits wound up to their stretch'd height!
>   . . . .
> 'Tis nothing but a politic conveyance,
> A sincere carriage, a religious eyebrow
> That throws their charms over the worldlings' sense. . . .
>   (I. i. 140–148, 160–162)[18]

It is relatively easy, for example, for Frank Gullman to charm Harebrain's senses. Although he places such implicit faith in his own powers of observation, hawkishly watching his wife for slightest signs of infidelity,[19] he is deluded by both the courtesan's tricks and his own perceptions. His comic blindness is made immediately evident when he chooses Gullman as a safe companion for his wife, for the girl immediately begins to instruct Mistress Harebrain in the arts of dissembling. Harebrain himself views the scene from a distance, but is not aware of the conversation the audience hears and is thus beguiled by the visual illusion of propriety. Gullman tells her pupil, "When husbands in their rank'st suspicions dwell, / Then 'tis our best art to dissemble well" (I.ii.74–75), while he remarks with complacent self-satisfaction, "She puts it home, i'faith, ev'n to the quick:/ From her elaborate action I reach that" (I.ii.96–97).

This kind of trick is repeated with a variation in the third act (III. ii). While his wife is committing adultery with her lover, Harebrain listens to her supposed conversation with Frank Gullman, which is actually a monologue by the latter. Since he hears, but does not see, what is happening, this "charming" of the senses complements the previous one in which he saw but did not hear. Moreover, he is deceived a third time, and in an episode in which he both sees and hears. The trouble is that he eavesdrops too late in the dialogue between Penitent Brothel and Mistress Harebrain to learn about their affair. He only listens to the end of Penitent Brothel's speech, the part which is trite moralizing:

> Live honest, and live happy, keep thy vows;
> She's part a virgin whom but one man knows:
> Embrace thy husband, and beside him none;
> Having but one heart, give it to but one.
>
> (IV. iv. 70–73)

After his wife's comic repentance—"I vow it on my knees, with tears true bred, / No man shall ever wrong my husband's bed" (IV.iv.74–75)—the foolish Harebrain rushes forward to exclaim rapturously: "Two dear gems this hour presents me with, / A wife that's modest and a friend that's right: / Idle suspect and fear, now take your flight!" (IV.iv.79–81)[20] This ironic epiphany, which culminates the action of the play's subplot, epitomizes Harebrain's comic blindness and muddled perceptions. He may have been tricked by Frank Gullman; but, as is clear from this last case, he is quite capable of deceiving himself.

Both Penitent Brothel and Harebrain are victims of their own follies (and, as cuckold and cuckolder they strike another of the play's comic balances); yet the question of perception here is relatively simple, basically a matter of moral blindness. In the case of Follywit and Sir Bounteous, however, this theme is presented by Middleton in a markedly more theatrical fashion, in such a way as to make his audience aware of some of the epistemological ambiguities of the drama itself. Follywit's art, more so than Frank Gullman's, is a dramatic one, and his wit, like the dramatist's, creates, in his own words, "pleasant witty comedy" (V.i.64). This is true not only in the scene in the last act in which he produces an "interlude" (V.i.26) for his uncle's feast, but also in his earlier ruses. After he and his cronies are introduced in disguise to Sir Bounteous as "Lord Owemuch" and his servants and are royally entertained, they don the theatrical disguise of "vizards" (II.ii.22) and "masking suits" (II.ii.23) to rob him. Later in the action, Follywit disguises himself in a courtesan's outfit and mask to fool Sir Bounteous a second time and, when he has stolen the jewels, the old man blames Frank Gullman.[21] But the question of theatrical illusion is most clearly and complexly defined in the play scene, which

is Follywit's masterpiece of trickery as well as the hubristic overexten-
sion of his art.

Follywit and his men, disguised as players, present themselves to
perform at Sir Bounteous' banquet. The young wit intends only to re-
cite the prologue to a play called *The Slip* and then escape with the
props he borrows from his gullible uncle, a gold chain, jewels, and a
watch (which later betrays him when it strikes the hour). He is forced,
however, in the midst of his getaway, to reenter the room and is given
an extemporaneous performance to explain away the entrance of a
real-life constable with his henchmen in custody. This act is so effec-
tive that the constable is unable to get the message across to Sir Bounteous that he has actually arrested real felons. Made a prisoner of the
theatrical illusion which Follywit constructs around him, he is left onstage, bound and gagged, as the "players" complete their escape. This
final trick of Follywit's is his most subtle. Sir Bounteous and Harebrain
see a certain madness in *The Slip*; but they are blind to the real madness, the way in which Follywit's play-within-a-play, essentially a
commedia dell' arte piece of virtuoso acting, transforms reality into
illusion, a process which takes place elsewhere in *A Mad World*—in
the three scenes in which Harebrain misinterprets the evidence of his
senses and in the young man's two previous theatrical deceits. The
most important illusion of all, then, is that *The Slip* is a true *artistic*
illusion, a real playlet. As its title suggests (a "slip" was a counterfeit
coin),[22] it is a fraud. After Follywit and the others have left the stage,
Sir Bounteous sees this. When Penitent Brothel states the obvious and
calls the players "counterfeit rogues" (V.ii.166), the old man says,
"Why, they confess so much themselves; they said they'd play / *The
Slip*; they should be men of their words" (V.ii.167–168). Follywit's
plan, of course, was that there be no play at all, only the prologue and
"the slip" which the actors execute in running off with the props.[23]

Precisely because, in this comedy, Middleton expresses the problem
of perception through various theatrical means, the relation of illusion
to reality comments on the nature of the dramatic art itself. Follywit
the artist confuses his spectators' sense of the real, a dramatic strategy
which becomes the stock in trade of tragicomic playwrights (including Middleton himself). In *A Mad World,* this particular maneuver
does not threaten the reality of the theater audience directly; still they
are forced to recognize a certain arbitrariness about the designations
"illusion" and "reality" or "playworld" and "real world." Their own
suspension of disbelief is reflected in that of Follywit's onstage audience; and the satirization of the naïveté of spectators, as in *The Knight*

of the Burning Pestle, begins to put them on the defensive. Specifically, their lack of control over their experience of the play is explicitly affirmed by the novel twist Middleton gives to the Plautine old man-young man rivalry; for, if the sophisticated spectators of this comedy identified with any character in the play, it would have been with Follywit, whose *savoir faire* was an idealized image of their own, and whose discomfiture would have come as a surprise. It may be, as Donne says to another sophisticated audience in his first *Paradox,* that their "wits are pleased with those jests, which cozen [their] expectations";[24] but the members of Middleton's audience are forced to recognize their intellectual limitations and feel that the epistemological obscurity which envelops the characters of his comedy affects them also, if only to a lesser degree. Middleton says "*A Mad World, My Masters*" to them, but he forces them to see that it is, finally, their own.

NOTES

1. Alfred Harbage, *Annals of English Drama: 975–1700,* rev. S. Schoenbaum (London, 1964), p. 92, sets 1604 and 1607 as the outside dates for this play. I accept his dating of Middleton's plays for the most part and place *The Phoenix, The Family of Love, Your Five Gallants,* and *Michaelmas Term* before *A Mad World* and *A Trick to Catch the Old One* after it. Cf. R. C. Bald, "The Chronology of Middleton's Plays," *Modern Language Review,* XXXII (1937), 33–43, and E. K. Chambers, *The Elizabethan Stage* (Oxford, 1923), III, 437–441.
2. See *A Mad World, My Masters,* ed. Standish Henning (Lincoln, Neb., 1965, "Regents Renaissance Drama Series"), p. x. I cite this text for this play, and for the other Middleton plays I use *The Works of Thomas Middleton,* ed. A. H. Bullen, 8 vols. (Boston, 1885–1886).
3. These words appear repeatedly in connection with Follywit's "comic pranks" (II.i.122) and Frank Gullman's deceits (see II.iv.89; II.v.4; III.iii.34; IV.v.124; V.ii.239, 261, 271–272).
4. In the first scene of the last act of this play.
5. Cf. *I Honest Whore,* IV.ii.129 ff. (in *The Dramatic Works of Thomas Dekker,* ed. Fredson Bowers, vol. 3 [Cambridge, 1955]). Ben Jonson, in *An Epistle to a Friend, to perswade him to the Warres,* II.31 ff., elaborates upon the text, "The whole world here leaven'd with madnesse swells" (in *Ben Jonson,* ed. C. H. Herford, Percy and Evelyn Simpson, vol. 8 [Oxford, 1947]).
6. In *Your Five Gallants,* Middleton also allows a morally superior character, Fitzgrave, to lord it over the play's fools; but the conclusion, like that of *A Mad World,* is an unmasking rather than a judgment scene. R. B. Parker, "Middleton's Experiments with Comedy and Judgment," in *Jacobean Theater,* ed. J. R. Brown and B. Harris (London, 1960), pp. 184–185, remarks: "by the time of *A Mad World, My Masters* Middleton has eliminated the good people completely from his comic world, and with them the need for moral indignation or over-severe punishment."

7. *Jacobean Tragedy: The Quest for Moral Order* (London, 1962); *The Moral Vision of Jacobean Tragedy* (Madison, Wis., 1960).
8. Cf., Alvin Kernan, *The Cankered Muse* (New Haven, 1959), p. 187.
9. Peter Ure, "Patient Madman and Honest Whore: The Middleton-Dekker Oxymoron," *Essays and Studies,* N.S. XIX (1966), 18–40.
10. Cf. II.i.50–68.
11. See III.iii.5–9. Sir Bounteous resembles the emblematic figure "Hospitalita" in Ripa's *Iconoloqia* (Venice, 1669), p. 266, who holds a cornucopia in one hand and extends an empty hand to the man on her left side who needs her assistance. He is also the "mad host" buffoon Northrop Frye names as a comic stereotype (*Anatomy of Criticism* [Princeton, 1957], p. 175).
12. Cf. the last line of *A Trick to Catch the Old One:* "Who seem most crafty prove ofttimes most fools" (V.ii.207). In *Measure for Measure,* Shakespeare alludes to the same phenomenon of recoil (although in grimmer circumstances) in a conversation between Lucio and the arrested Claudio:

    Lucio. Why, how now, Claudio! Whence comes this restraint?
    Claudio. From too much liberty, my Lucio, liberty.
    As surfeit is the father of much fast,
    So every scope by the immoderate use
    Turns to restraint. Our natures do pursue,
    Like rats that ravin down their proper bane,
    A thirsty evil, and when we drink we die.
            (I.ii.128–134, in *Shakespeare: The Complete Works,*
            ed. G. B. Harrison [New York, 1948])

13. This is comically parallel to Mistress Harebrain's initial conversion from faithful wife to adulteress.
14. He is called "Once-III" at the start of this scene in the play's quarto. A similarly comic change opposite to his takes place in the christening party scene in *A Chaste Maid in Cheapside* (III.ii) in which Puritan ladies get drunk and make sexual advances at the first males who come into reach.
15. *The Plays and Poems of George Chapman: The Comedies,* ed. T. M. Parrott (London, 1914).
16. Cf. Madeleine Doran, *Endeavors of Art* (Madison, Wis., 1954), pp. 364–365. I disagree with both Brian Gibbons (*Jacobean City Comedy* [Cambridge, Mass., 1968], p. 110) and R. B. Parker (p. 185) who see the didactic sections of this play as non-ironic. Compare the succubus scene in this play with the scene in *The Family of Love* (III.vi.) in which Lipsalve and Gudgeon mistake each other for devils.
17. *The Poems of Joseph Hall,* ed. A. Davenport (Liverpool, 1949), p. 12.
18. In *Michaelmas Term,* Middleton gives the art of deception a quasi-diabolical coloring in Quomodo and his "familiar spirits" (so named in the *Dramatis Personae*) Shortyard and Falselight, who "with subtle art beguile the honest eye" (I.i.86). The disguises in this earlier play have epistemological overtones; for in the city world of *Michaelmas Term* the real and the illusory are complexly interwoven. Cf. Ruby Chatterje, "Unity and Disparity in *Michaelmas Term,*" *SEL,* VIII (1968) 349–363.
19. See III.i.10–16.
20. Middleton puns on the word "friend," which also means "lover."
21. The audience watches Follywit "become" a woman in III.iii. As in the conclusion of Jonson's *Epicoene,* in which the "silent woman" is revealed to be a boy in disguise, they are made acutely conscious of the convention

of the performance of female roles by boys as well as of the fact that, in a very real sense, character *is* the disguise or mask worn in drama, an art form in which each figure on stage is a "fained personage" (*The Second Part of the Return from Parnassus,* l. 566, in *The Three Parnassus Plays,* ed. J. B. Leishman [London, 1949]). Since, in this private theater play, all roles, male and female, would have been played by the child actors, here, and in the scene in which the succubus appears in Mistress Harebrain's shape, Middleton complicates the disguise theme in such a way as to create a genuine epistemological uncertainty on the part of the audience. Follywit's disguising as Frank Gullman, whom he has not seen, also exploits the conventionality of the costume of the courtesan and the gulling, of course, has a self-consciously theatrical character. Follywit's remark, after fooling his uncle's servant with the disguise, "by faith, a good induction" (IV.iii.29) sets off the scene with Sir Bounteous as a kind of play-within-a-play.

22. See Bullen's note in *The Works of Thomas Middleton,* III, 353.
23. A similar trick is found in the play-scene (V.i) of Middleton's *Henqist, King of Kent; or The Mayor of Queenborough.*
24. *The Complete Poetry and Selected Prose of John Donne,* ed. Charles M. Coffin (New York, 1952), p. 280.

Washington University, St. Louis

RICHARD M. KELLY

CHESTERFIELD'S *LETTERS TO HIS SON*: THE VICTORIAN JUDGMENT

"They teach the morals of a whore and the manners of a dancing master,"[1] said Samuel Johnson of the Earl of Chesterfield's *Letters to His Son*. With such advanced publicity one may wonder why Mrs. Grundy allowed the noble Lord into the Victorian period. Mrs. Eugenia Stanhope's collection of the letters, which went through twelve editions between 1774 and 1803, was readily accessible to the early Victorians. In 1845 Lord Mahon's scholarly edition of the letters stimulated a renewed interest in Chesterfield. Five years later Sainte-Beuve edited a small volume entitled *Letters, Sentences and Maxims by Lord Chesterfield*. In 1853 Mahon published a supplementary volume containing additional Chesterfield letters. W. E. Browning in 1875 published *The Wit and Wisdom of the Earl of Chesterfield* which, like Sainte-Beuve's volume, was intended for popular consumption. The first collection of Chesterfield's letters to his godson, edited by the Earl of Carnarvon, appeared in 1890. The next year saw the publication of G. B. Hill's *Lord Chesterfield's Worldly Wisdom*. John Bradshaw's edition of the letters in 1892, an incomplete version of Mahon, was the last purportedly thorough collection in the nineteenth century. It was followed in 1901 by Sir Charles Strachey's edition, the most complete and accurate of all. In addition to the preceding works there were many miscellaneous collections of Chesterfield's letters in magazines and anthologies.

There can be no question, then, that the Victorians not only allowed Chesterfield into their age, but also kept him very much alive through their careful scholarship and literature. Their response to him, however, raises some interesting questions. How did the Victorians respond to the morality of his character and writings? What does the Victorian response reveal about the Victorians themselves? And how did the reputation of the Earl develop during the nineteenth century? In an attempt to answer these questions, this essay will examine the critical reaction of representative Victorians, drawn from a broad range of interests, backgrounds, and professions.

Since the Victorian judgment of Lord Chesterfield frequently either extends or rejects the eighteenth-century estimate of him, a brief summary of the Earl's reputation in his own day is in order. Roger Coxon in *Chesterfield and His Critics* summarizes the critical response of the Earl's contemporaries to the *Letters*: "Probably no English writer has been more injured by this effect of adverse criticism than the Earl of Chesterfield. The *Letters to His Son* were published during the period of a moral reaction against the laxity of the preceding half-century, and, though too buoyant to be actually submerged, were carried out to sea on an angry wave of criticism."[2] The most damaging criticism the Earl received was at the hands of Samuel Johnson. From the famous letter in which Johnson rejects Chesterfield's belated offer of patronage and from Johnson's previously quoted dictum about the letters, Chesterfield's reputation acquired a permanent stigma.[3] The terseness and wit of Johnson's remark made it memorable, and critics in the nineteenth century enthusiastically quoted it, though, ironically, a number of them replaced the word *whore* with a chaste dash. Throughout the rest of the century lesser writers proceeded to follow Johnson's lead in attacking the Earl. William Crawford, Thomas Hunter, and Jackson Pratt were followed by Cowper who, in the *Progress of Error,* portrays Chesterfield as a moral desperado:

> Thou polish'd and high-finish'd foe to truth,
> Grey-beard corrupter of our list'ning youth,
> To purge and skim away the filth of vice
> That, so refin'd, it might the more entice,
> Then pour it on the morals of thy son,
> To taint *his* heart, was worthy of *thine own!*
> Now, while the poison all high life invades,
> Write, if thou canst, one letter from the Shades.[4]

As late as 1798 Chesterfield's character was still under fire. In a parody of the *Letters* Horace Walpole, writing as a mother to her daughter, explains that as Chesterfield's appetite for fame and approbation was both intense and indefatigable, he would assuredly not have omitted all the virtues of the heart, had he not been convinced that virtue was never rewarded with public applause. Walpole concludes that manners have displaced morals: *"The Graces, the Graces!* on them alone is founded his lordship's whole plan."[5]

Critics in the eighteenth century clearly prepared the way and set the tone for the following generation's vigorous crusade against sham and humbug. The Victorian critic who attacked Chesterfield was not simply pointing a finger at the decadence of the preceding age but was castigating the insincerities of conformity, the moral pretension, and the evasion of his own day. The intense heat which the *Letters* generated in the moral fiber of the Victorian mind came largely from a spirit of self-criticism. As Walter Houghton has recognized, the most admirable quality of the Victorian mind at its best was "its readiness to submit society to close critical analysis and to judge it in the light of Western culture."[6] Houghton points to two lines of attack which the Victorians took against hypocrisy, both based upon a common "love of truth." One group of thinkers, he argues, emphasize the *truth,* the need to think freely and independently; the other group, represented by Carlyle, emphasize the *love* of truth. For the latter a society of sincere, truth-loving people is more important than the ideas they express.[7] In other words, they value truth of character more than knowledge. As will be seen by the comments of critics like Carlyle and Lord Brougham, Chesterfield's *Letters* serve as a springboard to attacks upon the moral character of the Earl him self, a character which the Victorians saw all too clearly in the social-minded Englishman of their own day who confounded morality with an expensive gig and the family coat-of-arms.

In a letter to Robert Mitchell in 1815, Carlyle compares Chesterfield's *Letters* to *Cicero de Officiis*: "It consists of letters addressed to his son, and if we compare the steady, affectionate, unbending precepts of the venerable Roman with the only work of a similar kind in our own times, *Chesterfield's Advice,* we shall blush for the eighteenth century!"[8] In another letter to Mitchell he explains in more detail why he dislikes the Earl's counsel:

> Lastly, I had recourse to Lord Chesterfield's advice to his son; and I think I never before so distinctly saw the pitiful disposition of this Lord. His directions concerning washing the face and paring the nails are indeed very praiseworthy: and I should be content to see them printed in a large type, and placed in frames above the chimney-pieces of boarding schools, for the purpose of enforcing the duties of cleanliness upon the rising generation. But the flattery, the dissimulation and paltry cunning that he is perpetually recommending, leave one little room to regret that Chesterfield was not his father.[9]

These comments by the young Carlyle anticipate his lifelong, intense crusade against hypocrisy and cant and his demand that a man be honest with himself and with others. Later writers were to convert Carlyle's judgment of Chesterfield into a powerful stereotype that to this day haunts his image.

More practical-minded and less inclined to make moral judgments than Carlyle, Macaulay is primarily concerned with Chesterfield's celebrity and scarcely at all with his ideas. Writing to Hannah Macaulay, he says, "I agree with your judgment on Chesterfield's 'Letters.' They are for the most part trash; though they contain some clever passages, and the style is not bad. Their celebrity must be attributed to causes quite distant from their literary merit, and particularly to the position which the author held in society." He elaborates further on: "Now, Chesterfield was, what no person in our time has been or can be, a great political leader and at the same time the acknowledged chief of the fashionable world; at the head of the House of Lords and at the head of the *ton;* Mr. Canning and the Duke of Devonshire in one."[10] Here is clear admiration, almost wistful envy, of the social and political stature the Earl achieved. Macaulay seems totally indifferent to the moral problems which Carlyle and later critics saw posed by the *Letters.* His labeling of most of the letters as trash is an evaluation of their literary merit and not a moral judgment of their teaching. As will be seen, Macaulay's attitude towards Chesterfield is atypical of the early Victorian period, and many years had to pass before authors could even separate the politician and statesman from the pernicious father of a bastard child and an abhorrent, cold-blooded author of a program of deceit.

The two writers who, more than anyone else, brought Chesterfield notoriety are Charles Dickens and Douglas Jerrold. In *Barnaby Rudge* (1840–1841) and *Punch's Letters to His Son* (1842) Dickens and Jerrold depict the Lord as a decadent, villainous aristocrat who carries the art of hypocrisy to new heights. Because of the wide appeal of Dickens' novel and of Jerrold's serial in *Punch* the Earl's reputation was profoundly damaged throughout the kingdom and beyond. Subsequent critics and editors, despite their dispassionate and scholarly attempts to arrive at an honest estimate of the Earl, could not completely eradicate the powerful impression left by Dickens' and Jerrold's caricatures. Commenting upon Dickens' travesty at the end of the Victorian era, Churton Collins says that "in the imagination of millions Chesterfield will exist, and exist only, in association with a character combining all that is worst, all that is most vile, most contemptible, most repulsive, in the traditionary portrait of him."[11]

Dickens' Sir John Chester, a caricature of Chesterfield, is a master of correct manners, a lover of gambling and drinking, a clothes horse, an arch-hypocrite, a despoiler of women, and a monstrous egoist bent on having society serve his best interests. Hardly believable, he is a wooden embodiment of the vices that Dickens saw threatening the social fabric of his own hard times. Despite the historical setting of the novel, Sir John Chester is very much a Victorian villain. Like Carlyle, Dickens saw in Chesterfield's *Letters* the perversions of moral character that the Earl, with studied care, would pass on to his son, thereby corrupting the next generation. In the controlled world of the novel, at least, Dickens could expose Sir John's hypocrisy and proceed to save his son, Ned, from its corrupting influence. Ned repudiates his father's doctrines: " 'I shall never repent the preservation of my self-respect, sir,' said Edward. 'Forgive me if I say that I will not sacrifice it at your bidding, and that I will not pursue the track which you would have me take.' "[12] Through Ned's firm stand against his father's influence, Dickens symbolically saves the next generation from a life built upon deceit and immorality. Mr. Haredale stands as still another obstacle to Sir John's wickedness. He is the familiar good man of the Dickens world, who, incapable of dishonor, maintains his own integrity while fighting vigorously to defend that of his niece, Emma. The benevolent Mr. Haredale, like Sir John, is another stock character of the Victorian novel and melodrama. His very presence implies that a good heart, a love of one's fellow man, and complete honesty are the real saving forces in a world beset by a wide range of destructive forces, from Utilitarianism to heartless industrialists.

It comes as no surprise that Sir John's favorite volume is Chesterfield's *Letters*: " 'Still, in every page of this enlightened writer, I find some captivating hypocrisy which has never occurred to me before, or some superlative piece of selfishness to which I was utterly a stranger.' "[13] Unlike Macaulay, who concerned himself only with the literary and biographical merits of the *Letters,* Dickens suggests here that their doctrines are pernicious because they are practical and therefore capable of destroying one's moral character. Just how corrupting the lessons are we see in the progressive deterioration of Sir John's proper façade.

In an encounter between Sir John and Mr. Haredale, which approximates an allegory of evil versus goodness, Sir John lectures his guest: " 'The world is a lively place enough, in which we must accommodate ourselves to circumstances, sail with the stream as glibly as we can, be content to take froth for substance, the surface for the depth, the coun-

terfeit for the real coin.' "[14] Later, when Haredale accuses him of
treachery and lying, Sir John rejects the term "lying": " 'Only a little
management, a little diplomacy, a little—intriguing, that's the word.' "[15]
And on the subject of marriage, a topic particularly sacred to the Victorians, Sir John's advice is equally odious. Eager to force his son to
marry Emma in an attempt to gain some money with which to support
his debauchery, he sets forth his materialistic views on marriage:
" 'Marriage is a civil contract; people marry to better their worldly condition and improve appearances; it is an affair of house and furniture,
of liveries, servants, equipage, and so forth.' "[16]

In *Punch's Letters to His Son,*[17] serialized in *Punch* during 1842,
Douglas Jerrold converts Chesterfield's "course of polite education"
into an art of hypocrisy offered not only as a parody but as a criticism
of moral principles in Victorian society. Again, as in *Barnaby Rudge,*
the Victorian emphasis upon sincerity, honesty, marital and paternal
love, chastity, true friendship, and sobriety underlies the satire. Mr.
Punch counsels his son to marry a dirty woman because "there's a fine
natural religion in dirt"; to employ a rhetoric of deceit in dealing with
other people; to discover the ruling passion and follies of his acquaint-
ances in order to blackmail them into his service; to employ flattery
when it serves to advance him in the social and economic scales; and to
gamble and drink freely, so long as such activity does not interfere
with the art of duplicity. At all costs, however, a reputation for honesty must be maintained: "What I wish to impress upon you, is the necessity of so uttering your verbal coinage, that to the superficial eye and
careless ear, it may have all the appearance, all the ring of the true
article. Herein lies the great wisdom of life."[18]

A long-time friend of Dickens, Jerrold shared with him the belief
that social reform is best begun with self-reform, society being in their
view only as moral as the human heart makes it. The character type of
Sir John Chester and Mr. Punch frequently reappears throughout the
works of both authors. Lord Chesterfield, or more precisely, the image
of him created by his contemporaries, provided Dickens and Jerrold a
stock character through whom they ridiculed the vices of their day.

In 1845, Lord Mahon made the first significant attempt to break
through the powerful stereotype and to present to the public an accurate, historical account of the Earl. Since Mahon's edition of the *Letters* is the single most important work of Chesterfield scholarship in the
period, his Preface deserves examination. After a glowing account of
the Earl's "brilliant" career, Mahon evaluates his character by the
strict standards of the Victorian ethic:

The defects of Chesterfield were neither slight nor few; and the more his contemporaries excused them,—lost as they were in the lustre of his fame,— the less should they be passed over by posterity. A want of generosity; dissimulation carried beyond justifiable bounds; a passion for deep play; and a contempt for abstract science, whenever of no practical or immediate use; may, I think, not unjustly be ranked amongst his errors. But, at the root of all, lay a looseness of religious principle. For without imputing to him any participation in the unbelief which his friend Bolingbroke professed, it is yet certain that points of faith had struck no deep root into his mind, and exercised no steady control upon his conduct. The maxims laid down in his familiar correspondence, even when right themselves, seldom rest on higher motives than expediency, reputation, or personal advantage. His own glory,—the false flame that flits over these low grounds,—however brilliant and dazzling from afar, will be found to lack both the genuine glow of patriotism, and the kindling warmth of private friendship. The country is to be served, not because it is our country, but inasmuch as our own welfare and reputation are involved in it: our friends are to be cherished, not as our inclination prompts, or their merits deserve, but according as they appear useful and conducive to the objects we pursue.[19]

One wonders, at this point, if the Earl described here resembles Sir John Chester and Mr. Punch more than he does the Philip Stanhope born in 1694. The Dickensian emphasis upon generosity and friendship, the familiar outcry against the Utilitarians' disregard of morality, and the strong sense of righteousness and patriotism in the 1840's are all found here. So many of the problems which Mahon uncovers, it seems, would have been solved if only the Earl had been a good Victorian Protestant.

Mahon proceeds to defend the Earl against one of the stock charges leveled against him by most of the earlier critics. After announcing that Chesterfield's character as an author will stand or fall by his letters and after praising their "clear, elegant, and terse" style, Mahon reviews the two chief lines of attack against them: "first, because some of their maxims are repugnant to good morals; and, secondly, as insisting too much on manners and graces, instead of more solid requirements. On the first charge, I have no defence to offer; but the second is certainly erroneous, and arises only from the idea and expectation of finding a general system of education in letters that were intended solely for the improvement of one man."[20] This observation is strikingly original and perceptive and was to influence considerably the judgment of subsequent critics who took the time to consider the *Letters* in reference not only to the age in which they were written, but also to the person to whom they were addressed.

Since Lord Mahon is too conscientious a scholar to bowdlerize his edition, he warns the prospective reader: "Only those persons whose principles are fixed, and whose understandings are matured, will be

able to read them with advantage,—to cull their good from their evil—
to profit by their knowledge and experience without the danger of im-
bibing their laxity of morals—and to such persons only does the Editor
commend them."[21] Even in this extremely cautious passage one must
note what the very task of editing the letters assumes—that there is
something worthwhile about them. Mahon affirms what Dickens' and
Jerrold's satires deny—that Chesterfield is historically important and
ought to be studied, that his letters are valuable both for their literary
merit and for the wisdom they contain for the sophisticated reader of
the day and of the future.

The contrasting attitudes of Lord Brougham and Abraham Hayward in their reviews of Mahon's edition clearly set forth two basic
points of view toward morality: Brougham judging Chesterfield by an
absolute standard of ethics and Hayward, from an historical-relativist
position, justifying the Earl's advice and behavior while admitting that
by an absolute standard both are immoral. In other terms, Brougham
condemns the *Letters* as a source of corruption for the youth of his day
and attacks the Earl as an immoral man unworthy of respect and certainly of emulation. Hayward, on the other hand, views the *Letters* as
revelatory of an earlier generation and therefore as documents of historical interest. Their "immorality" is more in the minds of Victorian critics,
he implies, than in either the Earl or the *Letters* themselves. Judged by
the specific time and circumstances of the period, then, neither the *Letters* nor the Earl can properly be condemned; rather, they may profit-
ably be understood and appreciated.

At the outset of Brougham's consideration of the morality of the
Earl and his writings he seems, like Hayward, to take an historical-
relativist approach, but suddenly the basis of his judgment shifts to the
typical Victorian absolutism that can tolerate no transgression of its
moral codes:

> These letters were addressed to a natural son—and that circumstance should
> be constantly kept in mind; it is needful to explain many things that are said,
> and the only apology for many omissions; but at the same time we must say
> that if any circumstances could aggravate the culpability of a father's calmly
> and strenuously inculcating on his son the duties of seduction and intrigue, it
> is the fact of that son's unfortunate position in the world being the result of that
> father's own transgression. And when one reflects on the mature age and laterly
> enfeebled health of the careful unwearied preacher of such a code, the effect
> is truly most disgusting. . . .[22]

Hayward reverts to Johnson's dictum about Chesterfield as the
source of the current prejudicial stereotype marring the Lord's reputation. He then defends the *Letters* against the charge that they inculate

immorality: "The advice to form a *liaison* with a married woman by way of apprenticeship in the art of pleasing, and the enquiries about *la petite Blot,* must be read in connexion with the persons and the time."[23] Reflecting the standards of his day, Hayward concedes that Chesterfield's advice was bad but that as a man he did not disregard virtue or principle just because he submitted to a "compromise with expediency." He also justifies Chesterfield's dissimulation on the grounds that artful prevarication is "absolutely indispensable for a diplomat, (Mr. Stanhope's intended profession) and the concealment every prudent man practices."[24] Thus Hayward sees as the virtue of prudence what many earlier critics condemned as hypocrisy. The only objection he shares with them is to the undue stress that Chesterfield places upon the social graces.

Writing five years after Hayward, C. A. Sainte-Beuve continued the trend of upgrading the character and writings of Lord Chesterfield. Like Hayward, he begins his defense by declaring Johnson's comment unfair: "Such a judgment is supremely unjust, and if Chesterfield, in particular instances, insists upon graces of manner at any price, it is because he has already provided for the more solid parts of education, and because his pupil is not in the least danger of sinning on the side which makes man *respectable,* but rather on that which renders him *agreeable.* Although more than one passage in these letters may seem very strange, coming from a father to a son, the whole is animated with a true spirit of tenderness and wisdom."[25] Sainte-Beuve, like Mahon, sees beyond the minor faults in the letters to the wisdom they offer future generations: "They are confidential letters, which, suddenly produced in the light of day, have betrayed all the secrets and ingenious artifices of paternal solicitude. If, in reading them nowadays, we are struck with the excessive importance attached to accidental and promiscuous circumstances, with pure details of costume, we are not less struck with the durable part, with that which belongs to human observation in all ages; and this last part is much more considerable than at a superficial glance would be imagined."[26]

Perhaps the most glowing, indeed, sentimental account of Chesterfield appeared in 1868, in Mrs. Oliphant's essay, "The Man of the World." Primarily interested in his character, she all but ignores his writings; and after a detailed examination of his career she concludes her essay in a manner that elevates the old image of Sir John Chester to tragic proportions: "It is as a polished trifler, a social philosopher, an instance of extreme cultivation, *finesse,* and falsehood, that the ordinary English reader looks upon Chesterfield; yet there he stands, sad as any prophet, stern as a Roman, patient as a Christian, forgiving all things, bearing all things. Strange, solemn, almost sublime ending to an unheroic life."[27]

A more convincing and analytical account of Chesterfield is provided by Leslie Stephen, who does not find him immoral but "as afflicted with a kind of colour-blindness which prevented him from paying attention to the moral side of things in general."[28] Stephen offers an explanation for the recurrent objection of the Victorians to the Earl's program of polite education: "Good manners are a delicate plant, which flourishes only in a calm atmosphere, being all the product of a state of society in a state of permanent equilibrium." He blames the socially ambitious middle class for the present disregard of the social graces: "Vulgarity is the product of a state of things in which the people in the gallery are trying to get into the stalls, and have only half succeeded." Stephen concludes that "the most necessary social art at the present day is to keep your neighbour at a distance without slapping his face, for who knows whether he is a gentleman or a swell-mobsman?"[29]

Stephen's observations curiously contrast with the earlier critics of the period and also with the following statement by a twentieth-century historian: "It was clear . . . that a revolution in manners had occurred during the first quarter of the nineteenth century. Older people who could recall the period just prior to the French Revolution were amazed at the change. Most of them rejoiced in the thought that low taste and coarse habits were fast disappearing. Only the exceptional person regretted that a certain honest and hearty vulgarity had also vanished."[30] True, the indelicate situations and frank language in novels like those of Fielding and Smollett kept these works out of many Victorian households. But although works by such authors were considered vulgar by "proper" Victorians, Stephen's argument suggests that the attempts of many members of the middle class to achieve social respectability by attending the right church on Sunday, by riding in a gig, and by appearing in furs at the opera constitute true vulgarity because such behavior debases the significance of aristocracy by foolish mimicry of its trappings. Chesterfield, then, because his very style of living and dealing with other people depends so heavily upon a refined sensibility and genuine aristocracy, has become irrelevant to the vulgar Victorians. In the words of Churton Collins, the Victorians "need the corrective—the educational corrective—of his refined good sense, his measure, his sobriety, his sincerity, his truthfulness, his instinctive application of aristocratic standards in attainment, of aristocratic touchstones in criticism."[31] On the other hand, recalling the parodic characters of Sir John Chester and Mr. Punch, one can recognize a markedly relevant Chesterfield, one the Victorians could enjoy because he reflects their common zeal to get ahead by outmaneuvering their peers. It is very likely that the Victorianism of the parodic Chesterfield accounts for his popularity.

During the 1870's the diplomat and statesman M. E. Grant-Duff wrote several essays on Chesterfield in which he advocates an educational program for budding statesmen. He quickly disposes of the moral issues in order to call attention to what he believes is the real value of the *Letters,* e.g., the practical advice they contain: "My object is, as I have said, a purely practical one. To examine, namely, how far his *Letters to his Son* can be made useful at the present day, and it fortunately happens that all his bad morality may, for that particular purpose, be left on one side."[32] He offers some modifications of Chesterfield's course of polite education and argues that his amended version of the letters be a "regular portion of the education of every Englishman who is likely to enter public life tolerably early." There is actually little that is new in Grant-Duff's project; he is merely heeding Johnson's advice that "take out the immorality, and the book should be put into the hands of every young gentleman."[33]

The sentimentalization of Chesterfield, begun by Mrs. Oliphant, is climaxed by the Earl of Carnarvon in his edition of Chesterfield's letters to his godson (1890). He dismisses the popular estimate of the Lord as inaccurate and sometimes (as in the case of Johnson, who, he argues, had a personal and political bias against the Lord) offers reasons for the distorted image given him. Actually, Carnarvon propagates a new stereotype of him as the man with a cynical, cold exterior but a generous, warm heart: "He was emphatically a man of the world, and for the most part he showed the hard and worldly side of his character; but it was also a kindly one with a depth of affection and devotion which makes his life to my mind a very pathetic combination of opposite feelings and qualities."[34] Assuming that genuine affection for his son and godson prompted his letter writing, Carnarvon probes beneath the impersonal social standards to the human heart: "The social standard which he had prescribed for himself, the cynical tone which he had adopted, and the inflexible self-control into which he had trained himself, in part perhaps disguised from himself, and certainly hid from others, the kindlier and softer feelings that had gradually grown up in a long and chequered career."[35]

In his essay on Chesterfield, Churton Collins summarizes the effect

Carnarvon's edition of the letters had on the Earl's reputation: "They had furnished, as all allowed, conclusive testimony that the severe sentence so long popularly passed on the author of these Letters, as a man, needs considerable modification. They had placed his character in a light far more favourable than it had ever been placed in before. They had shown that, if in the traditionary estimate of him more than justice had been meted out to his defects and errors, less and much less than justice had been done to his shining qualities."[36] Collins corroborates Carnarvon's judgment that these new letters reveal an aspect of Chesterfield's character never before seen with such clarity: "They show how much amiability, kindliness, humanity, seriousness, existed in one whose name has become a proverb for the very opposite qualities."[37] He vigorously disagrees, however, with Carnarvon's contention that these letters reveal Chesterfield to be a reformed rake. Collins argues that the Earl's morality remains consistent and reprimands Carnarvon for assuming the justice of the popular verdict on the earlier letters. Collins says that Chesterfield "was a man of the world and a philosopher, consistent alike in his precepts and in his principles."[38]

Collins offers two reasons for Chesterfield's unpopularity among his countrymen. First, "he is the most aristocratic of writers" and secondly, he is "the most essentially un-English."[39] Collins sees the Earl as a kind of French aristocrat whose writings simply do not translate well into the Victorian vernacular. The only objection Collins makes to Chesterfield's morality concerns the contempt with which he speaks of women. But even in his disapproval Collins detects the possibility that he might be reacting to a Victorianized Chesterfield: "We are so much in the habit of reading other ages in the light of our own, and of assuming what would apply to a man who acted and thought in a particular way among ourselves, would apply to a man who acted and thought in the same way a century ago, that we very often arrive at most erroneous conclusions."[40] This observation evolves from and is the culmination of nearly a century of Chesterfield criticism.

The last major edition of Chesterfield's letters to his son in the nineteenth century was by John Bradshaw, in 1892. Like almost all of the critics since 1845, Bradshaw's point of view is strongly influenced by the historical estimate of Lord Mahon and by the relativist position of Abraham Hayward. Almost paraphrasing Mahon, Bradshaw defends the maxims because the letters "were not written as a complete system of education, but they were intended to remedy the principal defects of a youth who, while requiring little or no incentive to book-learning, was almost incurably awkward."[41] And following Hayward's thesis, he explains the incompatibility of Chesterfield's wholesome advice to his son to develop purity of character and the Lord's own low, selfish motives on the grounds that such was the "authorized practice in all continental countries, and the impurity of our own Court at the time. . . ."[42] Like Stephen, Bradshaw views Chesterfield as more amoral than immoral and perhaps for this very lack of a strict religious principle, as a man ahead of his time in religious toleration, evinced in his liberal views of the bill for the naturalization of Jews. Bradshaw concludes his introduction by quoting Grant-Duff's suggestion that the letters be a part of the education of every Englishman who is likely to enter public life at an early age.

Maurice Quinlan, in his history of English manners from 1700 to 1830, observes that

> While she ruled, Mrs. Grundy was an extremely strict arbiter of manners. But she ruled by public fiat, for, despite the jibes of a Dickens or a Thackeray, the Victorians were proud of their social conservatism. This is particularly observable in the works of the minor writers, who, like the forgotten authors of other periods, sometimes reflect the temper of their age better than the major literary figures. Most Victorians felt that their customs and habits were notably superior to those former times. Although they were sentimental about many things, they did not hanker for a return of "the good old days" of their ancestors. To them the eighteenth century was a wicked era. At other periods in history nations have boasted of their tolerance, their wisdom, or their progressiveness. It was a distinguishing feature of the Victorian age that people gloried in their moral superiority.[43]

The varied responses of the authors dealt with in this paper, particularly those writing before 1845, partially support Quinlan's statement. But the preceding survey of critical reactions to Chesterfield's *Letters* demands that two important qualifications be made to Quinlan's contention. First, although there is unquestionably a sense of moral superiority in authors like Carlyle, Dickens, and Jerrold, it is the sense of superiority that the role of a satirist demands. Furthermore, these men are not so much attacking the moral decadence and hypocrisy of the eighteenth-century statesman as they are converting him into a Victorian in order to criticize themselves. Secondly, Quinlan's generalization overlooks the changing attitudes of these same Victorians. As this essay reveals, the critical response to Chesterfield moved through various stages, including righteous indignation, qualified and biographical understanding, relativist justification, sentimentalization, and outright praise and admiration. There are too many factors contributing to the death of Mrs. Grundy and the rebirth of Lord Chesterfield to be dealt with here, but the effects of the transformation inhere in the criticism surveyed. If the picture of Lord Chesterfield through the Victorian looking glass is protean, it is so because of the many distortions in the glass itself, and Chesterfield's changing image is sometimes more fascinating than its historical source.

NOTES

I am indebted to the University of Tennessee Graduate School for a summer grant, which enabled me to complete this study.

1, *Boswell's Life of Johnson,* ed. George Birkbeck Hill. 6 vols. (Oxford, 1934), I, 266.
2. *Chesterfield and His Critics* (London, 1925), p. 1.
3. Boswell's footnote on this comment sets forth the main attacks upon Chesterfield's *Letters* which were taken up by later critics: "That collection of letters cannot be vindicated from the serious charge of encouraging, in some passages, one of the vices most destructive to the good order and comfort of society, which his Lordship represents as mere fashionable gallantry; and, in some others, of inculcating the base practice of dissimulation, and recommending, with disproportionate anxiety, a perpetual attention to external elegance of manners." *Boswell's Life of Johnson,* I, 266.
4. *The Poetical Works of William Cowper,* ed. H. S. Milford (London, 1926), pp. 24–25.
5. *The Works of Horace Walpole.* 5 vols. (London, 1789), IV, 355–356.
6. *The Victorian Frame of Mind* (New Haven, 1957), p. 425.
7. *Ibid.,* p. 425.
8. *Early Letters of Thomas Carlyle,* ed. Charles Eliot Norton. 2 vols. (London, 1886), I, 33–34.
9. *Ibid.,* I, 69–70.
10. George Trevelyan, *The Life and Letters of Lord Macaulay.* 2 vols. (New York, 1877), I, 286–287.
11. John Churton Collins, *Essays and Studies* (London, 1895), p. 200.
12. *The Works of Charles Dickens.* 30 vols. (New York, n.d.), XXV, 300.
13. *Ibid.,* pp. 215–216.
14. *Ibid.,* p. 119.
15. *Ibid.,* p. 124.
16. *Ibid.,* p. 300.
17. *The Writings of Douglas Jerrold.* 8 vols. (London, 1851–1858), V (1853).
18. *Ibid.,* pp. 35–36.
19. Introduction to *The Letters of Philip Dormer Stanhope, Earl of Chesterfield,* ed. Lord Mahon. 5 vols. (1845–1853), I, xii.
20. *Ibid.,* pp. xviii-xix.
21. *Ibid.,* p. xxx.
22. *Quarterly Review,* CXXVI (1845), 260.
23. *Edinburgh Review,* LXXXII (1845), 439.
24. *Ibid.,* pp. 439–440.
25. Introduction to *Letters, Sentences and Maxims by Lord Chesterfield,* ed. C. A. Sainte-Beuve (New York, n.d.), p. 19. [Introduction written in 1850.]
26. *Ibid.,* p. 8.
27. *Blackwood's Edinburgh Magazine,* CIII (1868), 533.
28. "Hours in a Library," *The Cornhill Magazine,* XXIV (1871), 97.
29. *Ibid.,* pp. 98–99.
30. Maurice J. Quinlan, *Victorian Prelude* (Hamden, Conn., 1965), p. 3.

31. *Essays and Studies*, p. 262.
32. *The Fortnightly Review*, XXV n.s. (1879), 825.
33. *Boswell's Life of Johnson*, III, 53.
34. Introduction to *Letters of Philip Dormer Fourth Earl of Chesterfield to His Godson and Successor*, ed. Earl of Carnarvon (Oxford, 1890), p. xxxii.
35. *Ibid.*, p. xxxii.
36. *Essays and Studies*, p. 194.
37. *Ibid.*, p. 196.
38. *Ibid.*, p. 220.
39. *Ibid.*, pp. 233–234.
40. *Ibid.*, p. 239.
41. Introduction to *The Letters of Philip Dormer Stanhope, Earl of Chesterfield, with the Characters*, ed. John Bradshaw. 3 vols. (London, 1892), I, xviii.
42. *Ibid.*, p. xix.
43. *Victorian Prelude*, p. 4.

The University of Tennessee

BEN HARRIS MCCLARY, ED.

MURRAYANA: THIRTY-FOUR ATROCIOUS ANECDOTES CONCERNING PUBLISHER JOHN MURRAY II

The House of Murray, which celebrated its two hundredth anniversary in 1968, is historically the most colorful English publishing establishment. Among its several titular heads, all named John Murray with one distinguished from the others by the appropriate Roman numeral affixed to the name, John Murray II stands out because of his flamboyant nature and because of his personal association with the literary "greats" of his time. It was this John who gave the world the major works of Byron, who made publishing history with the prices he paid his authors in the early days of the nineteenth century, who first published the *Quarterly Review* and who never avoided an opportunity to call attention to himself and to his achievements.

In 1891, commissioned by John Murray III, Samuel Smiles produced the two-volume biography of the second John entitled *A Publisher and His Friends*: *Memoir and Correspondence of the Late John Murray, with an Account of the Origin and Progress of the House, 1768–1843*.[1] A valuable collection of material on the nineteenth-century publishing scene, the work is, as might be expected, highly sympathetic toward its subject, the result being a rather saint-like image which does not always fit the outlines drawn in the letters and other private statements of Byron, Thomas Moore, John Gibson Lockhart, Washington Irving, and the numerous contemporaries who were a part of Murray's circle.

John Murray I having died in 1793, young John and the family bookshop were left in the charge of Samuel Highley, who had been a business associate of the elder Murray. Highley's unimaginative book-selling leadership resulted in apprentice John's dissolution of the relationship in 1804 when he came of age. Immediately the young man launched into a career as both bookseller and publisher, the latter being a profession as yet imperfectly developed. In this capacity he initiated works ranging from current drama in book form to a best-selling English cookbook and was recognized, by 1807 when he married Miss Anne Elliot, the daughter of a deceased Edinburgh book dealer, as a prominent figure in the book trade, his connections including in Scotland Constable & Co. and Walter Scott and in London a group of influential Tories, such men as John Wilson Croker, William Gifford, and John Barrow, who were organizing in opposition to the Whiggish *Edinburgh Review*. With John Murray II as the founding publisher and Gifford as the editor, the first issue of the *Quarterly Review* appeared in February 1809, the work of Murray's Tory coterie.

In 1812 the Murrays moved from the Fleet Street address where the first John had opened his bookshop to the heart of aristocratic Mayfair, 50 Albermarle Street, the present address of the firm. *Quarterly Review* contributors continued to meet to talk about future plans, and the publisher's expanding gallery of authors gathered to discuss business and to gossip. The drawing room at the new address became "a sort of literary lounge" where lucky visitors might expect to talk with Byron and, if he were in town, Scott. The Murrays' dinner parties, where "conversation never failed" from seven to midnight, were similar to those "Lintot used to give to Pope and Gay and Swift; and Dilly, to Johnson and Goldsmith."[2]

At his own social events as well as abroad in society, John Murray II had a passion for broadcasting his projected plans, all the while name-dropping with wild abandon, a tendency which caused a contemporary to characterize him as a person who "chattered incessantly."[3] This vocal exuberance sometimes got him into trouble: "Murray's own leaky lips"[4]—to use the alliterative words of John Gibson Lockhart who became *Quarterly Review* editor in 1826—too often made premature announcements of future hopes or told stories better left untold. These same lips he used to "butter"[5] generously his successful authors and his clientele in an effort to keep as many people as possible happily writing and buying his books. Referring to her business dealings with Murray, mild Jane Austen described him in 1815 as "a rogue of course"; then she hastily added, "but a civil one."[6] He was a product of the Romantic Age, a studied opportunist, a spirited publisher who, perhaps more than any of his contemporaries, was able to cope with the literati of his time, figures of such explosive nature as Lord Byron, Lady Caroline Lamb, and young Benjamin Disraeli.

John Murray II was called by many names. To Byron he was "the *avaξ* of publishers";[7] Carlyle dubbed him "the Charon of Albemarle Street";[8] Thomas Moore saw him as the "great Bibliophola Tryphon."[9] To friend and enemy alike he was "the prince of aristocratic bibliopoles"[10]—Washington Irving used such a royal title in praise,[11] but Wordsworth assumed a bitter tone when he declared that Murray was "too great a personage for any one but a count, an aristocrat, or most fashionable author to deal with."[12] Situated in elite Mayfair, Murray himself appreciated the role most frequently assigned to him: "Emperor of the West."[13] All of these references took into account his prominent position in the book trade. He was also, a later biographer tells us, known as "The Playboy of the Publishing World."[14]

His "playboy" image was firmly set by the late 1820's. The Murrays' drawing room was, more than ever, the meeting place of the best of literary society, as were their frequent dinner parties.[15] And even in professional matters there was a "playboy" flair to John's activities. Having failed in a most spectacular fashion (to the extent of £26,-000) in an attempt to establish a daily newspaper, *The Representative,* which would rival *The Times,* Murray launched in 1828 another speculative venture, his Family Library, a multivolume series of new books by well-known authors, with Lockhart as the general editor. Meanwhile, his health fluctuated (Lockhart later declared that Murray's main physical disability was gout brought on by high living)[16] as business worries plagued him more and more. That he was drinking heavily was a fact, and it was rumored that he was "entangled" (a popular society word) with women of doubtful reputation. To an experienced blackmailer, John Murray II must have looked like a ripe plum.

Charles Molloy Westmacott, "the principal blackmailing editor of his day,"[17] focused his attention on the publisher in 1828. Of dubious parentage, Westmacott had worked his way into the London literary world by associating himself as a hack-writer with various scurrilous muck-raking ventures. Using the pseudonym "Bernard Blackmantel," he published several satirical works including *English Spy; or, Characteristic Sketches and Scenes of the Present Age,* but by 1827 he had abandoned this pen name and was advertising himself as "The Editor of *The Age,*" a weekly which could only be described as a scandal sheet. Listing some of the contents of *The Age* on September 14, 1828, the editor included "anecdotes for the man of the town—*bon mots* for the witty— . . . and *on dits* for the scandal-lovers." Then he added: *"Double entendres* may sometimes be found amongst us; but they are not *very* bad; all folks are not supposed to know the *meaning* of such jokes; and what is *hid* need not be *revealed.*"[18] Coming from Westmacott, the last clause was a threat rather than a statement. So notorious as a blackmailer was this man that Edward Bulwer devoted a section of his *England and the English* to an exposé of his work, including an explanation of Westmacott's operational procedure: he "writes to you—'Sir, I have received some anecdotes about you, which I would not publish for the world if you will give me ten pounds for them.' "[19]

If this were what happened to John Murray II, he apparently did not pay, for scattered through *The Age* during 1828 and 1829 are thirty-four atrocious anecdotes concerning the publisher.[20] Entitled "Murrayana," the series is a conglomeration of gossip, half-truths, misstatements, and fabrications—all put together for the purpose of reducing its subject in the mind of the reader to a clownish entrepreneur whose success was in spite of ineptitude, stupidity, and immorality. To achieve this image of Murray, the author dealt with selected factual bits, incorporating some actual and believable names of individuals for verisimilitude, but his usual technique was to plant seeds for the reader to cultivate. Even clearly false anecdotes (as, for example, XXXIV, indicating that Murray wished to use an umbrella to avoid getting wet while taking a shower bath) played a psychological trick by robbing the publisher of some of his dignity through the ludicrous situations in which he was pictured. The innuendo against Mrs. Murray (XIII) is perhaps the most obvious "seed" in the entire packet. References to Cavendish Square and King, Maddox, and Upper Baker Streets (IX, XII, XXIX, XXVII) imply or seem to imply that these were locations which Murray frequented for the purpose of debauchery, sexual or otherwise, but this alleged misconduct was probably as elusive to documentation in 1829 as it is today. Lost in time (if, indeed, they ever had a significant meaning) are such identifications as the "French gentleman" (XXV) and the "friend" with whom Murray was walking "in the neighbourhood of Dartford" (XXX).

The reader in the early 1970's must view "Murrayana" with even more skepticism than did his counterpart of the late 1820's. Untrustworthy though it is, Westmacott's image of Murray is an interesting counterbalance to Smiles' picture of the publisher, but more important than what it says about Murray is its genre value: few examples of the Literature of Blackmail get into print.

Murrayana

ANECDOTE I.—Some four of five years ago Murray received a letter, bearing the Winchester post mark, and the signature of George Winton, which informed the bibliopole, that the writer was then employed in preparing a life of Pitt, from authentic documents, and that it was his intention to give the publication to John, if it suited his inclination. The "absolute" gentleman, however, not having ever heard of any such person as George Winton in the literary world, and imagining that the communication came from some needy author, or gentleman of the press, sat down, in a humour not the most placid, to answer, what he conceived to be a most impertinent note from a perfect stranger. The reply was couched in Jack's usual polite and polished style, and stated, among other reasons for not undertaking the task, "that there were so many lives of the great statesman already concocted, by persons wholly incompetent to the task—all drawn up from 'unquestionable documents,' though bearing falsehood on the face of them —that he would require some less questionable character than Mr. George Winton, as a security for the outlay of his money." This laconic note was forthwith dispatched to the post-office, as the bookseller could not delay one moment in answering so presumptuous a correspondent. In a short time afterwards, BARROW, of the Admiralty,[21] called in at Murray's, and the letter was shown him, while Jack, with a self-approving chuckle, told him the nature of his reply. "Are you mad or tipsy?" said Barrow, "the letter is from THE BISHOP OF WINCHESTER, Mr. PITT's favourite tutor!" Poor Jack! 'Twas worth a Jew's-eye to have seen his face at the unexpected announcement. However, no time was to be lost; post-horses were immediately ordered, and down to Winchester drove the agonized bookseller, at the rate of ten miles an hour, in order to arrive before the mail. In this he fortunately succeeded, and waiting in the neighbourhood of the post-office until the bags were delivered, he applied, with trembling limbs and beating heart, for a letter for George Winton; he was lucky enough to procure it, and immediately returned to Albemarle-street with the precious epistle.[22] The joke got wind, and never had poor mortal such badgering to bear for some months afterwards as Mister Murray, bookseller and publisher.

ANECDOTE II.—When Murray kept the shop, which is now in the possession of Mr. Underwood, Fleet-street,[23] he had a large share in the sale of medical as well as general literature. A schoolmaster of the name of ———applied one day at the establishment, for a copy of CAESAR'S COMMENTARIES, and had the pleasure of being attended to by Absolute himself, who, having vainly rummaged the shelves for the book wanted, addressed the applicant, book in hand, as follows:—"Sir," said he, "I cannot find a copy of CAESAR'S COMMENTARIES, but I have brought you the last edition of HEBERDON's,[24] which, I suppose, will answer as well!" Jack did not know the difference!

ANECDOTE III.—When John was in Scotland, in the year 1806, he went on a tour of Aberdeen, accompanied by the late Mr. Hunter, of Blackness.[25] In the course of the journey, a particularly fine and extensive view of the German Ocean was pointed out to him, when he asked his companion, with his usual discernment—"God bless me! DOES GERMANY LIE OVER THERE?"

ANECDOTE IV.—"Absolute" met the Rev. Mr. Gilly, now a Prebendary of Durham, shortly after the publication of that gentleman's very interesing work on the present condition, &c. &c. of the VAUDOIS.[26] "It is a very clever work of yours, Sir," said he, "very clever indeed; it has put me quite on the fidgets as to the fate of these poor VAUDOIS—I think they were almost as badly used as the WALDENSES." "Sir," said Gilly, "they are the Waldenses—Waldenses is only Latin for Vaudois." "Latin," said Jack, "by G— it was Greek to me."

ANECDOTE V.—John being seated at dinner in a large party at Aberdeen, a *sheep's head* was one of the dishes: upon being asked if he knew what it was, he replied, "To be sure I do; *it is a HAGGIS!*" and the day after this a *haggis* was presented at table, which John as knowingly pronounced to be a *sheep's head*! ! !

ANECDOTE VI.—When Lord Byron was about to leave town for that country where his life became a sacrifice, Murray could scarcely be induced to talk on any other subject than the Noble Lord's departure.[27] Jack had an eye to his money bags; and, of course, no person can blame him for that. On one occasion he was grumbling loudly to his friend D'Israeli[28] on the never ending topic, when Croker[29] walked into the great bibliopole's shop. "I have advised him, and advised him repeatedly, to remain in London," were the words which struck the Secretary's ear, who looked at the speaker for a moment or two attentively, and then in his own peculiar manner—half lisp, half growl—exclaimed, "Murray, my old fellow, I have read of a man in scripture who was once advised by a certain long-eared animal,[30] but I could never discover that his remonstrance was in the slightest degree attended to."

ANECDOTE VII.—"What an extraordinary language Hebrew is," said Jack to Dr. Phillpots[31] one day. "I can't, for the life of me, make out even a letter of it. I suppose it must be very hard to learn." "Not very difficult," said the Doctor, "but a Hebrew book has one peculiarity which distinguishes it from all others, it is read backwards." "Stop," said Jack, "none of your gammon; read *backwards,* indeed; not a bit of it. I saw the Duke of Sussex[32] one day reading it in his front drawing-room."

ANECDOTE VIII.—John Murray was dreaming of the immense fortune that he was to make by the *"Representative,"* and annoying every man, woman, and child with his immeasurable boastings about that abortive off-spring of his imagination.[33] He was in the habit of going daily to Clowes's Office,[34] where the "Rip" was printed, and comparing it with the other Morning Papers. One forenoon he went there, as usual, and taking up the

Times, he, after an attentive perusal, flung it on the ground, and trampling it beneath his feet, exclaimed "Before one month, the *Times* shall be as low in public estimation as this copy, which I honour by treading on, now is." Alas! John, where is your *"Rip,"* and your £15,000?[35]

ANECDOTE IX.—When our hero set up the "Rip," alias the *Representative* newspaper, to eclipse the Old *Times,* it is well known that he had no less than six Editors in seven successive days. During these annoying changes, John was seen one evening wandering in the neighbourhood of Cavendish Square, and working his way along in a zigzag fashion, or, as Commodore Trunnion[36] would express it, upon tack and half tack, by a certain humane person, who feeling for his situation enquired if he wanted a coach. "No, d—me Sir," hiccupped John, "I want an Editor!"[37]

ANECDOTE X.—When Murray appointed Dundas his first secretary, he told him that he did so from a feeling of loyalty—"For," said he, "Dundas was a favourite name with Majesty, and if you behave yourself well, you shall be a prime favourite with the KING of the Booksellers."[38]

ANECDOTE XI.—John was, a few weeks ago, talking to Mr. Gillies[39] on things in general, newspapers, books, the Russian war, and Stinkomalee[40] —when he suddenly inquired of his friend whether he had seen a little book, lately published, on German literature. He was replied to in the affirmative, and was asked in his turn whether he understood German. "I do not, I am sorry to say," answered John, "but I sometimes amuse myself by playing on the German flute."

ANECDOTE XII.—Every one knows that our hero visits a certain house, in a certain street not far from Westminster Hall. King Street,[41] we believe, is its appellation; and it is as generally known that whenever he goes there, it is after a double potation of the refreshing grape-juice. The lady who reigns as mistress of the mansion had frequently told John, that nothing could be more disagreeable to her than the peculiar odour which wine gives the breath, and repeatedly requested that he would—were it but for once—pay her a visit sober.

On one occasion Jack was upset in a pool opposite the Treasury buildings,[42] which were then repairing, and dripping with sweets, made the best of his way to his old quarters. Astonishment made the lady exclaim, "my dear John, how you *do* smell!"—"What," replied our hero, "is there no way of pleasing you? If I do smell," looking at his muddy inexpressibles, "you cannot, at all events, say it is of claret to-night."

ANECDOTE XIII.—When Mrs. Elliott[43] and John were————But perhaps this anecdote may not be authentic; we shall enquire between this and our next Number.

ANECDOTE XIV.—The hero of these, our amusing historiettes, as well as many others of the natives, was much puzzled by a Greek inscription, which used to figure conspicuously (and perhaps now does) on a large white building (now a billiard room) in Welbeck-street, Cavendish-square. The word, if we recollect right, was διαταλαιπορου.[44] After in vain trying to decypher it, JOHN came to the sage conclusion, that it must be German for auctioneer. The rooms were then used as a furniture warehouse.

ANECDOTE XV.—Lord BYRON was one day admiring a beautiful statue, by CANOVA, just imported, and said, "All that it wants is to speak—it would then be a divinity."[45] The observation of his Lordship struck MURRAY as being very fine, and accordingly he determined to use it on the first opportunity. Being at a sale a short time after, CHRISTIE[46] was loud in his praises of a very handsome commode. "It is really very beautiful," said the actioneer. "Aye," said MURRAY, "all it wants is to speak, it would then be a divinity." The company laughed at the extravagance of JACK'S compliment. "Yes," said he, indignantly, "laugh as you like—blockheads as you are, you are little aware that is an observation I heard from the great Lord BYRON."

ANECDOTE XVI.—JOHN met a friend the other day in the Strand, who complained of the weather, observing, "Though it is so cold, I think the wind is Westerly." "Yes," said JOHN, "the wind is in the West, but still there is some of the East with it."

ANECDOTE XVII.—John was once upon a jury at the Westminster Sessions, when a poor creature who had starvation in his looks, was tried for horse stealing. The tender heart of the great bibliopole was touched by the misfortunes of the prisoner, which were clearly apparent as the trial proceeded, and he was determined to save him, if possible, from the gallows. "Gentlemen," said John to his brother jurymen, when they had retired to consult, "it is evident from what we have heard, that the prisoner has committed the crime imputed to him, but we should feel for the distresses of our fellow-creatures. If we return a verdict of guilty, he will certainly be hanged. I therefore propose that we find him guilty of the minor offence, namely, that of manslaughter." It is needless to say, that his humane advice was not attended to.

ANECDOTE XVIII.—So determined is Murray to prove that Lord Byron was a moral poet, and worthy of the monument about to be erected in his memory,[47] that he has actually commenced an action against an individual for reprinting some of the few moral passages that his Lordship's works contain.[48]

ANECDOTE XIX.—When John was an apprentice, he was asked one day who was the greatest and most voluminous author of the day. Jack, after considering some time, replied, "Why, Index, to be sure." Some have attributed this joke to the facetious Joe Miller, and put the word "Finis" into *his* mouth, but ours is the genuine anecdote.

ANECDOTE XX.—When Murray was a miscellaneous vendor of books and stationary, in Fleet-street, that is, before he aspired to the rank of an "absolute" publisher, a gentleman applied to him one day for a copy of Beckford's Calip Vathek, which is rather a scarce book. After searching his shelves for some time in vain, he returned to his customer, and with one of his winning smiles declared, "that he could not put his hand on Caleb

Vathek; but if Caleb Williams would do as well, that work was at his service."[49]

Anecdote xxi.—George Banks, Esq.[50] was one day in conversation with Jack in Albemarle-street, who was listening intentively to a description of some of the curiosities which the former gentleman had seen in the course of his travels. In speaking of the statue of Memnon, Mr. Banks was endeavouring to explain to Murray of what an enormous size the figure must be, when the ear, which is above ground, was the height of six-feet. "Six devils," exclaimed the bibliopole, "I know that Memnon is a giant; but no living man, giant or no giant, has an ear six-feet high. That bam won't answer for a cunning fellow like me."[51]

Anecdote xxii.—When Murray resided at Wimbledon,[52] he had the following Notice printed and exhibited on a board placed in a conspicuous part of the grounds. We are authorized to say that the composition is from the able and classical pen of the great Bibliopole himself:—

NOTICE
Whoever is found trespassing on these grounds will be *shot* and *prosecuted*.

Whether the intention was ever put into practice or not our informant does not mention.

Anecdote xxiii.—A short time since a foreigner who had been making some purchases at Murray's shop in Albemarle-street, was recognised by a friend and introduced by him to "Absolute." As soon as he had left the house, Jack inquired what countryman he was. "He comes from Geneva," said the friend. "I *knew* from his talk," said our hero, "that he was a Dutchman." The gentleman endeavoured to correct Jack's mistake, but in vain. "I know very well," said he, "that Geneva is Hollands, and Hollands is Dutch, and a Dutchman he is, or I'll be————."

Anecdote xxiv.—Jack went on one occasion, through mere curiosity, to hear a lecture on Natural History. The Professor was engaged in treating the varieties of the Genus Pica, and made use of the following words: —"The Genus Pica," said he, "is our pie." "That's a lie," said Murray, loud enough for the whole assembly to hear him, "for if Pica was pie, it would be entirely spoiled." He left the room instantly, declaring that from that moment he would never set foot in any lecture-room again.

Anecdote xxv.—A French gentleman, who had been introduced to Murray last summer, and treated by him (as, to do him justice, is his constant practice) with the greatest hospitality, was invited to spend a day with Jack and a party of his friends at Richmond. The day was peculiarly bright and clear, and, before dinner was served up the host and his foreign friend sauntered about the pretty green lawn at the rear of the Star and Garter Hotel,[53] where the company were to be entertained. Murray pointed out and explained the different picturesque objects which are to be seen from that delightful spot, and expatiated, in his own impressive and intelligent manner, upon the river Thames, the clusters of trees, the cottages scattered upon the river's banks, and in short every feature of the scenery which makes the neighbourhood of Richmond so delightful. Among the rest of the objects, he pointed out "a speck in the horizon," Windsor Castle, and of course informed the stranger that it was one of the Royal palaces. Curiosity and desire of information induced his companion to inquire whether the Castle was an ancient one. Murray's reply was singular:—"It *was* ancient *formerly,* Sir," said Jack, "but Mr. Wyattville[54] has been lately repairing it!"

ANECDOTE XXVI.—One day recently—we forget the precise day—was oppressively hot, and Murray felt the effects of the sun as annoying as most residents of London. Several refrigerants were tried by him, such as hock, cold brandy and water, soda water, ginger beer, lemonade, &c. but all to no purpose; the more he tried to expel the caloric by potations, the more fiercely it afflicted him. Captain Parry[55] happened to call on John, and found him in a state of feverish excitation. "This is the hottest day, Parry," said Murray, wiping his forehead, "that I ever felt." "It is warm, indeed," was the reply; "how stands the thermometer?" "Thermometers be d——d," said Jack, "hang me if the heat is not *ten degrees above Fahrenheit!*"

ANECDOTE XXVII.—Our worthy bookseller was making the best of his way home one night, a short time ago, in a state which must not be mentioned to ears polite, but in that state which Jack is in every night of his life; and missing an angle in Upper Baker street,[56] he tumbled head-over-heels into an area, where he alighted up to the neck in a large vessel of soap-suds, in which the family linen had been washed the day before. After a good deal of difficulty, he was extricated from his perilous situation by the aid of a neighbouring watchman and a gas-lighter's ladder and conducted home with a bruised body and a pair of clouded optics.[57] The following day he gave directions that he should be denied to every person who might inquire for him; but Wilson Croker, who wanted Murray to discount a fifty pound bill for him, would *not be denied*, and he forced his way into Jack's bed-room, where he found him with his head wrapped in a flannel, the very picture of despair. The principal business which brought the Secretary there being finished, he inquired the cause of Murray's indisposition, and was told, *in confidence,* the mishap he had met with. "My dear friend," said the sufferer, "I tumbled into a wash-tub, broke one of my ribs, I believe, battered my head, and, from want of room to breathe in, was nearly smothered." "That *is* strange," replied the Secretary with one of his own sardonic smiles; "that *is* strange, that you should be nearly smothered, when, by your own account you were so peculiarly fortunate as to have tumbled into an *airy.*"

ANECDOTE XXVIII.—Cadell was talking with Murray a few days since about the great success and extensive sale of Blackwood's Magazine, and the general popularity of its political opinions.[58] "True," said Murray, "there is but one periodical that can compete with it; I need not tell you the one I mean: but the only thing that Blackwood's Magazine wants to make it a *Quarterly* is, that it should be published every three months!"

XXIX.—JACK MURRAY, returning from Epson Races in an open barouch, with his fair friend of Maddox-street,[59] and having lost the turnpike ticket (a Hebrew collector, but not "one without guile,") demanded repayment, to which Jack was reluctantly forced to yield, upon which John Wilson Croker, his companion observed, that it was a "Jew trick." "Yes," added Jack Murray, "it is so, and it is Jew-dish-us (judicious) also." The Hebrew collector was seen to blush, for the first time in his life, at this puerile attempt of the "Emperor of the West."

ANECDOTE XXX.—Not many weeks ago, the hero of our facetiæ was walking with a friend in the neighbourhood of Dartford,[60] when they encountered an object but rarely seen—a dead jackass. Murray philosophised over the inanimate animal in a style which would have done credit to Laurence Sterne himself, and thus ended his pathetic oration:—"But my friend there is no use in talking, the animal is dead, but it is only what I shall be myself some day hereafter."

XXXI.—A country gentleman who keeps some good hunters, and an excellent pack of fox-hounds, was telling Murray one day that he had been so unfortunate as to lose his own favourite horse, who had strayed from the stables, and accidentally slipping from the bank into the river, flooded at the time, was drowned. "And what have you done with the carcase?" enquired the bibliopole. "Given it to the hounds," was his friend's reply. "There you acted foolishly," said Jack; "had it been my case, I should have hung the carcase up in the stable as a warning to the remainder of the horses, by which they would learn such as quit their stalls without leave are likely to come to an untimely end."

XXXII.—When the intention of Don Pedro to bestow the hand of his daughter Donna Maria de Gloria, upon his brother Don Miguel, was first made known in this country, Murray heard of it, of course, and was extremely puzzled to discover how it could be managed. It was explained to him that the only difficulty in effecting the object was the consent of the Pope, which was obtained, that Pontiff having agreed to grant the parties a dispensation. Still Murray was incredulous, and at last he settled down into a decided non-belief; "For," said the sagacious bookseller, "no Pope that ever lived had it in his power to make a woman her own aunt!"[61]

XXXIII.—John had a very handsome watch some time ago, but parted with it because he said he could never get it to keep time. "D—n it," said he, "it is sometimes a quarter, sometimes twenty-five minutes different from all other watches, and yet I take more pains with it than many would do. I set it myself by a sun-dial every day that the sun shines." "Had you not better set it by the clock at the Horse Guards, you will then have the true time,"[62] said a friend to him. "True time," said Jack, "why, you silly fool, can the sun-dial be wrong! do you imagine the sun don't know what time of day it is."

136   BEN HARRIS MCCLARY

XXXIV.—Our hero was recommended at one time, by his physician, to use a shower-bath, for a headache which annoyed him. "I have but one objection," said he, "and that is, that I am almost sure to catch cold when I get wet; but if you insist upon it, I suppose I must submit; but will you allow me to take my umbrella with me!"

NOTES

This article is part of a research project made possible by a grant from The American Council of Learned Societies, summer 1967.
1. Hereafter cited as Smiles.
2. So declared American George Ticknor who visited the Murray "literary exchange" in June 1815 and recorded his pleasant experiences there. *Life, Letters, and Journals of George Ticknor* (Boston, 1876), I, 58, 62–63, 68. Murray's drawing-room group is usually considered as being the genesis of the Athenaeum Club. See Ian Jack, *English Literature, 1815–1832, Vol. X: The Oxford History of English Literature* (Oxford, 1963), pp. 27–28; Reginald Colby, *Mayfair: A Town Within London* (New York, 1966), pp. 118–120.
3. Charles C. F. Greville, *The Greville Memoirs: A Journal of the Reigns of Kings George IV and William IV*, ed. Henry Reeve (London, 1875), I, 280.
4. Quoted in Myron Franklin Brightfield, *John Wilson Croker* (Berkeley, Cal., 1940), p. 186.
5. See *The Letters of Richard Ford, 1797–1858*, ed. Rowland E. Prothero (New York, 1905), p. 165.
6. *Jane Austen's Letters to Her Sister Cassandra and Others*, ed. R. W. Chapman (Oxford, 1932), II, 425.
7. *The Works of Byron: Letters and Journals*, ed. Rowland E. Prothero (London, 1904), II, 224.
8. Quoted in Smiles, II, 355.
9. *Memoirs, Journal, and Correspondence of Thomas Moore*, ed. Lord John Russell (London, 1853), II, 210.
10. James Grant, *Portraits of Public Characters* (London, 1841), II, 1.
11. See Pierre M. Irving, *The Life and Letters of Washington Irving* (New York, 1864), I, 432.
12. Quoted in R. Ellis Roberts, *Samuel Rogers and His Circle* (London, 1910) p. 168.
13. West *End* of London. See Anecdote XXIX.
14. George Paston [Emily Morse Symonds], *At John Murray's: Records of a Literary Circle* (London, 1932), p. 6.
15. Charles MacFarlane described two typically riotous dinner parties in the late 1820's in *Reminiscences of a Literary Life* (London, 1917), pp. 19–20, 68–69. In *Theodore Hook and His Novels* (Cambridge, Mass., 1928, pp. 203–204), Myron Brightfield quoted an account of a party during which the inebriated Murray chased Hook around the table.
16. Letter to H. H. Milman, dated 1830. Presently in Murray Archives.
17. Michael Sadleir, *Blessington-D'Orsay: A Masquerade* (London, 1933), p. 138. Sadleir is the only research scholar who has devoted any time to Westmacott, his interest being confined to the editor's attacks on the reputation of Countess Blessington in 1831–1832. (See *ibid.*, pp. 138 sqq.,

241–242.) Earlier Sadleir had told the Blessington story from Bulwer's viewpoint in *Bulwer: A Panorama* (London, 1931), pp. 336–346. See also "Charles Molloy Westmacott" in William Bates, *The Maclise Portrait of Illustrious Literary Characters with Memoirs* (London, 1898), 236–242. There is a drawing of the subject opposite p. 236.

18. Sept. 14, 1828, p. 294.
19. (London, 1833), II, 235.
20. Anecdotes I–II, Aug. 31, 1828, p. 275; III–V, Sept. 7, p. 286; VI–VIII, Sept. 14, p. 294; IX–X, Sept. 21, p. 302; XI–XIII, Sept. 28, p. 310; XIV–XVI, Oct. 19, p. 335; XVII–XIX, Nov. 9, p. 355; XX–XXI, Nov. 23, p. 370; XXII–XXIV, Dec. 7, p. 286; XXV–XXIX, June 7, 1829, p. 182; XXX–XXXIV, Aug. 16, p. 262.
21. Later Sir John Barrow (1764–1848), Secretary of the Admiralty and constant friend and literary adviser to Murray. See *Dictionary of National Biography*. Hereafter cited as *DNB*.
22. The correct name and title of the author was Sir George Pretyman Tomline, Bishop of Winchester (1750–1827). *Memoirs of the Life of the Right Hon. William Pitt* was published by Murray in 1821 and ran through four editions before the end of 1822. "Much was expected of the work owing to Tomline's unique opportunities to knowledge, and the fact that Pitt's correspondence was in his possession; but," says the *DNB* (quoting Murray's *QR* [XXXVI, 286]), "Tomline altogether disappointed public expectations by the scanty use he made of Pitt's letters." LVII, 16.
23. Thomas and George Underwood, Booksellers, 32 Fleet Street. Pigot & Co.'s *Metropolitan Alphabetical Directory for 1828* (London [1827]), p. 403. After Murray's removal, the Fleet street business had been bought by the Underwoods who finally failed in 1831. See Smiles, I, 234.
24. The reference is apparently to W. H. Heberden's *Commentaries on the History and Cure of Diseases,* translated from his father's Latin text in 1802. It was extremely popular and has recently been published in facsimile.
25. Alexander Gibson Hunter, the partner of Archibald Constable in Edinburgh. Constable & Co. were "courting" Murray at this time because they wanted him to serve as agent for the *Edinburgh Review* in London. For a description of the tour, see Smiles, I, 70–71. Thomas Constable in his history of his father's business activities, *Archibald Constable and His Literary Correspondence* (Edinburgh, 1873), I, 159–160, tells of Hunter's death on March 9, 1812.
26. William Stephen Gilly (1789–1855) had published in 1824 *Narrative of an Excursion to the Mountains of Piedmont, and Reaches among the Vaudois, or Waldenses, Protestant Inhabitants of the Cottian Alps* (London). *DNB, XXI,* 377.
27. "John Murray's Byronic prestige" (George Bernard Shaw's term used in a letter to Daniel Macmillan, Sept. 11, 1934, quoted in Charles Morgan, *The House of Macmillan* [London, 1943], p. 132) was a fact from 1812 when John II began publishing *Childe Harold's Pilgrimage.* Byron "used" his publisher for his own purposes, but John II and his successors have been amply repaid. By 1828 Murray had organized a fabulous collection of Byroniana and had put Tom Moore to work on a highly publicized edition of the letters and journals. The Murrays have "the finest Byron collection in existence," according to Leslie A. Marchand, *Byron: A Biography* (New York, 1957), I, xiv.

28. Isaac D'Israeli (1766–1848), father of the later prime minister. A wealthy Jewish bibliophile who spent much of his time in the British Museum Reading Room and at Murray's. See *DNB,* V, 1022–25.

29. John Wilson Croker (1780–1857), outspoken Tory politican and one of the most frequent contributors to *QR*. See *DNB,* V, 123–132. His long and close relationship with John Murray II makes up a large part of Myron F. Brightfield, *John Wilson Croker* (Berkeley, Cal., 1940).

30. Reference to Balaam's ass. Numbers 22:21–33.

31. Henry Phillpots (1778–1869), formerly a fellow of Magdalen College, Oxford, later (1830–1869), Bishop of Exeter. *DNB,* XLV, 222–225.

32. Augustus Frederick, Duke of Sussex, sixth son of George III, was an avid collector of expensive books, his private library amounting to over 50,000 printed volumes and many Hebrew and other ancient manuscripts. *DNB,* I, 729–730.

33. In late 1825 Murray invested heavily in a daily newspaper of which he was to be a partner with young Benjamin Disraeli (who had thus anglicized his name). The first issue appeared on Jan. 25, 1826. Disraeli proved to be an unstable partner (he later caricatured Murray in his novel *Vivian Grey*), and Murray's frequently voiced intention of rivaling the London *Times* was never realized. The last issue was published on July 29. See Smiles, II, 180–218.

34. *The Representative,* Jan. 25, 1826, stated: "Printed and Published by Thomas Cope at the Printing Office of Mr. Clowes, in Northumberland-court, Strand. Advertisements and Communications for the Editor to be sent to the Offices of the *Representative,* No. 25, Great George-street, Westminster, or No. 46, Fleet-street." William Clowes was the printer of the *QR* and many of Murray's quality books. Cope's personal file of *The Representative* is in the Colindale Newspaper Library of the British Museum.

35. Murray reckoned his losses at closer to £26,000. Smiles, II, 215.

36. Commodore Hawser Trunnion, a one-eyed naval veteran in Smollett's *Adventures of Peregrine Pickle.*

37. Murray's biggest problem with his newspaper was securing a competent editor. As Smiles, II, 210–211, told this story, Murray was hurrying home, deep in thought about the editorship, when he motioned a greeting to an acquaintance. Mistaking the gesture for a beckon, the friend approached him and asked what he wanted. Seizing the question and the moment, the publisher flabbergasted the pedestrian by screaming into the cold night air: "I want an editor! I want an editor!"

38. The royal reference is perhaps to Sir David Dundas (1735–1820), highly regarded by the reigning family. See *DNB,* VI, 184. In his private memoirs Charles MacFarlane told of an attempt to help anonymously William Godwin financially which originated in "King John's drawing room. . . . And if King John had not babbled over his cups, and if his head clerk and 'Fidus Achates,' Mr. Dundas, had not tattled, Godwin would never have known whence the money came." P. 100.

39. Robert Pearse Gillies (1788–1858) was editing the *Foreign Quarterly Review,* being sponsored by the London firm of Truettel & Wurtz, Truettel, Jr., & Richter. *DNB, XXI,* 369–370.

40. A word coined by Theodore Hook, a frequenter of Murray's drawing room (see above, note 15), referring to the University of London and the controversy surrounding its founding.

41. King Street, in 1828, was a continuation of Whitehall from the point where,

a little south of the Treasury, that thoroughfare forked, making Parliament and King Streets. The Greater London Record Office, The County Hall, London, S.E.1, does not have sufficient residency listings to allow for speculation as to possible identity of the individual referred to here.

42. The sewer plans of the Westminster Commission of Sewers in the Greater London Record Office show a well-developed system of enclosed sewers in the 1820's. The "pool" in question, if there is any validity to this anecdote, must have been, as the text suggests, open temporarily.

43. Perhaps sly innuendo aimed at Mrs. Murray, using the *Mrs.* to suggest an older more experienced woman than a mere Miss.

44. Translated as "through hardship." The Archives Department of the Westminster Public Library has two drawings (Ashbridge 160/WEL) of this building, in the style of an Egyptian mausoleum. They are dated *c.*1823 and indicate that it was then the studio of Peter Edward Stroehling, portrait painter and miniaturist who died during or shortly after 1826. No trace of the building remains. Westmacott's Greek, undoubtedly a corrupt form of the original inscription, can be loosely translated as "through enduring toil."

45. Perhaps a reference to Byron's well-known verse appreciation of Canova's bust of Helen.

46. James Christie, the younger (1773–1831), auctioneer. *DNB,* IV, 283–284. Christie's, the historic firm of auctioneers, is still at 8 King St., St. James's, London, S.W.1.

47. On June 7, 1828, a committee met at John Murray's to consider taking subscriptions for a monument to Byron. On May 22, 1829, the committee wrote to Thorwaldsen, the sculptor, offering £1500 for a likeness of Byron to be placed in Westminster Abbey. Modeled in Rome, it was shipped to England in 1831, but it remained in the customs house as the Abbey refused to accept it year after year. In 1843 Trinity College, Cambridge, accepted the statue, placing it in the center aisle of the Library. Richard Edgcumbe, *History of the Byron Memorial* (London, 1883), *passim.*

48. For the sum of £3885, John Murray had purchased at auction the Byron copyrights which he did not already own (Smiles, II, 305–306). These copyrights Murray did not hesitate to defend by legal action, but there is no evidence of his going to this extreme.

49. William Beckford's *Vathek, An Arabian Tale* was first published in English in 1786. William Godwin's *Adventures of Caleb Williams,* a propaganda novel having to do with crime and detection, was published in 1794.

50. Probably George Bankes (1788–1856) whose father was a trustee of the British Museum and an authority on aspects of ancient history. See *DNB,* III, 120–121. The Memnon reference is to the colossal statue at Thebes.

51. On Nov. 23, 1828, in addition to "Murrayana," *The Age* carried the following quotation as a separate article:

"We have frequently said, and still more frequently thought, that our old friend, JACK MURRAY, of the Murrayana, Esq., was not equal in wisdom to the seven wise masters. Indeed, his chaplain, Parson EDWARDS, admitted something of the same kind to us the other day. 'My master,' said the widow-bewitching Welshman, 'is half his time muzzy, half his time asleep, and the other half an ass.'

"Though this is true, yet, in matter of business, he is, as JOHNSON said of GOLDSMITH, 'an inspired idiot.' He caught GIFFORD first, then BYRON, and now LOCKHART. The first put him at the head of all periodicals (the Quarterly is worth to old Muzzy at least £4000 a-year) the second made him the fashionable and the successful publishers—and now the Scot has started for him the FAMILY LIBRARY, which if all tales are true, will be as great a hit as either of the others. There were six THOUSAND subscribed the first day; and beyond doubt, the Life of BUONAPARTE deserved it. If the thing goes on with the same spirit, it must knock BROUGHAM, and the Useful Knowledge scamps, and all such small deer, out of the market as clean as a whistle. MUZZY is doing the genteel thing on the occasion—forking out £500 a volume to the scribes, and employing FINDEN and CRUIKSHANK and other prime fellows as his artists. That after all is the way to do the thing as it ought to be. JACK may order in more champagne, but when he next gets hoozy on hock, he should not let BEN D'ISRAELI be of the party, to take down his talk. No—JOHN—no—that sallow Hebrew has been the devil to your good fame. Get drunk with CROKER, if you like—the Right Honourable will not blab, because he owes you money—or with BARROW, for he will be as soon drunk as yourself, and will forget in the morning—but 'ware VIVIAN GREY. Stick to the Family Library—and to family duty—(no objection, however, to an occasional call in Maddox-street)—and you will do well."

The following week, letting "Murrayana" rest, *The Age* had this feature note: "Old JACK MURRAY is, after all, a good natured fellow at heart: he observed to LOCKHART last week, in speaking of our MURRAYANA, 'Never mind the wags of the AGE; you know, LOCKHART, their sale is only about ten thousand copies, and if we choose, we can reply to them in the Quarterly, which amounts to nearly seventeen.' "

52. Since the time of John Murray II, the family has usually maintained a country house at Wimbledon. See Paston, *At John Murray's,* p. 17.

53. The Star and Garter Hotel, situated at the top of Richmond Hill opposite the main gate of Richmond Park, was a regular resort for royalty and society from all over Europe. The view from lawns in the rear of the hotel was one of the most famous in the country, including then Windsor Castle. It was here years later that George Bernard Shaw set the scene for Act II in *The Doctor's Dilemma.* The hotel is now the Star and Garter Home for Disabled Sailors, Soldiers and Airmen. Miscellaneous Papers, Public Library, Richmond-Upon-Thames, Parkshot, Richmond, Surrey.

54. Architect Sir Jeffrey Wyattville had been working on Windsor Castle since 1824. *DNB,* LXIII, 191.

55. William Edward Parry (1790–1855), the arctic explorer, had already (in 1827) gone farther north than any other civilized man would go until 1876. The journals of his three voyages to achieve this goal had been published with great success, running into numerous editions, by Murray. See *DNB,* XLII, 392–392.

56. Upper Baker Street was a short block running up to Regent's Park. This street was a highly respectable address, including among its residents the venerable Mrs. Sarah Siddons at No. 27 and Countess de St. Martin at No. 39. Records in City of Westminister Central Library, Marylebone Road, London, N.W.1.

57. John Murray II had only one good eye. An accident during his early school years cost him the use of one eye, but there was no disfiguration.

58. *Blackwood's Edinburgh Magazine* was founded in 1817 as a Tory rival to the *Edinburgh Review,* an avowedly Whiggish periodical. Robert Cadell (1788–1849) had been a partner of Constable's in Edinburgh, but in 1826 went on his own and became Sir Walter Scott's publisher. See *DNB,* III, 630–631.

59. See above, note 51. A careful study of the residents of Maddox Street as indicated in the 1828 Rate Book, Archives Department, Westminster City

Library, Buckingham Palace Road, London, S.W.1, offered no likely identification for this individual.
60. In Kent, approximately seven miles west of Gravesend.
61. In 1826 Don Pedro I, Emperor of Brazil and King of Portugal, abdicated
    the Portugese crown in favor of his seven-year-old daughter, Maria da
    Gloria, who for political reasons was betrothed to her twenty-five-year-old
    uncle, Don Miguel. He was appointed regent in July 1827 and proclaimed
    king in 1828. H. V. Livermore, *A History of Portugal* (Cambridge, 1947),
    414–421.
62. "The clock contained in the cupola of the Horse Guards, was unrivaled for
    accuracy in the eighteenth century, and was taken for an authoritative
    timekeeper as Greenwich time is observed to-day." Information Leaflet
    available at Headquarters, Horse Guards, Whitehall, London, S.W.1.

Wesleyan College, Georgia

B. J. LEGGETT

DANTE, BYRON, AND TENNYSON'S ULYSSES

The generally accepted view that Tennyson's characterization of Ulysses was derived essentially from Dante's *Inferno* had its origin in Tennyson's own testimony that "there is an echo of Dante"[1] in "Ulysses" and his note in the Eversley Edition which quotes some thirty lines from Canto XXVI of the *Inferno*. Other sources for "Ulysses" have been suggested, principally Homer and Shakespeare, but the prevailing view is that it is not the Homeric Ulysses that we hear in the poem, rather Homer's Odysseus as reinterpreted by Dante.[2] Shakespeare's Ulysses, in the opinion of some scholars, may have contributed to the imagery of lines 22–24 of "Ulysses,"[3] and Douglas Bush has suggested a further parallel between these lines and *Hamlet,* IV, iv, 32–38,[4] but these are no more than faint echoes, and although Bush asserts that Tennyson "saw himself in part as a Hamlet,"[5] the traditional view of the poem as based solidly on Dante's portrayal of Ulysses has persisted virtually unchallenged.

Such an assumption is entirely consistent with traditional interpretations of the poem. Critics who have accepted Tennyson's own statement that the poem represents "the need of going forward, and braving the struggle of life"[6] have found ample support for this theme in Ulysses' heroic speech in the *Inferno*. In fact, many of the readers who follow Tennyson's view are no doubt influenced to some degree by their knowledge of Dante's Ulysses and their assumption that he is mirrored in Tennyson's hero. W. B. Stanford, for example, feels that it was Dante who revolutionized the interpretation of Ulysses by depicting him as a "man possessed by an irresistible desire for knowledge

143

and experience of the unknown world." This interpretation, he suggests, inspired modern presentations like Tennyson's "Ulysses": "The poem, as Tennyson himself remarked, gave expression to his own feelings 'about the need of going forward and braving the struggle of life. . . .' "[7] Douglas Bush follows the same line of argument: "The Greek world had no room for a mind and soul questing after the unknown, and Tennyson's conception, derived from Dante, becomes a noble expression of his belief in 'the need of going forward, and braving the struggle of life.' "[8]

Some modern readers have, however, uncovered disturbing elements in the poem which run counter to Tennyson's assessment as well as the interpretations based on it. W. H. Auden disputed the Tennysonian reading of "Ulysses" in his introduction to a selection of Tennyson's poems: ". . . what is *Ulysses* but a covert . . . refusal to be a responsible and useful person, a glorification of the heroic dandy?"[9] Paull Baum has also attacked the traditional view of the poem:

One does not brave the struggle of life by carving fresh adventure and "new things" or by sailing beyond the sunset. One does not brave the struggle of life by abandoning one's wife or indulging one's desire of travel, by following knowledge like a sinking star, by resigning prudence, the useful and the good, the sphere of common duties, the offices of tenderness—to one's son. This is the philosophy of escape. We feel that Ulysses has somewhat deceived himself—or that Tennyson is confused about it. The magnificent language does not quite conceal the muddled thinking.[10]

But while Baum concludes that the inconsistencies in Tennyson's portrayal of Ulysses represent "muddled thinking," E. J. Chiasson proposes the thesis that the poet *deliberately* portrayed "a type of human being who held a set of ideas which Tennyson regarded as destructive of the whole fabric of his society."[11] It is true that the poem ends with a burst of heroic oratory, but "the person who speaks this language is the person whom Tennyson has introduced to us as connubially insensitive . . . contemptuous of duty and the softer affections, proud in his relationship with the gods, disingenuous and contemptuous toward his own son and toward his own people; a man who pursues life with a thoroughgoing indiscrimination, and who reaches at best a vague and undirected respect for the life of intellect."[12]

It is not surprising, then, that traces of the Byronic Hero have been detected in Tennyson's Ulysses, identified by Baum in Ulysses' "pride, self-confidence, even boastfulness, his 'hungry heart' for more 'life' . . . and his rather grandiose rhetorical language,"[13] by Stanford in his "mood of peevish discontent with normal life . . . his romanticized description of himself as 'always roaming with a hungry heart,' and . . . his determination 'to drink life to the lees,' "[14] and by Chiasson in his "social irresponsibility, pursuit of sensation, and adoration of the naked intellect."[15] Yet, curiously, even the critics who find a Byronic spirit in the poem assume that Tennyson's conception of Ulysses is taken from Dante, and they are forced to justify or explain away the Byronic echoes, as Baum does when he states that "the Byronic was probably not intended for our ears, perhaps not entirely clear in the poet's," and that spellbound by the charm of the poem, we "forgive the deception."[16] But this is to assume that the Byronic echoes are intrusions into a poem based primarily on Dante, and it is this assumption that has obscured somewhat the true lines of Tennyson's portrait of Ulysses. Although Tennyson certainly borrowed from Dante the incident of the last voyage and some of the phrasing of Ulysses' heroic address to the mariners, I am convinced that Byron's influence in the poem is almost as pervasive as Dante's, perhaps even more important in providing the key to an understanding of Tennyson's persona. More specifically, I believe it can be shown that Canto III of *Childe Harold's Pilgrimage* is a significant source for the theme, imagery, and language of "Ulysses," as well as for the characterization of Ulysses himself. To substantiate such a claim, which may seem extravagant in view of the long-standing tradition of Dante's preëminence as a source, I wish to examine in detail the Byronic elements in Tennyson's portrait of Ulysses before moving on to an examination of the passage in *Childe Harold* III which, I believe, helped give shape to Tennyson's treatment of the Ulysses legend.

In a well-known passage from a letter of 1813 Byron gave expression to the impulse and temperament which define, to some extent, the Byronic Hero:

The great object of life is sensation—to feel that we exist, even though in pain. It is this "craving void" which drives us to gaming—to battle—to travel—to intemperate, but keenly felt pursuits of any kind, whose principal attraction is the agitation inseparable from their accomplishment.[17]

This statement might serve equally well as a description of the motivating philosophy of Tennyson's hero. Ulysses' lust for intense feeling and his indulgence in sensation for its own sake are so evident from the opening passage of the poem that they scarcely need documentation. He "cannot rest from travel," but must "drink / Life to the lees."[18]

> ... all times I have enjoy'd
> Greatly, have suffer'd greatly, both with those
> That loved me, and alone; ...
>
> (ll. 7–9)

Like the Byronic Hero, Ulysses here makes no real distinction between joy and pain; the adverb *greatly* in its repetition suggests that the quality of the experience is determined primarily by its intensity; it is better to have suffered greatly than not to have felt at all. Ulysses' absorption in experience is such that he feels himself "a part of all that I have met."[19] "Always roaming with a hungry heart," he has, finally, "become a name." It is a name, the syntax of the passage suggests, synonymous with the quest for vital experience. To satisfy a perpetual hunger, "Life piled on life / Were all too little." It is only the new and forbidden, "Beyond the utmost bound of human thought," which satisfies. Once mastered, experience becomes dull and unprofitable, and thus it is that

> all experience is an arch wherethro'
> Gleams that untravell'd world, whose margin fades
> For ever and for ever when I move.
>
> (ll. 19–21)

This last passage recalls another aspect of the Byronic Hero's quest to absorb himself in a world of feeling—his continual frustration in discovering that meaningful experience is always just beyond his reach:

The Byronic Hero of Sensibility feels too positive a sense of identity to be able to commit himself. . . . In one sense, since this self-assertion frustrates any total commitment, it brings about what Professor Lovell calls "the failure of a quest," and it is the disappointment of his failure which Werther expresses when he says, "When we hurry toward it . . . , everything is as before, and we stand in our poverty, in our own narrowness, and our soul languishes for the refreshment which has eluded our grasp."[20]

Ulysses' arch image suggests the same kind of paradox. The "gleams" of the "untravell'd world" encourage Ulysses' quest for new and fresh experience, but the futility of the quest is assured by the very fact that it is only in being untraveled that the new world is attractive. It is therefore inevitable that Ulysses must pursue "the margin [that] fades / For ever and for ever when I move." New, therefore meaningful, experience is forever outside the bounds of the arch of mastered experiences, and it is this dilemma which faces Ulysses as the monologue opens. The ultimate goal of his previous travels was Ithaca, but Ithaca is now "barren," and Ulysses "an idle king":

> . . . and vile it were
> For some three suns to store and hoard myself,
> And this gray spirit yearning in desire
> To follow knowledge like a sinking star,
> Beyond the utmost bound of human thought.
>   (ll. 28–32)

The concluding passages of "Ulysses," especially the lines addressed directly to the mariners, obscure somewhat the Byronic motives which lie behind the final voyage, for here the pursuit of sensation, "life piled on life," is coupled somewhat ambiguously with heroic action, and Ulysses' goal becomes identified with "some work of noble note." However, as a number of critics have pointed out, the tone of the poem undergoes a distinct change with line 44:

> There lies the port; the vessel puffs her sail:
> There gloom the dark broad seas. My mariners,
> Souls that have toil'd, and wrought, and thought with me—
> That ever with a frolic welcome took
> The thunder and the sunshine, and opposed
> Free hearts, free foreheads—you and I are old;
> Old age hath yet his honour and his toil;
> Death closes all: but something ere the end,
> Some work of noble note, may yet be done,
> Not unbecoming men that strove with Gods.
>   (ll. 44–53)

It is impossible to miss the new oratorical tone, the flattering references to men "that strove with Gods." The self-analysis of the opening passages is now gone, and the poem has shifted from interior to exterior monologue.[21] Consequently, one is justified in placing more emphasis on the first three paragraphs of the poem (ll. 1–43) in attempting to arrive at some understanding of the forces that motivate Ulysses' actions. The final paragraph, laced with the heroic oratory designed to rouse the mariners "made weak by time and fate," is less reliable as an index to his character.

Related to Ulysses' longing for an intense life of feeling, suggested in the first two paragraphs of the poem, is his Byronic discontent with the life of common humanity, what Chiasson has characterized as "social irresponsibility." It is on this point that readers of "Ulysses" are most sharply divided, since it is directly related to Tennyson's assertion that the poem expresses the need to brave the struggle of life. One difficulty lies in the critics' arbitrary and necessarily subjective views of what braving the struggle of life involves, an issue that can never be wholly resolved. But, leaving moral judgments aside, it is clear that Ulysses himself does not view the struggle in terms of his responsibilities as a king, or even as a husband or father. It may be, as some have argued, that the anticipated adventures do indeed amount to some kind of personal struggle, but even a casual reading of the poem suggests that his motives are almost identical with those of the Byronic Hero of *Childe Harold* III, whose quest, in Ernest J. Lovell's words, is "to throw off that humanity which plagued him and to achieve a self-oblivion free of both ennui and despair."[22] Except for the reference to sin, the following stanza from *Childe Harold* III is an apt description of the mood revealed by Ulysses' self-analysis, although Harold is looking backward, Ulysses forward:

> And thus I am absorbed, and this is life:—
> I look upon the peopled desert past,
> As on a place of agony and strife,
> Where, for some sin, to Sorrow I was cast,
> To act and suffer, but remount at last
> With a fresh pinion; which I feel to spring,
> Though young, yet waxing vigorous as the Blast
> Which it would cope with, on delighting wing,
> Spurning the clay-cold bonds which round our being cling.
>   (III, 73)[23]

The motivation behind Ulysses' monologue is clearly to break the "clay-cold bonds" which link him to the still hearth and barren crags, the aged wife, and the savage race. In the much-debated third paragraph (ll. 33–43) Ulysses, in effect, frees himself from all the ties that bind him to society. He renounces not only his public duties, "the sceptre and the Isle" and the labor "to make mild / A rugged people," but, even more significant, "the sphere / Of common duties" and the "offices of tenderness," which are now viewed as the exclusive property of Telemachus, who must assume even the responsibility to "pay / Meet adoration to my household gods." Ulysses' break with the world of man and the public, private, and sacred duties of that world is now effected, and like "self-exiled Harold," who has become "restless and worn" in "man's dwellings," he "wanders forth again."[24]

In treating Childe Harold's alienation from society, Andrew Rutherford remarks that "no conflict is involved because 'mankind' is lumped together as a homogeneous mass of dullness and stupidity, to be easily rejected by the great or sensitive soul; and this rejection is based simply on a firm conviction of his own spiritual superiority."[25] This is perhaps the most satisfactory explanation for the patronizing attitude Ulysses displays toward mankind in general. He characterizes his countrymen as a "savage race / That hoard, and sleep, and feed, and know not me." His only reference to Penelope is as "an aged wife," and his attitude toward Telemachus betrays the same sense of spiritual superiority: "He works his work, I mine." Telemachus is "blameless," "centered in the sphere / Of common duties," "decent not to fail," but, the implication is, Ulysses is of a different order of mankind. His greater capacity for feeling and acting lifts him above these rather mundane virtues, which are expressed, as John Pettigrew has pointed out, in essentially negative terms.[26] Ulysses' contempt for ordinary humanity, of which Telemachus is a part, is emphasized not so much by any one direct statement as by the tone of the entire third paragraph. As Pettigrew suggests, ". . . Ulysses' indifference to the kind of work left to Telemachus and to the kind of value represented by him is admirably stressed by the 'un-Tennysonian' extreme abstractness and poverty of the diction and the flat, flabby rhythms, qualities emphasized by the richness and surface vigor in the surrounding paragraphs."[27] The tone of the entire passage justifies the even stronger conclusion of Paull Baum that Ulysses' description of Telemachus has an "air of condescension with a tinge of contempt,"[28] a contempt, one might add, not so much for Telemachus himself as for the "sphere of common duties" he represents. For the Byronic Hero, in Thorslev's view, "has been 'fated,' set apart from other men, alienated from the social world of which he would otherwise gladly be a part."[29]

The sea voyage which is emblematic of both Ulysses' alienation from society and the gratification of his lust for "life piled on life" is, at the same time, a means of achieving the self-oblivion which was one object of the Byronic Hero's quest: "The soul can flee, / And with . . . the heaving plain / Of ocean . . . mingle—and not in vain" (*Childe Harold* III, 72).[30] Ulysses' purpose is "To sail beyond the sunset, and the baths / Of all the Western stars, until I die."[31] What emerges, then, at the end of the poem is the same paradox that lies at the heart of the Byronic Hero's desire to lose himself in a welter of raw sensation: "To mingle with the Universe" (*Childe Harold* IV, 178). Thorslev sees this trait as the most influential legacy of the Byronic Hero:

This agonized Hero of Sensibility was Byron's legacy to the literature of the age which succeeded him—not the healthy, ironic but life-affirming message of his great satire. Until almost the end of the century, both in England and on the Continent, Byron was remembered primarily as the author of *Childe Harold,* not of *Don Juan.* The agonized Hero of Sensibility appears again and again in the literature of the succeeding age: sometimes morbidly analytic of his own emotional and spiritual states, and in his *Weltschmerz* longing for some engagement to absolute truth which will rid him of his painful self-consciousness; longing to "mingle with the Universe," but being continually frustrated in his desire by the reassertion of his skeptical, sometimes cynical, and sometimes remorseful ego.[32]

To view Tennyson's Ulysses as one of the inheritors of Byron's legacy is to come to some understanding of the inconsistencies involved in a quest simultaneously for "life piled on life" and death; a desire simultaneously for "some work of noble note" and freedom from a position of nobility; a longing for a "newer world" and a complete break with the world which was the goal of his life's energies. Ulysses' affinities with the Byronic Hero account for the compulsive self-analysis which informs his monologue, his disdain for his countrymen, his wife and his son, and his spiritual arrogance. But, it should be noted, Ulysses' affinities with the Byronic Hero "explain" the complexities and paradoxes of his personality in a quite limited way—by relating them to a clearly defined and influential character-type whose model is Byron's Childe Harold. The close parallels between the two characters indicate a strong Byronic influence at work, but to rest the matter here is to indicate nothing more than a temperament and a tradition exercising its force. There is, however, evidence that Tennyson's debt to Byron was more direct, that, in fact, while Dante's *Inferno* may be called the "source" for "Ulysses" in a strict sense (if the poem had its beginnings in Dante's account of Ulysses' final voyage), it was Byron's *Childe Harold* which provided its informing theme, imagery, and tone.

In stanzas 42–45 of Canto III of *Childe Harold* Byron considers a class of men to which Tennyson's Ulysses belongs. Such men are characterized by "a fire / And motion of the Soul" which

> once kindled, quenchless evermore,
> Preys upon high adventure, nor can tire
> Of aught but rest . . . .
>
> (III, 42)

His own example of such a man is Napoleon (the setting for these stanzas is Waterloo), but he includes in this class

> Conquerors and Kings,
> Founders of sects and systems, to whom add
> Sophists, Bards, Statesmen, all unquiet things
> Which stir too strongly the soul's secret springs, . . .
>
> (III, 43)

Like Ulysses, these men cannot rest from travel:

> Their breath is agitation, and their life
> A storm whereon they ride, to sink at last,
> And yet so nursed and bigoted to strife,
> That should their days, surviving perils past,
> Melt to calm twilight, they feel overcast
> With sorrow and supineness, and so die;

> Even as a flame unfed, which runs to waste
> With its own flickering, or a sword laid by,
> Which eats into itself, and rusts ingloriously.
> (III, 44)

Not only has Byron sketched here the outline of a type of character who later appeared as Tennyson's Ulysses, but the two episodes are remarkably close thematically. Byron's assertion that "Quiet to quick bosoms is a Hell" (III, 42) becomes the informing theme of Ulysses' monologue, which, moreover, follows so faithfully at times Byron's imagery and phrasing that one must assume a direct link between the two works.

The sword image with which Byron concludes stanza 44 is only one instance of Byron's influence on Tennyson's metaphorical language. It reappears in the second paragraph of "Ulysses":

> How dull it is to pause, to make an end,
> To rust unburnish'd, not to shine in use!
> As tho' to breathe were life.
> (ll. 22–24)

The source of this passage has usually been identified as Shakespeare's *Troilus and Cressida*:[33]

> ... Perseverance dear my lord,
> Keeps honor bright; to have done, is to hang
> Quite out of fashion, like a rusty mail
> In monumental mockery.
> (III, iii, 150–153)

But, as W. B. Stanford has noted, the contexts of the passages in Shakespeare and Tennyson show significant differences.[34] It is Byron who furnishes the Tennysonian context, the adventurer whose days have melted to "calm twilight," who feels "overcast with sorrow and supineness" like "a sword laid by, / Which eats into itself, and rusts ingloriously." Furthermore, Ulysses' language implies that his analogy may be to a sword, rather than the rusty mail of Shakespeare's image. One would, it seems to me, make this identification in reading the poem, although perhaps only because it is a more common analogy and because "to shine in use" suggests an implement rather than something worn.[35]

One might, however, ignore the link between the two images were it not reinforced by further echoes in "Ulysses" of the four-stanza passage of *Childe Harold*. To cite a further instance, Byron accounts for the restlessness of his hero-wanderers in these terms:

> there is a fire
> And motion of the Soul which will not dwell
> In its own narrow being, but aspire
> Beyond the fitting medium of desire; . . .
>
> (III, 42)

Ulysses refers to

> this gray spirit yearning in desire
> To follow knowledge like a sinking star,
> Beyond the utmost bound of human thought.
>
> (ll. 30–32)

The parallels here extend even beyond the identity of the sentiment expressed to include the phrasing ("Beyond the fitting medium"—"Beyond the utmost bound") and the end-rhymes (*fire, aspire, desire—desire, star*). This is one of only two instances of a rhyming couplet in "Ulysses," the other being the concluding two lines of the poem (in neither case is there full rhyme; the concluding rhymes are *will, yield*), and it may well be that the off-rhyme in lines 30–31 was influenced by Tennyson's recollection of the Byron passage. Furthermore, Tennyson's image of the sinking star in line 31, associated as it is with the "gray spirit" of line 30, condenses both elements of Byron's phrase "fire and motion of the Soul," although it may also owe something to the stars which appear to Ulysses in Dante's account of the final voyage. If Tennyson's "sinking star" is a corresponding metaphor for Byron's "fire and motion of the Soul," then the syntactical ambiguity of line 31, noted by several critics,[36] is clarified. The syntax does not make clear if the phrase "like a sinking star" modifies *follow* or *knowledge*; however, the Byron analogue would indicate that the phrase modifies *follow* rather than *knowledge,* for it recalls Byron's description of the unbounded, fiery flight of the unquiet soul.[37]

Further elements of the four stanzas in *Childe Harold* seem to have exerted an influence on the shaping of "Ulysses" even if their effect is less readily observed. In stanza 45 Byron describes the fate of the man who has surpassed common humanity:

> He who ascends to mountain-tops, shall find
> The loftiest peaks most wrapt in clouds and snow;
> He who surpasses or subdues mankind,
> Must look down on the hate of those below.
> Though high above the Sun of Glory glow,
> And far beneath the Earth and Ocean spread,
> Round him are icy rock, and loudly blow
> Contending tempests on his naked head,
> And thus reward the toils which to those summits led.

Traces of Byron's imagery of mountain tops and icy rock, suggesting the sense of alienation and desolation which the superior man experiences, may be seen in the initial setting of "Ulysses," in which the king is placed among the "barren crags" by a cold hearth. But the spatial imagery also reinforces, as it does in Byron, a sense of spiritual superiority, the height of the superior man's noble station, from which he metes and doles "unequal laws unto a savage race, / That hoard and sleep, and feed, and know not me." The hatred for the spiritually elite exhibited by ordinary humanity in Byron is transformed by Tennyson into contemptible indifference, but the emphasis remains on the gulf separating the man of insight and feeling from the common herd.

If it is inconsistent that this sense of alienation from humanity should be expressed by a man who later declares, "I am a part of all that I have met," it is an inconsistency shared by Byron's persona, who anticipated Ulysses' statement with "I live not in myself, but I become / Portion of that around me" (III, 72).[38] It is evident that in both the Byronic Hero and Ulysses the identification of the self with the external world is qualified by the exclusion of the remainder of mankind. It is rather with the elements of nature that the two characters seek some kind of fusion. In stanza 44 of *Childe Harold* III the final act of self-oblivion is depicted in terms of a stormy shipwreck, and this symbolic dissolution of man into the elements of nature looks forward to Ulysses' resolve to "sail beyond the sunset, and the baths / Of all the western stars, until I die," and his intimation that "the gulfs will wash us down."

One final example serves to indicate the extent to which even the most characteristic element of Ulysses' personality, his weakened physical prowess combined with a strength of will, owes something to Canto III of *Childe Harold*. Ulysses' concluding outburst of oratory, addressed to the mariners, has been termed by one critic "the poem's most original feature":[39]

> 'Tis not too late to seek a newer world. . . .
> Tho' much is taken, much abides; and tho'
> We are not now that strength which in old days
> Moved earth and heaven; that which we are, we are;
> One equal temper of heroic hearts,
> Made weak by time and fate, but strong in will
> To strive, to seek, to find, and not to yield.
> (ll. 59, 65–70)

The passage contains, certainly, the most memorable lines of the poem, but its originality is open to question. Although the context is not identical, the following lines from *Childe Harold* combine too much of Ulysses' language and feeling to be ignored as a source:

> 'Tis too late!
> Yet am I changed; though still enough the same
> In strength to bear what Time cannot abate,
> And feed on bitter fruits without accusing Fate.
> (III, 7)[40]

Ulysses reverses Byron's judgment that it is indeed too late to seek a newer world, but he echoes at one point (1. 59) Byron's phrasing as well as Byron's concern with time and fate, his resolve not to yield to these forces, and his assessment of his present state ("Tho' much is taken, much abides" is essentially a restatement of the idea of "Yet am I changed, though still enough the same").

There are differences in emphasis and direction here, as in the other examples I have cited, and, viewing each pair of corresponding passages in isolation, one might well question whether *Childe Harold* III exerted a significant influence on the formation of "Ulysses"; however, the accumulation of parallels and verbal echoes and the similarities of the contexts in which these occur provide, it seems to me, convincing evidence for Byron's imprint on the poem. This is not to suggest that "Ulysses" is no more than a reworking of certain themes and episodes of *Childe Harold,* or even that Tennyson was consciously following Byron as a source. What is suggested is that Tennyson's conception of the character of Ulysses and the theme and tone of his monologue are more heavily indebted to Canto III of *Childe Harold* than has previously been thought.

It would not be necessary to insist so emphatically on Byron's presence in the poem were it not for the weight of the traditional belief that Tennyson's Ulysses is "unmistakably the Ulysses of Dante."[41] While I should not wish to minimize the importance of Tennyson's reliance on Dante, a debt which has been amply recorded by numerous critics, the evidence presented here should serve as a corrective to the judgment that Tennyson's conception of Ulysses is derived solely from Dante. What Tennyson certainly derived from Dante was the legend of a quest-hero, "tardy with age," who, in a rousing address to his mariners, dedicated himself to the pursuit of knowledge and virtue:

> 'O brothers!' I began, 'who to the west
> Through perils without number now have reach'd;
> To this the short remaining watch, that yet
> Our senses have to wake, refuse not proof
> Of the unpeopled world, following the track
> Of Phoebus. Call to mind from whence ye sprang:
> Ye were not form'd to live the life of brutes,
> But virtue to pursue and knowledge high.'[42]

This quest motif is central to Tennyson's poem, but, as Robert Langbaum has observed, the "informing image and emotion [of the corresponding passages in Ulysses] are not in Dante—the *gray* spirit indicating an old man's tired yearning, and the *sinking* star directing the yearning toward disappearance, extinction":

> What is incidental in Dante, that Ulysses is old, caught Tennyson's imagination to become the central fact from which his meaning emerges. There is no sign of diminished vigour in Dante's Ulysses. He is destroyed, as a matter of fact, as punishment for his too vigorous presumption in daring to sail beyond the limits assigned to man. The tempest that destroys him is the disaster he has risked in going adventuring. But even before embarking, Tennyson's Ulysses holds out death in one form or another as the inevitable goal of the journey.[43]

What is more, the qualities of mind which most nearly define Tennyson's Ulysses—a tendency toward self-analysis, indulgence in experience as an escape from despair, a sense of spiritual superiority and the disdain for common humanity and for society which this entails—are not present in Dante's account. Baum, who argues for the importance of Dante as a source, admits at the same time that Dante's influence did not extend far into Tennyson's characterization of Ulysses:

> Not only is the moralizing all Tennyson's, or nearly all, but the fuller characterization of Ulysses—his pride as well as his restless eagerness, and his determination
> >   *To strive, to seek, to find, and not to yield*
> which was denied to Dante's Ulisse because he must end in the Malebolge of Hell.[44]

T. S. Eliot has suggested the essential distinction between the two accounts: "The story of Ulysses, as told by Dante, reads like a straightforward piece of romance, a well told seaman's yarn; Tennyson's Ulysses is primarily a very self-conscious poet."[45] It is this self-conscious role which clearly distinguishes Tennyson's Ulysses from Dante's, and allies him with Byron's Childe Harold.

The evidence of Byron's influence on "Ulysses" also serves to justify to some extent the anti-Victorian and Byronic readings of the poem which have predominated in recent years. Baum's once controversial conclusion that the poem expresses "the philosophy of escape" rather than the "need of going forward and braving the struggle of life"[46] is reinforced by Ulysses' affinities with Byron's Childe Harold, and Chiasson's even harsher view of Ulysses as "a hard, self-contained individual, contemptuous of his people, impervious to the softer affections, the sheer incarnation of 'Renaissance' *superbia*"[47] is also rendered more acceptable in light of the Byronic tradition into which the poem may be placed. Chiasson's further contention that the poem should be read as "a dramatic portrayal of a type of human being who held a set of ideas which Tennyson regarded as destructive of the whole fabric of his society"[48] is, however, more difficult to accept, even in view of Ulysses' parallels with the Byronic Hero. The reader who is familiar with the widely accepted view of Tennyson's "divided will" set forth by E. D. H. Johnson,[49] among others, should not find it necessary to interpret the poem as a deliberate attempt to exploit Ulysses as an anti-Victorian villain. Johnson has shown that in poem after poem Tennyson exhibits themes and moods which are at odds with the expressed content of his material. It is for this reason, he states, that "many of the poems which seem to be indisputably the products of Victorian literary convention have an extra dimension which, once recognized, relates them to the deeper sources of the author's poetic vision."[50]

It is Johnson also who reminds us that Tennyson's relatively uneventful life "made him more reliant than most English poets on literary sources for inspiration."[51] Byron's strong influence on Tennyson's early poetry is generally acknowledged, and although Charles Tennyson holds that the Byronic phase did not extend far beyond Byron's death,[52] the evidence is that he remained a source of inspiration throughout Tennyson's career.[53] The famous description of the fourteen-year-old Tennyson who, on hearing the news from Missolonghi, ran out to the edge of a brook, threw himself to the ground, and carved on the sandstone the words "Byron Is Dead"[54] suggests the depth of the young man's attachment to a figure who was for him the embodiment of the poet. It should not be altogether surprising, then, that the mature poet turned to Byron in a more oblique way in the poem begun almost immediately after Tennyson heard the news from Vienna that Hallam was dead.

NOTES

I am grateful to the Graduate School of the University of Tennessee for providing the summer grant which enabled me to complete this article.
1. Hallam, Lord Tennyson, *Alfred, Lord Tennyson: A Memoir by His Son* (London, 1897), II, 70; hereafter cited as *Memoir*.
2. W. W. Robson states that "Tennyson's Ulysses is Homer's Odysseus felt through Dante" ("The Dilemma of Tennyson," in *Critical Essays on the Poetry of Tennyson*, ed. John Killham [London, 1960], p. 156). W. B. Stanford, who has traced the Ulysses theme from Homer to modern poets, says of the poem: "Homer's voice is the least significant here. The *Odyssey* provides some phrases and the scenery . . . and the *dramatis personae*. From his opening words, however, this Ulysses is clearly not the social-minded, home-loving prince of the Homeric poems" (*The Ulysses Theme: A Study in the Adaptability of a Traditional Hero* [Oxford, 1963], p. 202). For other statements of Tennyson's debt to Dante see Paull Baum, *Ten-*

nyson Sixty Years After (Chapel Hill, 1948), pp. 92–95; Robert Langbaum, *The Poetry of Experience* (New York, 1963), pp. 90–91; Elton E. Smith, *The Two Voices: A Tennyson Study* (Lincoln, Neb., 1964), pp. 124–128; Douglas Bush, *Mythology and the Romantic Tradition in English Poetry* (New York, 1963), p. 209; Edgar Hill Duncan, "Tennyson: A Modern Appraisal," *Tennessee Studies in Literature,* IV (1959), 19; Clyde de L. Ryals, "Point of View in Tennyson's Ulysses," *Archiv für das Studium der neueren Sprachen und Literaturen,* CXCIX (Oct. 1962), 232–234; Charles C. Walcutt, "Tennyson's 'Ulysses,'" *Explicator,* IV (1945–46), Item 28; John Pettigrew, "Tennyson's 'Ulysses': A Reconciliation of Opposites," *Victorian Poetry,* I (Nov. 1963), 31–32.

3. See Jerome H. Buckley, *Tennyson: The Growth of a Poet* (Boston, 1960), p. 269n; Bush, p. 210n; and Stanford, p. 203.
4. "Tennyson's 'Ulysses' and 'Hamlet,' " *Modern Language Review,* XXXVIII (1943), 38.
5. *Ibid.,* p. 38.
6. *Memoir,* I, 196.
7. Stanford, p. 202.
8. Bush, *Mythology and the Romantic Tradition in English Poetry,* p. 209.
9. *A Selection from the Poems of Alfred, Lord Tennyson* (Garden City, N. Y., 1944), p. xx.
10. Baum, p. 303.
11. "Tennyson's 'Ulysses'—A Re-Interpretation," *University of Toronto Quarterly,* XXIII (1953–1954), 403.
12. Chiasson, pp. 407–408.
13. Baum, p. 300.
14. Stanford, p. 202.
15. Chiasson, p. 408.
16. Baum, pp. 300, 303.
17. *The Works of Lord Byron, Letters and Journals,* ed. Rowland E. Prothero (London, 1904), III, 400.
18. Quotations from "Ulysses" are from *The Works of Alfred, Lord Tennyson,* Eversley Edition, ed. Hallam, Lord Tennyson (London, 1908). Because of readers' familiarity with the poem and because of its brevity, I have not cited line numbers for short quotations included in the text of the article.
19. In *The Byronic Hero: Types and Prototypes* (Minneapolis, 1962), Peter Thorslev states, "All of these heroes have souls of sensibility. . . . Often they long for some kind of absorption in the universe around them . . . and above all they have almost infinite capacities for feeling" (p. 188).
20. Thorslev, pp. 142–143.
21. Although several critics have noted the shift from interior to exterior monologue, there is some disagreement on whether it takes place at line 33 or line 44. I would argue for the latter because of, among other things, the shift to second-person pronouns and terms of direct address, missing in the first 43 lines. See Pettigrew, pp. 40–41, for a résumé of the discussions of this problem.
22. *Byron: The Record of a Quest* (Hamden, Conn., 1966), p. 122.
23. Quotations from *Childe Harold's Pilgrimage* are taken from *The Works of Lord Byron, Poetry,* ed. E. H. Coleridge (London, 1904). I equate Childe Harold and the Byronic Hero on the authority of Thorslev, who observes in *The Byronic Hero: Types and Prototypes* that Childe Harold is "the first important Byronic Hero and the prototype of all the rest" (p. 128).
24. See stanzas 15 and 16 of *Childe Harold* III.

25. *Byron: A Critical Study* (Stanford, 1961), p. 55.
26. Pettigrew, p. 40.
27. Pettigrew, pp. 39–40.
28. Baum, p. 301.
29. Thorslev, p. 137.
30. In Thorslev's view, "Harold longs . . . for [the] obliviousness of self, [the] annihilation of the ego" (p. 144). Lovell's *Byron: The Record of a Quest* is in part a treatment of this theme. See especially Chapter V, "The Wordsworthian Note and the Byronic Hero."
31. The difficulty of reconciling the braving of the struggle of life with the desire for extinction has been noted by a number of critics. Robert Langbaum, who finds in the poem the same longing for oblivion that informs most of T. S. Eliot's early poetry, states that "weariness and longing for rest is the emotional bias" of "Ulysses," "though here the emotion is couched in the contrasting language of adventure, giving an added complexity of meaning to the poem" (p. 90). Edgar Hill Duncan, who reads the poem as a personal allegory, holds that it is "paradoxically, a pursuit of death, and the Happy Isles, symbolically in the poem and in Tennyson's consciousness, are in one of their meanings the Heaven which Arthur Hallam's soul now inhabits" (pp. 26–27). John Pettigrew, commenting on the concluding passage of the poem, finds that it "reveals a great deal more than a man going forward and braving the struggle of life, for its atmosphere is redolent of death, and death is associated now not with Ithaca, as it was earlier in the poem, but with the world beyond it and with the voyage" (p. 42).
32. Thorslev, p. 144.
33. See note 7 above. John Pettigrew agrees that the lines echo the passage in *Troilus and Cressida,* although he points as well to the passage in *Childe Harold* (p. 44 and 44n). His is the only reference I have been able to discover which links the four stanzas in *Childe Harold* to "Ulysses" in any way, although he does so only incidentally in compiling a list of echoes in the poem, which includes in his view Homer, Virgil, St. Mark, *Hamlet, Macbeth,* Shelley, and Milton.
34. See Stanford, p. 203.
35. Needless to say, Tennyson may have had both passages in mind, for they serve to reinforce one another. Douglas Bush ("Tennyson's 'Ulysses' and 'Hamlet'") has located yet another passage in Shakespeare (*Hamlet,* IV, iv, 32–38) which employs a similar image:

> What is a man,
> If his chief good and market of his time
> Be but to sleep and feed: A beast, no more.
> Sure he that made us with such large discourse,
> Looking before and after, gave us not
> That capability and godlike reason
> To fust in us unus'd.

36. The ambiguity of the line is discussed by Baum, p. 300, Pettigrew, p. 39, and Jay L. Halio, " 'Prothalamion,' 'Ulysses,' and Intention in Poetry," *College English,* XXII (1961), 393.
37. The phrase could modify both *follow* and *knowledge* only if one assumes that the object of the quest takes on the quality of the quest itself. That is, one might paraphrase the passage "to follow knowledge in the same manner that one follows a sinking star," in which case the metaphor applies both to

the journey and the object of the journey. The emphasis remains, however, on the actions of the persona and not on a characterization of knowledge.

38. This parallel has been pointed out by Bush (*Mythology and the Romantic Tradition in English Poetry*, p. 209n) and Pettigrew (p. 44n). Byron's statement does not occur in the four-stanza passage to which Tennyson most frequently alludes, but some twenty-seven stanzas later.
39. Stanford, p. 204.
40. Again, this passage is not contained within the stanzas which seem to have exerted the most influence on "Ulysses," but its close proximity argues for its inclusion as a source.
41. Robson, p. 156.
42. I quote from the translation of the *Divine Comedy* by Henry F. Cary, which Tennyson almost certainly knew. See Pettigrew, p. 32.
43. Langbaum, p. 91.
44. Baum, p. 94.
45. "Dante," in *Selected Essays* (New York, 1950), p. 211.
46. Baum, p. 303.
47. Chiasson, p. 405.
48. Chiasson, p. 403.
49. *The Alien Vision of Victorian Poetry* (Hamden, Conn., 1963).
50. Johnson, p. 22. Johnson also observes that "Tennyson's genius was most at home when employed on traditional legends of proven narrative and moral interest, which could yet be made exemplificatory of deeper implications for the reader who cared to look below the surface" (p. 66).
51. Johnson, p. 15.
52. Charles Tennyson, *Alfred Tennyson* (New York, 1949), pp. 33–34.
53. Jerome H. Buckley labels the persona in "Locksley Hall" a Byronic Hero, although he feels Byronism is rejected at the end of the poem (Buckley, pp. 76–77). He also calls the persona in *Maud* a "Byronic antihero" (p. 141).
54. See Charles Tennyson, p. 33.

The University of Tennessee

JOSEPH J. EGAN

THE FATAL SUITOR: EARLY FORESHADOWING IN
TESS OF THE D'URBERVILLES

In the opening pages of *Tess of the d'Urbervilles* Hardy draws the picture of the novel in miniature when he introduces this seemingly casual description of the Vale of Blackmoor and the folklore associated with it: "The district is of historic, no less than of topographical interest. The Vale was known in former times as the Forest of White Hart, from a curious legend of King Henry III.'s reign, in which the killing by a certain Thomas de la Lynd of a beautiful white hart which the king had run down and spared, was made the occasion of a heavy fine" (p. 10).[1] Philip Mahone Griffith has commented perceptively on the relevance of the local tradition of the hunted animal to the life-fate of Hardy's heroine: "The presence of the legend foreshadows Tess's pathetic 'fall' and ultimate fate: she is the White Hart of Blackmoor Vale. When she finally returns from Flintcomb-Ash Farm to relieve her destitute family, shortly before capitulating to her seducer, Alec d'Urberville, again, she walks through the Vale and is reminded of the 'harts that have been hunted here.' "[2] The purpose of the present study is to continue this method of critical approach to the aesthetic design of the early part of the novel by showing that in "Phase the First—The Maiden" Hardy also utilizes vegetative imagery, together with vivid metaphorical passages and further hints of the legendary, to foreshadow the essential elements in the Tess-Alec relationship.

The gradual change which the progress of the fruitful season brings to the Trantridge countryside delicately parallels the "transformation" that Tess, the maiden, undergoes in the vicinity of The Slopes, the Stoke-d'Urberville estate. The "fine and picturesque country girl," with "all her bouncing handsome womanliness" (p. 12), arrives at The Slopes in early June, when Nature is alive with fertility and growth; is seduced in September, the time of ripened tenderness which closes the cycle of natural flowering; and leaves Alec in late October, with the knowledge at heart that she has "harvested" a bitter fruit in her "fall" from maidenhood. The summer scenes are especially rich in symbolic foreshadowing, the vegetative imagery suggesting significant aspects of the human drama unfolded in the novel. Thus, on his first meeting Tess during her preliminary visit to The Slopes, Alec offers her a tour of the grounds that takes them eventually "to the fruit-garden and green-houses, where he asked her if she liked strawberries":

D'Urberville began gathering specimens of the fruit for her, handing them back to her as he stooped; and, presently, selecting a specially fine product of the 'British Queen' variety, he stood up and held it by the stem to her mouth.
'No—no!' she said quickly, putting her fingers between his hand and her lips. 'I would rather take it in my own hand.'
'Nonsense!' he insisted; and in a slight distress she parted her lips and took it in.
They had spent some time wandering desultorily thus, Tess eating in a half-pleased, half-reluctant state whatever d'Urberville offered her. When she could consume no more of the strawberries he filled her little basket with them; and then the two passed round to the rose trees, whence he gathered blossoms and gave her to put in her bosom. She obeyed like one in a dream, and when she could affix no more he himself tucked a bud or two into her hat, and heaped her basket with others in the prodigality of his bounty.

(p. 34)

The sexual reference implicit in the images of the strawberry, lips, and basket and in the frank, almost sensual idea of fertility evoked by the red abundance of the fruit and roses suggests not only the physical truth of Alec's seduction of Tess, but also the fact of his emotional-psychological domination. He relentlessly manipulates her, "half-pleased, half-reluctant," to his will; he insists and overwhelms her virginal simplicity and passionate self alike, with his masculine assertiveness, the bewildered, vulnerable girl being able only to accept "whatever d'Urberville offered" and to obey "like one in a dream." As she returns homeward by van at the end of her first encounter with Alec, we are given this final, pathetically ironic, portrait of Tess in bloom:

Then she became aware of the spectacle she presented to their surprised vision: roses at her breast; roses in her hat; roses and strawberries in her basket to the brim. She blushed, and said confusedly that the flowers had been given to her. When the passengers were not looking she stealthily removed the more prominent blooms from her hat and placed them in the basket, where she covered them with her handkerchief. Then she fell to reflecting again, and in looking downwards a thorn of the rose remaining in her breast accidentally pricked her chin. Like all the cottagers in Blackmoor Vale, Tess was steeped in fancies and prefigurative superstitions; she thought this an ill omen—the first she had noticed that day.

(p. 36)

This wound of "ill omen," whose connotations are ultimately psychical, as well as sexual, portends the tragic results of Tess's "pursuit" by Alec, the "one who stood fair to be the blood-red ray in the spectrum of her young life" (p. 34); it also parallels the wounds she later gives him, first during the threshing operations at Flintcomb-Ash Farm when she strikes him with one of her heavy leather gloves and "the blood began dropping from his mouth upon the straw" (p. 275) and then near the close when she stabs him to the heart.

In addition to this fruit and floral imagery, there is yet another means of dramatic foreshadowing in the first "phase" of *Tess,* namely, the wild ride Alec gives Tess in his "highly varnished and equipped" gig (p. 42) on the occasion of her journeying to The Slopes to become keeper-in-residence of its fowl-farm:

Having mounted beside her, Alec d'Urberville drove rapidly along the crest of the first hill, chatting compliments to Tess as they went. . . . Rising still, an immense landscape stretched around them on every side; behind, the green valley of her birth, before, a gray country of which she knew nothing except from her first brief visit to Trantridge. Thus they reached the verge of an incline down which the road stretched in a long straight descent of nearly a mile. . . . She began to get uneasy at a certain recklessness in her conductor's driving.
'You will go down slow, sir, I suppose?' she said with attempted unconcern.
. . . .
'Why, Tess,' he answered . . . 'it isn't a brave bouncing girl like you who asks that? Why, I always go down at full gallop. There's nothing like it for raising your spirits.'
. . . .
Down, down, they sped . . . . The aspect of the straight road enlarged with their advance, the two banks dividing like a splitting stick; one rushing past at each shoulder.
. . . .
He loosened rein, and away they went a second time. D'Urberville turned his face to her as they rocked, and said, in playful raillery: 'Now then, put your arms round my waist again, as you did before, my Beauty.'
. . . .
'Will nothing else do?' she cried at length, in desperation . . . .
'Nothing, dear Tess,' he replied.
'Oh. I don't know—very well; I don't mind!' she panted miserably.

(pp. 43–45)

In the context of the future "union" between this man and woman, the fevered, undulatory "driving" episode, where the "inexorable" Alec gives Tess "the kiss of mastery" (p. 45) in her moment of confused surrender and of entrance into an unknown "gray country," functions both as a figurative prophecy of the girl's sexual initiation, climaxed amid the gloom of "The Chase," and as a symbolic statement of the effect Alec has on the subsequent course of her life as a woman. Associated with "irregularity of motion" (p. 43) from the start, Alec continually plunges Tess "downhill"—indeed he dwells at "The Slopes"—through his reckless behavior towards her, a behavior that finally dooms them both.

When Tess leaves Trantridge in October to rejoin her family, Alec conveys her in his carriage over the same route they had traversed the previous summer. Tess now issues a heated warning to her seducer, who has accused her of deliberate compliance with his sensual requests: " 'How can you dare to use such words!' she cried, turning impetuously upon him, her eyes flashing as the latent spirit (of which he was to see more some day) awoke in her. *'My God! I could knock you out of the gig!' "* (p. 65; italics are mine). These words return us at last to the realm of legend, for Tess's threat merges, in "Phase the Sixth," with the tale of the d'Urberville Coach to form a dark presage of the mutual destruction that concludes the lives of these unhappy people, the present-day actors in the family's legendary drama: " 'It is that this sound of a non-existent coach can only be heard by one of d'Urberville blood, and it is held to be of ill-omen to the one who hears it. It has to do with a murder, committed by one of the family, centuries ago. . . . One of the family is said to have abducted some beautiful woman, who tried to escape from the coach in which he was carrying her off, and in the struggle he killed her—or she killed him—I forget which' " (p. 293). Thus, through metaphors drawn from the fields and folklore of his native "Wessex" and woven together into an impressive his vision of the tragic concurrence of circumstance, passion, and pattern of foreshadowing, Hardy, the fictive artist, is able to intensify human frailty.

NOTES

1. New York, 1965. All citations made in the text to *Tess of the d'Urbervilles* will be from the Norton Critical Edition, ed. Scott Elledge.
2. Philip Mahone Griffith, "The Image of the Trapped Animal in Hardy's *Tess of the d'Urbervilles*," *Tulane Studies in English*, XIII (1963), 88.

Slippery Rock State College

FORREST E. HAZARD

THE ASCENT OF F 6: A NEW INTERPRETATION

Michael Ransom, the central figure in Auden and Isherwood's *The Ascent of F 6,* has been generally regarded as the victim of a mother-fixation, a lust for power, or both.[1] That interpretation is probably sound for much of Act I. For Ransom recoils unheroically from the grosser aspects of physicality, shuns the entanglements of moral commitment, and undertakes the conquest of the mountain for selfish personal reasons. Nevertheless, there is considerable evidence throughout the play, and especially in Act II, which suggests that the authors intended to portray not a failure but a modern version of the mythical hero. The purpose of this essay is to demonstrate that intention. As external evidence, I shall cite statements about Ransom which Auden and Isherwood made outside the play both before and after they wrote it. As internal evidence, I shall show that the details about his youth mark Ransom out as an embryonic hero already in the early stages of his career and, furthermore, that although in Act I he feels abnormally repelled by the untidiness of life and accepts the leadership of the climbing expedition for the wrong reasons, he perceives in Act II the moral dilemma into which his weakness has led him and works out what the authors considered a heroic solution.

Discussing this play in an interview, Auden acknowledged that Ransom was modeled after T. E. Lawrence and then added the following remarks about the major action of the plot: "The ascent of the mountain is a symbol of the *geste,* it can also be a symbol of the act of aggression."[2] One meaning of *geste* is a heroic achievement; and that, rather than an act of aggression, was apparently what the au-

165

thors meant Ransom's climb ultimately to represent, notwithstanding the unidealistic motives with which it was undertaken. For in 1934, not long before they must have begun working on *F 6*, Auden wrote that Lawrence's life was an "allegory of the transformation of the Truly Weak Man into the Truly Strong Man, an answer to the question 'How shall the self-conscious man be saved?' . . ." The answer Lawrence found was that "action and reason are inseparable; [that] it is only in action that reason can realize itself, and only through reason that action can become free." Though he had to struggle hard with the temptation to lose himself in "blind action," he "conquered it . . . resolutely. . . ."[3] Lawrence, Auden felt, exemplified "most completely what is best and significant in our time, our nearest approach to a synthesis of feeling and reason, act and thought. . . ."[4] More recently in *Exhumations* Isherwood declared that "my friends and I found [Lawrence] . . . fascinating. He was the myth-hero of the 'thirties. Auden and I consciously tried to recreate him in our character of Michael Ransom in *F. 6*."[5]

The play itself also seems consistent with these views. For Ransom must not only meet the challenge of self-conciousness which Lawrence had to face as "myth-hero of the 'thirties," but also must be heroic at most of the other points in his career. The mythic hero, for example, often has an antagonistic twin brother, in most respects his opposite, who symbolizes the primary threat and challenge to heroic development.[6] Ransom similarly has such a twin in his brother James, and the two of them have always been markedly different both in character and appearance. As a baby James was "bigger, prettier, the doctor's pride, / Responding promptly to the nurse's cluck"; Ransom was "tiny, serious and reserved."[7] James "cannot live an hour without applause," and his mother has lavished it upon him; whereas from Ransom she has withheld affection and "all that could infect / Or weaken" so as to make him "truly strong" (p. 138).

Ransom is like the mythic hero in other ways as well. As a young boy he "Kept a tame rook" (p. 139). Taming a rook is one example of the mutually beneficial relationship which must be established between man and animal, mind and body, intellect and unconscious—in short, between the symbolically masculine and feminine principles of creation—if civilization is to progress.[8] Other evidence of his heroic nature is also mentioned. He is "said to be an authority on Goya" and to have "Translated Confucius during a summer" (p. 140). He has blue eyes (p. 139), which are popularly associated with a superior intelligence. He "Drinks and eats little" (p. 140) and for amusement plays chess (p. 130).

At times, however, he admittedly appears unheroic. Early in the play he expresses an obsessive revulsion from the taint of corruption in every act, no matter how well intentioned ("the web of guilt that prisons every upright person . . . myself not least"), and from the pervasive untidiness of ordinary existence: "Under I cannot tell how many of these green slate roofs, the stupid peasants are making their stupid children" (p. 118). Indeed he finds life so burdensome that he broods on death as a welcome release: "O, happy the foetus that miscarries and the frozen idiot that cannot cry 'Mama'! Happy those run over in the street today or drowned at sea, or sure of death tomorrow from incurable diseases!" (p. 119). But such feelings are not uncommon in the embryonic hero. With the growth of his intellect and its love of order, he becomes virtually nauseated by messiness of any kind, whether moral or physical.[9] This nausea is one horn of the dilemma with which the hero must wrestle. The more he holds aloof from moral engagement and the physical messiness of normal life, the more alienated and nauseated he becomes. On the other hand, the farther he moves in the opposite direction, the closer he comes to the other horn of the dilemma. That horn is the risk of being corrupted by the evil which Ransom's twin brother stands for: the oppressive use of power over others (or, as it is phrased in this play, "the exercise of the human will" [p. 154]). Lesser men are defeated by this dilemma. But heroes must solve it.

In his essay "Criticism and a Mass Society" (1941) Auden explored this dilemma in detail. His conclusions are especially illuminating here because they agree with the solution Ransom reaches in Act II. An "open" society, Auden asserted, is based on the assumption that men vary markedly in virtue and ability; they are equal only in their inborn tendency toward evil. It is, therefore, the duty of the elite to educate the masses and urge them to live wisely. But no one, however superior, may impose his views on the others by force, even for their own good. Such a society has to be democratic so that once the masses have the best information and guidance available, they may make their own decisions—and suffer for them if they make them badly. And the elite must not withdraw and stand aloof when the masses demonstrate by their poor judgment that they are slow to learn.[10] In the following passage Auden defined this responsibility of leadership as it applies to the literary critic, but it is clear that he considered it binding as well on all of the other leaders in an open society, including such men as Ransom:

> Accepting his responsibility, he will see his position of influence as an accident, an inheritance which he does not deserve and which he is incompetent to administer. For though it is absolutely required of a man that he should intend to help others, the power to do so is outside his control. No man can guarantee the effect upon others of the acts he does with the intention of helping them. Indeed all he knows for certain is that, since his actions are never perfect, he must always do others harm, so that the final aim of every critic and teacher must be to persuade others to do without him, to realize that gifts of the spirit are never to be had at second hand.[11]

Ransom reaches essentially the same conclusion at the monastery, where the expedition pauses for rest. In a glowing crystal brought in by one of the monks, all the climbers but Shawcross, who cannot bear to look, find the elements of their personalities which if not mastered will destroy them or at least seriously limit their development. Ransom sees a mass of people pleading for a leader whom they can follow with blind obedience. He is tempted to answer this plea. The world, the abbot explains, always depends on such leaders to maintain order because they alone realize that all men are evil and therefore have to be governed. But "woe to the governors, for, by the very operation of their duty, however excellent, they themselves are destroyed. For you can only rule men by appealing to their fear and their lust; government requires the exercise of the human will: and the human will is from the Demon" (pp. 149–154).

Like all potentially great men Ransom, the abbot continues, is confronted by what he calls the Demon's second temptation, "the temptation of pity"[12] (Ransom has long since overcome the Demon's first temptation, i.e., the temptation to believe that human nature is good rather than evil). Since the masses cannot or will not understand and control the evil side of their nature themselves, one is tempted out of pity to use his will to conquer the Demon for them by ordering or forcing them to be good. To help Ransom overcome the second temptation, the abbot invites him to remain at the monastery as a religious ascetic and abnegate the will completely (pp. 152–154).

Ransom's decision, which apparently represents the authors' way out of this moral dilemma, is (1) to decline the abbot's invitation because to accept it would constitute an unheroic withdrawal from practical affairs, and (2) to reduce the exercise of the will to the minimum consistent with engagement: "I recognise my purpose. There was a choice once, in the Lakeland Inn. I made it wrong; and if I choose again now, I must choose for myself alone, not for these others" (p. 155). Though he is in favor of turning back, Ransom now considers it his duty to continue as leader of the expedition if the others, properly informed, decide to push on. His error at the Lakeland Inn was his failure to explain the political consequences of the expedition and his selfish motive for undertaking it. As a result the decisions of the others to follow him were not responsible, informed acts but acts of blind allegiance to a magnetic, wilful leader.

Therefore, when the radio reports that the Ostnians are threatening to win the race to the summit, Ransom, eager to correct his fault as a leader, takes a vote on whether to continue the climb, telling his followers beforehand that he considers it a fool's game if the mountaineering is not correctly carried out (pp. 155–157). What he means by correct mountaineering becomes clear when he and Shawcross discuss the methods the rival expedition is using to advance so rapidly. The Ostnians are hammering pitons into the face of the mountain and "hauling each other up like sacks!" They are not mountaineers, Shawcross complains; they are soldiers on a forced march. Realizing that their own expedition as well must sacrifice correct principles to speed if they are to win the race to the summit, Ransom argues that it is wrong to continue: "Ian, you're the purist: is this your idea of climbing? No time for observations; no time for reconnoitre?" (p. 156). The authors' point seems to be that one should begin any important undertaking of his own free will and proceed slowly enough to understand its full significance each step of the way, with the leader serving only as a helpful guide; otherwise one becomes a soldier blindly taking orders on a forced march.

But when the other climbers disagree, Ransom replies with resignation: "Very well then, since you wish it. I obey you. The summit will be reached, the Ostnians defeated, the Empire saved. We have betrayed ourselves. We start at dawn" (pp. 156, 157). If he refuses to continue as their leader, he is guilty of withdrawing from the group and standing aloof because he believes they have made an unwise decision. And if he orders them to turn back, he runs into the opposite ditch by imposing his will upon them, i.e., by forcing them to be good. In view of the outcome of the vote and his status as one of the elite, the only heroic course open to him is to lead on to the summit.[13]

Having resolved on that course, Ransom chooses Gunn to accompany him on the last lap of the climb because Gunn embodies the qualities which Ransom needs as a complement to his own if he is to pursue his heroic course. The other climbers are out of the running.

Lamp was caught by the avalanche (p. 162). Dr. Williams is too old and too fat (p. 167). As for Shawcross, Ransom concedes that he "is steady, reliable, a first-class climber. . . ." But he cannot face the danger of F 6 voluntarily (p. 166). In part, facing F 6 means coming to terms with the untidiness of life, including not only the difficulties of democratic government but also the depressing imperfections of man's physical nature, without forgetting one's heroic goal. Shawcross cannot bring himself to do this. He is too ascetic, too intolerant of the unorthodox, strong only in his obedience to authority. Earlier at the monastery he refused to look into the crystal because he felt that "We aren't meant to know these things" (p. 150). Now he rebuffs Dr. Williams' inquiries about his health and scorns Gunn's appetite (p. 160). Still, he desperately wants to conquer F 6 and hopes Ransom will order him to try (p. 166). But if Ransom gives that order, he succumbs to the Demon's second temptation (the temptation of pity) and ceases to act heroically.

Gunn too has faults, but they are at the opposite end of the spectrum from Shawcross'. Shawcross recoils from messiness and uncertainty; Gunn thrives on them. As a climber Gunn is "only a brilliant amateur, a novice with an extraordinary flair" (p. 166); moreover, he is a practical joker and a kleptomaniac (p. 145). But by taking him along instead of Shawcross, Ransom, as it were, corrects the imbalance in his own nature which earlier caused him to view the grosser physical aspects of life with profound disgust and long for death as an escape from them. Furthermore, he avoids the temptation to use force. For Gunn, unafraid of F 6 (p. 166), can face it of his own free will.

The last scene of the play describes the delirium into which Ransom sinks before dying on the summit and the effects of his achievement on England and Ostnia. Having abided by the vote to continue the climb, having chosen Gunn to accompany him on the last lap, and having reached the summit, he has combined action with reason in the manner which Auden considered appropriate for the elite in an open society. Using different metaphors, the delirium retells this victory and prefigures its spiritual consequences. In this version Ransom encounters his twin brother, who appears as a dragon (the shape this shadow figure often assumes),[14] and defeats him in a contest. Then as a reward Ransom's spirit is apparently taken to God.

But before the delirium begins, the chorus, by way of a prologue, outlines several parts of the hero myth which the delirium is to treat immediately thereafter in more detail, among them the wasteland to be redeemed, the dragon to be overcome, and the reward to be given the conquering hero:

> For the Dragon has wasted the forest and set fire to the farm;
> . . . .
> O, when shall the deliverer come to destroy this dragon?
> For it is stated in the prophecies that such a one shall appear,
> . . . .
> Our elders shall welcome him home with trumpet and organ,
> Load him with treasure, yes, and our most beautiful maidenhead
> He shall have for his bed.   (p. 174)

Then comes the delirium. On the summit a veiled figure signals with her hand, and James appears as the dragon amid a fanfare of trumpets (pp. 174, 175). Here he symbolizes the cultural values of the wasteland, especially the excessive use of the will, which Ransom as hero must transcend. The contest takes the form of a chess game, with the followers of the two contestants serving as their chessman. Having agreed to answer any questions that Mr. and Mrs. A. (average citizens) would care to pose, James and his group are asked: "Why is my work so dull?" "Why doesn't my husband love me any more?" "Why have I so little money?" and "Why were we born?" The responses, full of shibboleths and references to the sacrifices of the climbers, are calculated to bully the questioners into silence (pp. 176, 177). The thematic purpose of this forum is to show the power orientation and general bankruptcy of the wasteland.

After the chess game has continued for a few minutes in silence except for the drum roll in the background and an occasional "Check," this strange turn of events brings the contest to its climax:

> Ransom (*looking for the first time towards the summit and seeing the figure*) Look!
> James Mate! I've won!
> (*The* FIGURE *shakes its head*)
> Ransom (*his eyes still fixed upon it*) But was the victory real?
> James (*Half rises to his feet, totters: in a choking voice*) It was not Virtue—it was not Knowledge— it was Power! (*Collapses*)   (p. 177)

Ransom, it should be noted, does not lay a hand on James. To overcome what James stands for, Ransom, like Christ tempted by Satan on the tower in *Paradise Regained* (IV, 551–580), rejects the use of oppressive force. If the hero is to master his shadow figure instead of becoming its instrument, he must rise above its methods.[15]

After mastering his shadow, the mythic hero often rescues and marries a beautiful maiden. Sometimes she wears a veil, the removal of which may underscore or take the place of her rescue. The marriage of the hero and the maiden symbolizes the union of the masculine and feminine principles of the universe, one instance of which occurs when the hero properly combines reason and action. From this marriage issues new life in such forms as a child, a better civilization, and the rebirth of personality or spirit on a higher level.[16]

Such a rebirth of the spirit, I believe, is the meaning of Ransom's encounter with the veiled figure on the summit. Having found his salvation from self-consciousness by absorption in action whose significance he understood, Ransom now meets his mother, who, young again as she was when he was a child, represents either the form in which God appears to him or the mediatrix who conducts his soul to God. When the veiled figure is accused of threatening normal order, Ransom *"rushes up to the summit and places himself in front of the* FIGURE, *with his arms outstretched, as if to protect it"* (p. 181). In his effort to protect the creative element of life against the hostile conservative spirit of things as they are, Ransom is crucified. The figure's veil falls away, and Mrs. Ransom is revealed *"as a young mother."*[17] *"He falls at her feet with his head in her lap,"* and she, stroking his hair, describes the "marriage" awaiting him: "in the castle tower above, / The princess' cheek burns red for your love, / You shall be king and queen of the land, / Happy for ever, hand in hand" (p. 182). Then the stage, after being slowly darkened, is gradually illumined by the sun rising over Ransom's dead body on the summit (p. 183).

Asked about the mother-image on the mountain top, Auden offered this explanation: "It seems to me that in man's search for God he erects before him a number of images. I believe that the mother-image is one of the last to be outgrown."[18] Auden seems to have been saying that though the imagery changes, what it stands for is constant and real. Perhaps it could be argued that he meant that the mother-image is a barrier between man and God and that since Ransom is unable to surmount it, he fails at the very end to become a Truly Strong Man. Ransom admittedly is weak at the beginning of the play and accepts the leadership of the expedition for unheroic reasons. But in view of his correct response later on to the challenge reflected in the crystal, his defeat of the dragon, and the rising sun (one of the most common symbols of rebirth), the interpretation which I have advanced seems more valid.

Finally, the remainder of the action is also consistent with the hero myth. The benefit conferred by the mythic hero is real but not lasting. Sooner or later it fails because the people, incapable of understanding the full significance of the hero's act, mistranslate its moral significance into a way of life which produces another wasteland.[19] Similarly, England and Ostnia are reconciled at the end of the play, if only for a while, by Ransom's death. At a broadcast with James and his group, for example, Blavek—leader of the Ostnian expedition—declares it an honor to have been defeated by such a man as Ransom. But the probable ephemerality of this friendly mood is fairly obvious in Stagmantle's fatuous comment: "As Monsieur Blavek has said, Sport transcends all national barriers and it is some comfort to realise that this tragedy has brought two great nations closer together—" (p. 185).

If, then, my interpretation of the play is correct, Michael Ransom—notwithstanding his serious error at the beginning of the climb—is ultimately not a failure but, as his name suggests, a hero, who, by avoiding aloofness from the untidiness of life at the one extreme and the oppressive use of the will at the other, for the time being redeems the people and their wasted land.

NOTES

1. See the following reviews, articles, theses, and books (listed in chronological order): E. M. Forster, "Chormopuloda," *The Listener*, XVI (Supplement, Oct. 14, 1936), vii; "Parnassus or F6?" *Times Literary Supplement*, Nov. 7, 1936, p. 902; Janet Smith, Review of *The Ascent of F 6*, in *The Criterion*, XVI, No. 63 (1937), 330; C. Day Lewis, "Paging Mankind," *Poetry*, XLIX (1937), 225, 226; Derek Verschoyle, "The Theatre," *The Spectator*, CLVIII (1937), 403; "Plays and Pictures," *The New Statesman and Nation*, XIII (1937), 368; A. V. Cookman, "The Theatre," *The London Mercury*, XXXV (1937), 619; Barbara Nixon, Review of *The Ascent of F 6*, *Left Review*, III (1937), 254; Mary Colum, "Life and Literature: The Drama," *Forum*, XCVII (1937), 355; George Jean Nathan, "Theater," *Scribner's Magazine*, CII (1937), 66; Kerker Quinn, "Poets into Playwrights," *The Virginia Quarterly Review*, XIII (1937), 618; Elizabeth Drew, *Discovering Drama* (New York, 1937), p. 210; Richard Hoggart, *Auden: An Introductory Essay* (New Haven, 1951), pp. 80–82; Justin M. Replogle, "The Auden Group: The 1930's Poetry of W. H. Auden, C. Day Lewis and Stephen Spender" (unpubl. diss., U. of Wis., 1956), pp. 142–145, 182, 183; John G. Blair, *The Poetic Art of W. H. Auden* (Princeton, 1965), pp. 101, 102; William J. Bruehl, "The Auden/Isherwood Plays" (unpubl. diss., U. of Pa., 1966), pp. 185–216; and William J. Bruehl, *"Polus Naufrangia*: A Key Symbol in *The Ascent of F6*," *Modern Drama*, X (1967), 163, 164.

   Hoggart and Bruehl offer the most extended analyses of the problem discussed in my paper.

   I agree with most of these critics that Ransom undertakes the conquest of F 6 with unheroic motives, but I contend that at the monastery he sees his error and corrects it.

174   FORREST E. HAZARD

2. Quoted by Howard Griffin, "A Dialogue with W. H. Auden," *Hudson Review*, III (1951), 583.
3. " 'T. E. Lawrence,' " *Now and Then*, No. 47 (Spring 1934), p. 30.
4. Ibid., p. 33.
5. (New York, 1966), p. 13.
5. Gertrude Jobes, "Correlative Deities" and "Twins," *Dictionary of Mythology, Folklore, and Symbols*, 3 vols. (New York, 1962); Erich Neumann, *The Origins and History of Consciousness*, trans. R. F. C. Hull, Bollingen Series XLII (New York, 1954), 93–100, 136, 181–186; Mary Esther Harding, *Psychic Energy: Its Source and Goal*, Bollingen Series X (New York, 1947), 291, 292; C. G. Jung, *Aion* (1959), IX, ii of *The Collected Works of C. G. Jung*, trans. R. F. C. Hull, eds. Herbert Read et al., Bollingen Series XX (New York, 1953 to date), 41, 42; C. G. Jung, *Symbols of Transformation* (1956), V of *The Collected Works of C. G. Jung*, 367, 368; C. G. Jung, *Two Essays on Analytical Psychology* (1953), VII of *The Collected Works*, 25, 52, 53, 65; C. G. Jung, *The Archetypes and the Collective Unconscious* (1959), IX, i of *The Collected Works*, 29, 284, 285; Jolan Jacobi, *The Psychology of Jung* (New Haven, 1943), pp. 102, 103; James Campbell, *The Hero with a Thousand Faces*, Bollingen Series VII (New York, 1949), 245, 246, 336, 337.
   By citing sources predominantly Jungian, I do not mean to imply that Auden and Isherwood were Jungians; they knew many schools of thought and were quite eclectic. The Jungian interpretation of the hero myth, however, seems both useful and valid here because it is consonant with traditional views, with which, as I hope to demonstrate in my paper, Auden and Isherwood agreed when they wrote *The Ascent of F 6*.
7. W. H. Auden and Christopher Isherwood, *The Ascent of F 6*, in *Two Great Plays*, by W. H. Auden and Christopher Isherwood, Modern Library Paperback No. 48 (New York, [1959]), p. 137. Page references in parentheses in my text are to this edition.
8. Jobes, "Animal," *Dictionary of Mythology, Folklore, and Symbols;* Mircea Eliade, "The Yearning for Paradise in Primitive Tradition," *The Making of Myth*, ed. Richard M. Ohmann (New York, 1962), pp. 88, 92. In "K.'s Quest," *The Kafka Problem*, ed. Angel Flores (New York, 1946), p. 48, Auden wrote that the hero succeeds where others fail because "he is willing to accept help from the humblest creature, the ant, the bird, etc., while his better endowed rivals believe that they can suceed by their own gifts alone. . . ." See also Stith Thompson, "Helpful Animal," *Motif-Index of Folk-Literature*, 6 vols. (Bloomington, Ind., 1955–58), VI, 378.
9. Erich Neumann, *Art and the Creative Unconscious*, trans. Ralph Manheim, Bollingen Series LXI (New York, 1959), 185–187, 194, 195.
10. *The Intent of the Critic*, ed. Donald A. Stauffer (Princeton, 1941), pp. 144, 145.
11. *Ibid.*, p. 146.
12. In "The Heresy of Our Time," *Renascence: A Critical Journal of Letters*, I (1949), 24, Auden wrote: "Behind pity for another lies self-pity and behind self-pity lies cruelty.
   "To feel compassion for someone is to make oneself their equal; to pity them is to regard oneself as their superior, and from that eminence the step to the torture chamber and the corrective labor camp is shorter than one thinks." See also Hoggart, p. 81.
13. Hoggart contends that at the monastery Ransom's "dilemma is discussed at length but still not fully faced" (p. 80). In *"Polus Naufrangia*: A Key

Symbol in *The Ascent of F6*," p. 164, William Bruehl argues: "This 'I obey you' is an unacceptable rationalization of the obsession that he really obeys. Furthermore, he knows that he is permitting his comrades to obey him. In the same breath he admits, 'We have betrayed ourselves.' Even this plural is not honest because Ransom alone is capable of betrayal: he alone has foreknowledge. Ransom, the exceptional leader, the people's hero, his comrades' idol, is exposed as a fraud." In a note on the same page Bruehl adds that "Ransom is obsessed with an unconscious need for his mother's love and approval."

I have offered an answer to this interpretation in my text. I would only repeat here that if Ransom orders his followers to abandon the climb, he succumbs to the Demon's second temptation and ceases to act heroically.

14. Campbell, *The Hero with a Thousand Faces*, p. 337.
15. In *Two Essays on Analytical Psychology*, pp. 52, 53, Jung asserts: "Logically, the opposite of love is hate . . . but psychologically it is the will to power. Where love reigns, there is no will to power; and where the will to power is paramount, love is lacking. The one is the shadow of the other: the man who adopts the standpoint of Eros finds his compensatory opposite in the will to power, and that of the man who puts the accent on power in Eros." The contest between Ransom and James seems to embody this principle.
16. Campbell, pp. 109–114; Neumann, *The Origins and History of Consciousness*, pp. 198–213; Jung, *Two Essays on Analytical Psychology*, pp. 195, 196, 208, 209, 226; Jung, *The Archetypes and the Collective Unconscious*, pp. 29, 200; Mary Esther Harding, *Psychic Energy*, pp. 145–153.
17. Campbell gives this description of the anima figure, which Mrs. Ransom apparently represents at this point in the play: "She is the paragon of all paragons of beauty, the reply to all desire, the bliss-bestowing goal of every hero's earthly and unearthly quest. She is mother, sister, mistress, bride" (pp. 110, 111). In *The Origins and History of Consciousness*, p. 212, Neumann writes as follows about this part of the heroic quest: "It is . . . impossible to find the treasure unless the hero has first found and redeemed his own soul. . . . This inner receptive side is, on the subjective level, the rescued captive, the virgin mother . . . who is at once man's inspiration, his beloved and mother. . . ."
18. Quoted by Griffin, p. 591. In his doctoral dissertation "The Auden/Isherwood Plays," p. 202, Bruehl says of this explanation that "It is a remark by Auden long after his conversion to Christianity, an event which would put the play in a wholly new perspective for him and confuse the issue for us who must judge the play in the terms of 1936." But since the explanation Auden gave seems consistent with my interpretation, I have not found it necessary to assume that he had become confused about his use of this image.
19. Campbell, pp. 217, 218.

Chicago State College

FEDERICO GARCÍA LORCA AND JUAN RAMÓN JIMÉNEZ: THE QUESTION OF INFLUENCES

In this article we should like to return to the question of the literary relations between Lorca and Jiménez. At this late date, we are of course not claiming the revelation that Jiménez influenced Lorca, a fact which all critics recognized very early, and perhaps even over-stressed. When Lorca began to write poetry around 1918, the acknowl-edged masters were Juan Ramón Jiménez and Antonio Machado. Around 1920, however, the younger poets like Gerardo Diego and Guillermo de Torre began to struggle to introduce the *ultraísta* move-ment in Spain, thus challenging the dominance of Jiménez and Machado. Although Jiménez continued to exert influences on Lorca's Generation of 1927, this influence manifested itself more permanently in the poetry of Jorge Guillén and Pedro Salinas. Lorca, Rafael Alberti, Vicente Aleixandre and Luis Cernuda all began to absorb the newer poetic currents of ultraism, surrealism and existentialism. Lorca's gradual separation from Jiménez is clearly documented in various pronouncements by the two poets. Thus far these materials have not been collected and presented in an orderly fashion. In regard to Jiménez, certain of his later writings and the recent literary diary of Juan Guerrero Ruiz, *Juan Ramón de viva voz,* are of especial value for our ascertaining his reactions to Lorca.

In 1921 Lorca published in Madrid his *Libro de poemas*, an exten-sive collection of lyrics written in Granada during the years 1917–1920. As Lorca said in a prologue, the book was "la imagen exacta de mis días de adolescencia y juventud . . . mi infancia apasionada"; in gen-eral, these poems of melancholy adolescence proved to be an atypical

177

phase in Lorca's poetry, in spite of their being overpraised later by
critics like Díaz-Plaja, who was striving desperately to emphasize the
traditional in Lorca. It is not surprising that there are echoes of Jiménez,
especially of such books as *Arias tristes* and *Pastorales*. The clearest
example, as many critics have pointed out, is Lorca's "Canción prima-
veral":

> Voy camino de la tarde
> entre flores de la huerta
> dejando sobre el camino
> el agua de mi tristeza.

The "Canción otoñal" has the same tone.

> Hoy siento en el corazón
> un vago temblor de estrellas,
> pero mi senda se pierde
> en el alma de la niebla.
> La luz me troncha las alas
> y el dolor de mi tristeza
> va mojando los recuerdos
> en la frente de la idea.

This note of tender sadness, of melancholy, was typical of the early
poetry of Jiménez. But we should be aware that only a very few of the
seventy poems of *Libro de poemas* show clear echoes of Jiménez.
Already, as Lorca declares, "¡Mi corazón es una mariposa . . . que
presa por la araña gris del tiempo tiene el polen fatal del desengaño."
Already, that is, the poet is feeling disenchantment and resignation,
sentiments to which Jiménez constantly refused to surrender. Obviously this note of time and disenchantment suggests Antonio Machado,
of whom there are many echoes in the book.

But, as the penetrating critic Angel del Río first pointed out, "Hay
(en el *Libro de poemas*) mucho más de lo que se cree de Rubén
Darío."[1] This influence of Darío is surprising when we consider that
the general influence of *modernismo* was waning rapidly by 1918. In
a *poema suelto* of 1918, however, Lorca remembered Darío specifically:

> Panidas, sí, Panidas;
> el trágico Rubén
> así llamó en sus versos
> al lánguido Verlaine . . . .

And in his first prose work *Impresiones y paisajes* Lorca echoed that
"La Marquesa Eulalia cesó de reír," a specific reference to one of
Darío's princesses. It is also well known that as late as 1934 Lorca
joined Pablo Neruda in Buenos Aires in an act of homage to Rubén
Darío.

In two lyrics of *Libro de poemas* Lorca clearly showed himself a follower of Darío. In "El macho cabrío" it is the early Darío of sensuality:

> ¡Salve, demonio macho!
> Eres el más intenso animal.
> Místico eterno
> del infierno carnal . . . .

And in "Lluvia" he imitates the Darío of the "Nocturno," even in the form of the alexandrines:

> La nostalgia terrible de una vida perdida,
> El fatal sentimiento de haber nacido tarde,
> O la ilusión inquieta de una mañana imposible
> Con la inquietud cercana del dolor de la carne.

It is significant that even at this time Lorca chose to imitate the sensuality of Darío and the satanism of Darío's follower Valle-Inclán, and not the new manner of Jiménez as exemplified in books like *Eternidades* and *Belleza.*

Although we have not seen it pointed out previously, Lorca is perhaps closest to Jiménez in a group of poems generally called "Suites," written around 1921. At this moment Jiménez's importance as a literary figure was probably at zenith, since he had published major works such as *Sonetos espirituales, Diario de un poeta reciencasado, Eternidades, Piedra y cielo* and the *Segunda antolojía poética.* In 1921 Jiménez became the guiding force behind the journal *Indice,* although technically Díez Canedo and Guerrero Ruiz served as "secretaries" and Jiménez remained anonymous. The journal was to be an organ for artists interested in the "exaltación del espíritu y por el gusto de las cosas bellas"[2]—that is, Jiménez was to exert his considerable influence. Now since Lorca was not established at this time, and since he had a great talent for sensing and following poetic directions, it is logical that he should contribute to Jiménez poetry, an action which would please the master.

In three numbers of *Indice,* Lorca published three groups of "Suites" of very short lyrics (a manner Jiménez had recently adopted), a total of twenty-two poems. In general, the lyrics are aesthetic, artistic and sufficiently philosophical to have impressed Jiménez. The very titles "Suite" and "Berceuse" suggest the aesthetic, normally thought alien to Lorca's temperament. In the lyrics there is a tendency to project grand symbols in a short poem in the manner of Jiménez. The poem "Acacia" reads as follows:

> ¿Quién segó el tallo
>   de la luna?
> (Nos dejó raíces
>   de agua.)
> ¡Qué fácil nos sería cortar las flores
>   de la eterna acacia!

Although here Lorca seems to be contemplating suicide as a means of interrupting the life process, the use of the flower as symbol suggests Jiménez's important lyric from *Piedra y cielo* in which the *margarita* is the universe itself.

> Sí—dice el día—No
> —dice la noche.—
> ¿Quién deshoja esta inmensa margarita,
> de oro, blanco y negro?
>
> ¿Y cuándo, di, Señor de lo increado,
> creerás que te queremos?

The "Suite de los espejos" is an ambitious series of lyrics, in which Lorca attempts to establish a philosophical pattern interweaving symbols such as Christ, Adam and Eve, Moon and Earth. In the poem "El gran espejo," the mirror is of course the universe.

> Vivimos
> bajo el gran espejo.
> ¡El hombre es azul!
> ¡Hosanna!

Lorca's use of the color blue to suggest enchantment or optimism is not typical of him, but is typical of Jiménez, for example, in the early poem "Dios está azul," which was later amplified in "Conciencia hoy azul" of *Animal de fondo*. Another example of the grand symbol in this series is "Rayos."

> Todo es abanico.
> Hermano, abre los brazos.
> Dios es el punto.

The development of the symbol of the mirror in a number of poems indicates in both poets a continuing preoccupation with self-absorption and the problem of reality, which each poet worked out in his own way. In another series of short lyrics apparently from these same years, Lorca is echoing Jiménez in various ways, especially in "Vista general."

> Toda la selva turbia
> es una inmensa araña
> que teje una red sonora
> a la esperanza.
> ¡A la pobre virgen blanca
> que se cría con suspiros y miradas!

The "red sonora" suggests the phrase "Soledad sonora," which Jiménez had in fact taken from San Juan de la Cruz but had made his own. And the "virgen blanca," with various modifications, was Jiménez's favorite symbol until his last years. At this stage of Lorca's development, in general Jiménez must have approved of his pupil.

During the years 1921–1924 García Lorca was rapidly developing his poetic talents in a traditional and a vanguard direction at the same time, but in both directions he was developing away from Jiménez. Around 1920 the young poets of Lorca's generation such as Gerardo Diego and Guillermo de Torre began to introduce the *ultraísta* movement in Spain, in rebellion against the dominance of Jiménez and Machado. In 1925 Torre declared bravely in his *Literatura europea de vanguardia*[3] that Machado was "lost in nostalgic backward looks and classic preoccupations," that Jiménez by his symbolist ideology, his elegiac tone and his excess of sentiment was still tied to the early 1900's —in short, both were unsuitable to lead the new movement. *Ultraísmo* as a movement ultimately foundered in Spain because of the lack of a leader, but from it Lorca developed his modern metaphor. Since the *ultraístas* tended to consider poetry as an elegant and ironic stylized play, Jiménez of course had only antipathy for the movement.

During the years 1921–1924 Lorca also began to exploit the popular materials of Andalusia in his *Poema del cante jondo*. Now of course Jiménez and Lorca were both Andalusians, but Jiménez had always cast a cold eye upon the popular—as he said, "A la minoría, siempre." Even when he had used the ballad form in *Pastorales* he had remained an impressionistic aesthete. But Lorca, following the bent of his genius, stylized the traditional *siguiriya* and *soleá* into an artistic form of permanency, a pattern unlike anything Jiménez ever did.

Yet it was just at this time in Lorca's development, around 1924, when Jiménez succeeded in exerting a specific and powerful influence on Lorca. During their travels around Spain, Jiménez and his wife Zenobia visited Granada and Lorca's family.[4] When Jiménez returned to Madrid he sent to Lorca's sister Isabel his distinct and unique ballad "Generalife." As Bernard Gicovate[5] has pointed out, the "Generalife" has the unmistakable ring of the *Romancero gitano*.

> Nadie Más. Abierto todo.
> Pero ya nadie faltaba.
> No eran mujeres ni niños
> no eran hombres: eran lágrimas.
> ¡Oh, qué desconsolación
> de traída y de llevada;
> qué llegar al rincón último,

en repetición sonámbula;
qué darse con la cabeza
en las finales murallas!

Admittedly Jiménez himself had antecedents for this manner. For example, compare these lines from "Desolación absurda," written by Julio Herrera y Reissig in 1902.

Noche de tenaces suspiros
platónicamente ilesos:
vuelan bandadas de besos
y parejas de suspiros . . .
y llevan su desconsuelo
hacia vagos ostracismos,
floridos sonambulismos
y adioses de terciopelo . . . .

Certainly Jiménez deserves credit for this specific influence on Lorca's *Romancero gitano,* but what is surprising is that Jiménez never specifically claimed this credit.

In addition to the form of the ballad, even in part of his mature poetry it is clear that Lorca found in Jiménez's earlier poetry certain colors and symbols which he proceeded to develop in his own fashion. From the profusion of colors which Jiménez used in his early impressionistic manner—white, gold, blue, mauve, violet and green—Lorca with his emphasis on the sensual logically chose green for development. Jiménez in his earlier poetry also used green to suggest the sensual, only a momentary phase in his work, for example, in a semipopular poem such as "El pajarito verde."

Morado y verde limón
estaba el poniente, madre.
Morado y verde limón
estaba mi corazón.

But the lyrics which interested Lorca were those like "La verdecilla," in which the sensuality of the lass is stressed: "Verde es la niña. / Tiene verdes ojos, pelo verde."

Of course it is well known that Lorca began with this idea in the "Romance sonámbulo," with the famous line. "Verde, que te quiero verde." But even in this ballad, in which green ultimately suggests, not mystery as many have thought, but the sexual instincts which pervade the world, Lorca is already pushing beyond the limits Jiménez would allow. And in the ballad of "Antoñito el Camborio," Lorca's "moreno de verde luna" is a tragic and doomed (though brilliant) figure, isolated from society and persecuted by it. By the time of *Poeta en Nueva York* Lorca is using green in a manner which Jiménez would call perverted. For example, at the end of the revolutionary poem "El niño Stanton," the poet concludes with this ugly image in green: "Iré penetrando a voces las verdes estatuas de la Malaria."

Lorca's treatment of the moon symbol followed this same direction away from its normal use in Jiménez. In Jiménez the moon had been a "pastora de plata," usually white or gold. In Lorca's "Romance de la luna, luna," the moon with her "polisón de nardos" is still a feminine figure. But, as we have seen, his "moreno de verde luna" is assuming his particular emphasis, the very color suggesting the not-normal sensuality. In his revolutionary poem "Crucifixión," from *Poeta en Nueva York,* the moon is closely connected with the libido symbol of the horse, in a strong image: "Era que la luna quemaba con sus bujías el falo de los caballos." By the time of the drama *Bodas de sangre* the moon symbol has become specifically a boy, who competes with the *Mendiga* as Death for the lives of the lovers in the play. With both the color green and the moon symbol, then, Lorca proceeded in a personal manner in a way entirely alien to Jiménez's concept of poetry.

But the final separation from Jiménez was initiated by Lorca himself in a poem in *Canciones,* written between 1921–1924. Part of the poems of *Canciones* are in the *ultraísta* manner, and a great number of them are of troubled and confused theme, which would have displeased Jiménez. The significant poem is in a section called "Tres retratos con sombra." The first portrait is of Paul Verlaine, and the shadow over Verlaine must concern secrets of his turbulent life. The third portrait, of Debussy, is concerned with narcissism. The second portrait is entitled "Juan Ramón Jiménez," and reads as follows:

> En el blanco infinito,
> nieve, nardo y salina,
> perdió su fantasía.
>
> El color blanco anda,
> sobre una muda alfombra
> de plumas de paloma.
>
> Sin ojos ni ademán
> inmóvil sufre un sueño.
> Pero tiembla por dentro.
>
> En el blanco infinito,
> ¡qué pura y larga herida
> dejó su fantasía!
>
> En el blanco infinito,
> Nieve. Nardo. Salina.

It is interesting that a critic like Vázquez Ocaña quotes this poem and concludes: "Y Federico, que siente dentro a Manrique, a Garcilaso, a Góngora, a Quevedo, decide quedarse con Juan Ramón, entre los vivos. . . ."⁶

Actually, we should say the opposite, for why is there a "shadow" over the portrait of Jiménez? Lorca, a poet of the five senses, is subtly criticizing Jiménez for losing himself in a thinned-out world of "white infinity." Without eyes, without movement, the poet "is suffering a dream." In other words, Jiménez has lost himself in an unseeing, passionless self-absorption alienated from life itself. Lorca never changed this opinion of Jiménez, but was generous enough to recognize his ultimate greatness. In 1936, in an interview he declared: "Hay dos maestros: Antonio Machado y Juan Ramón Jiménez. El primero, en un plano puro de serenidad y perfección poética. Poeta humano y celeste. El segundo, gran poeta turbado por una terrible exaltación de su yo, increíblemente mordido por cosas insignificantes, con los oídos puestos en el mundo, verdaderamente enemigo de su maravillosa y única alma de poeta."⁷ Recently, Luis Cernuda in a long and merciless essay on Jiménez pushed Lorca's idea beyond any reasonable limits by insisting that Jiménez by his incredible self-concern ultimately destroyed his talent.⁸

In 1928 Jiménez seems to have replied to Lorca in one of his stinging *Caricatura líricas,*⁹ one of a series Jiménez wrote over the years. Although Lorca had just published his immensely successful *Romancero gitano,* there is no suggestion of praise in the *Caricatura.* Jiménez still finds him in a blind alley with no way out: "No quiere dejar el caño de sus musarañas." Lorca has crashed, like a big fly against a windshield, against the closed sunset. When Jiménez looks toward Lorca's future, he sees no clear escape. "¿Por qué boca de pozo, alcantarilla, cañería ha salido?" And to Lorca's earlier criticism that Jiménez was "without eyes," Jiménez concludes that Lorca, "como un hospiciano que no ha visto nada en el mundo, llega a casa a la hora total . . . una azucena de tela en la mano." Thus almost every sentence of the clever caricature has a pejorative phrase which cuts deeply. Jiménez gradually refused to recognize any poetry concerned with the senses only.

By 1930 Lorca had won his permanent place in Spanish literature with the fame of the *Romancero gitano,* and as proof of his maturity in that year he wrote and delivered his critical essay "Teoría y juego del duende." In the essay Lorca plays grandly in literature past and present to develop his idea of the *duende,* or daemon, as the permanent source of his poetic inspiration. According to Lorca, there are three sources of inspiration, in ascending order: the muse, the angel, and the daemon. Among the artists inspired by the daemon, Lorca brings together such varied names as Socrates, Descartes, Quevedo, the Count of Lautréamont, Goya, the *cantaora* Pastora Pavón and the *torero* Juan Belmonte. And surprisingly, he also includes Santa Teresa and San Juan de la Cruz. But in speaking of the angel, the second level of inspiration, he says significantly: "Cuando ve llegar a la muerte, el ángel vuela en círculos lentos y teje con lágrimas de hielo y narciso la elegía que hemos visto temblar en las manos de Keats . . . y en las de Bécquer y en las de Juan Ramón Jiménez. Pero, ¡qué horror el del ángel si siente una araña, por diminuta que sea, sobre su tierno pie rosado!"[10] Obviously Lorca is repeating the subtle criticism of his earlier poem.

Much later, in an essay entitled "Angel y duende," Jiménez replied specifically to Lorca's essay. Said Jiménez: "Federico García Lorca, el cárdeno poeta granadí, paisano como yo del duende y del ángel, escribió una preciosa 'Teoría y juego del duende,' llena por todas partes de chispa duendiosa algo anjelista. [Pero] es claro que el duende de Granada no es como el duende de Sevilla, Moguer, Cádiz . . . Granada es la montañesca mística escondida." And Jiménez continued ominously: "Pero no hablo del ánjel en el sentido azucenesco melodioso, como Federico García, ni le doy al duende el aire malsano de caño que él le da. Mi duende y mi ánjel de mi parte andaluza no tienen categoría de divinos ni de malditos, no son malos ni buenos."[11]

During the late 1920's and 1930's an important source pertinent to our purpose here is Guerrero Ruiz's diary *Juan Ramón de viva voz,* covering basically the years 1928–1935, in which Guerrero has given us an honest (if sometimes chilling) picture of Jiménez the man and his opinions. During these years, Jiménez was seeing his disciples of the Generation of 1927—Lorca, Guillén, Alberti, Salinas, Aleixandre—attempt to assert their own individuality. Jiménez's pronouncements on Lorca indicate that he was willing to write him off as a bad follower. In 1930, Jiménez opined, "entre los irresponsables, Lorca [es] el más desorientado actualmente."[12] Actually, Lorca had just written (but had not published) his great book of surrealist poetry, *Poeta en Nueva York.* In 1931 Jiménez commented disgustedly, "lo de Federico García es ya el truco permanente, una cosa muy floja."[13] With this comment Jiménez seems to be excluding parts of the *Romancero gitano*; what had specifically triggered his outburst was one of Lorca's wilder surrealist pieces called "Dos amantes asesinados por una perdiz."

Since Lorca's *Romancero gitano* achieved international fame, Jiménez continued to discuss it, but his low opinion of the book as a

whole indicates that he claimed little basic influence on it. He conceded
that "de Federico García Lorca hay cinco o seis romances magistrales
en el *Romancero gitano,* que traen un elemento granadino a la poesía
española y son lo mejor de su obra. Si Lorca hubiera hecho cien
romances gitanos de calidad, ya tenía segura la gloria; pero luego ha
derivado a otros caminos que no son el suyo, dondé se ha extraviado.
. . ."[14] But he went on to add: "No hay que olvidar la influencia que a
través de Dalí ha recibido Lorca de la pintura moderna, de Chirico,
Derain y otros; cuando Lorca describe unos paños en un romance los
está viendo a través de la pintura de Chirico. . . ."[15] This influence of
Chirico by way of Salvador Dalí is of course surrealist and Freudian,
both schools alien to Jiménez's concept of poetry. In summing up,
Jiménez concluded: "Lorca, lo mejor que ha hecho es el *Romancero
gitano,* pero éste tampoco tiene espíritu, es otra Andalucía de pandereta, vista de otro modo, pero de pandereta, poesía externa, brillante,
vista de otro modo, pero sin espíritu. . . ."[16] In this negative criticism,
Jiménez, as have the Spanish critics in general, is obstinately setting
Lorca up as a poet of the people, then attacking him for being only a
popular poet. Actually, the *Romancero gitano* is vanguard poetry
in which Lorca in both design and execution of the book is brilliantly
utilizing popular forms to project his own personal psychological
themes.

Therefore, if Jiménez thought the *Romancero gitano* was an "Andalusia for tourists," we can imagine his rejection of Lorca's other major
work, including surrealist poems like the "Oda a Salvador Dalí," the
great book *Poeta en Nueva York* and the *Diván del Tamarit.* In an
interview in 1938, Jiménez at least referred to *Poeta en Nueva York.*
"El otro día," he said, "me preguntaron Vds. si yo no veía una
diferencia esencial entre la poesía última, verso libre, de García Lorca
y la del *Romancero gitano.* Yo quiero esplicar . . . que las imájenes
locas parecen más locas en verso descuidado que en verso regular. En
realidad, la forma domina un poco la locura."[17] In later years, Jiménez
apparently made no further pronouncements on Lorca; after all, these
are fairly conclusive. Ricardo Gullón's *Conversaciones con Juan Ramón
Jiménez* of recent date could probably have been an important source,
but Gullón deliberately deleted strongly adverse opinions of Jiménez.
It is probably significant that there is almost nothing on Lorca.

In summing up, certainly we can say that in a few of Lorca's earliest
poems there is a recognizable influence, an echo of the tender melancholy of Jiménez's early poetry. Later Lorca seemed to adapt certain
symbols and chromatic preoccupations of Jiménez, but always trans-

formed them into his own particular emphases. In general, probably the influence of Jiménez was overshadowed by that of other poets nearer in temperament to Lorca. Lorca followed the early Darío of sensuality in one moment; he also followed Ramón del Valle-Inclán, also a consistent *modernista,* in his emphasis on the satanic, the rebellious and the foreboding. Lorca is like Antonio Machado in his tragic outlook, in his existential attitude toward life. As Angel del Río concluded, "en lo substantivo apenas cabe concebir dos genios poéticos más opuestos que el del autor de los *Sonetos espirituales,* toda aspiración vertical a una pura belleza sin contorno, y el poeta del *Cante jondo,* toda sensualidad, color, patetismo dramático."[18] This is correct as far as it goes. Jiménez himself, Graciela Palau, his biographer, and Díaz-Plaja have gone further to insist that Lorca was a poet of the people, then have attacked the shortcomings of his poetry because it was only popular poetry. Lorca himself rejected the notion that he was a popular poet, but in vain. It is encouraging that recently a Spanish critic like Manuel Durán has attempted to see Lorca as "Poeta entre dos mundos," the traditional Spanish and the modern European, and Durán has even dared to suggest that Lorca might be an Andalusian more universal that Jiménez.[19] As we have seen, Jiménez was incapable of appreciating or even tolerating the turbulent, the despairing and the revolutionary in a great deal of Lorca's poetry, so that it is clear Jiménez disowned any influence from an early date. Let us hope that the poetry of both Lorca and Jiménez, admittedly very different, can continue to exist side by side, but it will of course be for posterity to decide this question.

NOTES

1. Angel del Río, "El poeta Federico García Lorca," *Revista Hispanica Moderna,* I (1934–35), 178.
2. See Graciela Palau, *Vida y obra de Juan Ramón Jiménez* (Madrid, 1957), pp. 219–221.
3. (Madrid, 1925), pp. 40–45.
4. See Graciela Palau, pp. 254–255.
5. "El 'Romance sonámbulo' de García Lorca," *Hispania,* XLI (1958), 300–302.
6. Fernando Vázquez Ocaña, *García Lorca* (Mexico, 1957), p. 148.
7. Federico García Lorca, *Obras completas* (Madrid, 1960), p. 1766.
8. Luis Cernuda, "Juan Ramón Jiménez," *Estudios sobre poesía española* (Madrid, 1958), pp. 119–135.
9. Juan Ramón Jiménez, "Caricaturas líricas," *Revista Hispanica Moderna,* I (1934–1935), 185.
10. Federico García Lorca, p. 44.
11. Juan Ramón Jiménez, "Angel y duende," *Pájinas escogidas* (Madrid, 1958),

p. 180. In these quotations we have followed the usual practice of Spanish critics in respecting Jiménez's peculiar orthography.

12. Ruiz, *Juan Ramón de viva voz* (Madrid, 1961), p. 55.
13. Ruiz, p. 162.
14. Ruiz, p. 216.
15. Ruiz, p. 216.
16. Ruiz, p. 435.
17. José Lezama Lima, *Coloquio con Juan Ramón Jiménez* (Havana, 1938), pp. 19–20.
18. Angel del Río, "Frederico García Lorca," *Revista Hispánica Moderna,* VI (1940), 252–253.
19. Manuel Durán, "García Lorca, poeta entre dos mundos," *Asomante,* XVIII (1962), 70–77.

The University of Tennessee

CONTRIBUTORS

KENNETH BALL, Assistant Professor of English at the University of Kentucky, has previously published on Joel Barlow in *Eighteenth-Century Studies.*

CARL W. COBB, Associate Professor of Romance Languages at the University of Tennessee, has presented his studies of Spanish literature in such journals as *Philological Quarterly* and *Hispania.* His *Federico García Lorca* appeared in 1967.

JOSEPH J. EGAN, Associate Professor of English in the Graduate School of Slippery Rock State College, has written a number of essays on Robert Louis Stevenson and other late nineteenth-century figures.

ALLISON ENSOR, Assistant Professor of English at the University of Tennessee, is the author of the recent *Mark Twain and the Bible.* His essays have appeared in *American Literature* and *Tennessee Studies in Literature,* among other journals.

FORREST E. HAZARD, Associate Professor of English at Chicago State College, has written elsewhere on W. H. Auden and Edward Albee.

RICHARD M. KELLY, Associate Professor of English at the University of Tennessee, has been represented in such journals as *University of Toronto Quarterly, Victorian Newsletter,* and *Studies in English Literature.* Two books of his, *The Best of Mr. Punch: The Humorous Writings of Douglas Jerrold* and a study, *Douglas Jerrold,* are scheduled to appear this year.

B. J. LEGGETT, Assistant Professor of English and in 1969–1970 Acting Assistant Dean of the Graduate School at the University of Tennessee, has published essays in several periodicals. His *Housman's Land of Lost Content* will be published this year.

BEN HARRIS McCLARY, Professor and Chairman of the Eng-

189

lish Department of Wesleyan College, Macon, Georgia, holds two degrees from the University of Tennessee and the D. Phil. from the University of Sussex. The most recent of his several books is *Washington Irving and the House of Murray: Geoffrey Crayon Charms the British, 1817–1856.*

ARTHUR F. MAROTTI, Assistant Professor of English at Washington University in St. Louis, has written frequently on Renaissance poets and dramatists, including Spenser, Donne, Middleton, and Jonson.

JOHN NIST, a graduate professor of English language and linguistics at Auburn University, is the author or editor of five books and a number of essays, including one on Chaucer in Volume XI of *Tennessee Studies in Literature.* In 1964 he was awarded the Machado de Assis Medal by the Brazilian Academy of Letters.

JOHN H. STROUPE, Associate Professor of English at Western Michigan University, has published in a variety of journals. He is coeditor of *Comparative Drama* and is now working on a book-length study of the dramatic use of the masque from Sophocles to Genêt.

LINDA W. WAGNER, Associate Professor of English at Michigan State University, has published verse and criticism in three books and a number of essays. One of her books is *The Poems of William Carlos Williams: A Critical Study.*

GUY R. WOODALL, Professor of English at Tennessee Technological University and a Ph.D. from the University of Tennessee, continues to publish on various phases of our first national period. One essay has recently appeared in *Studies in Bibliography,* and the study here included is his second to appear on Robert Walsh in this journal.

NATHALIA WRIGHT, Professor of English at the University of Tennessee, is the author of such well-known books as *Melville's Use of the Bible, Horatio Greenough: The First American Sculptor,* and *American Novelists in Italy.* Among the many works she has edited, the most recent is *Volume I: Journals and Notebooks, 1803–1806* of *The Complete Works of Washington Irving.*

NOTICE TO CONTRIBUTORS AND SUBSCRIBERS

Although the present editors will continue, beginning in 1971 with Volume XVI, *Tennessee Studies in Literature* will have as its Managing Editor Professor Richard M. Kelly, who will be assisted by Professor Allison Ensor. All manuscripts should now be addressed to the Managing Editor, *Tennessee Studies in Literature,* McClung Tower 306, University of Tennessee, Knoxville, Tennessee 37916. Inquiries regarding subscriptions and other business matters should be addressed as before to the University of Tennessee Press, Communications Building 293, University of Tennessee, Knoxville, Tennessee 37916.